Beyond the Dream

Awakening to Reality

THOMAS HORA, M.D.

Second Edition

A Crossroad Book
The Crossroad Publishing Company
New York

1996

The Crossroad Publishing Company
370 Lexington Avenue, New York, NY 10017

First published as
Beyond the Dream: Discourses on Metapsychiatry and Spiritual Guidance
by PAGL Press, Orange, Calif., copyright © 1986
by Thomas Hora, M.D.

Printed in the United States of America

Library of Congress Cataloging-in-Publication Data

Hora, Thomas.
    Beyond the dream : awakening to reality / Thomas Hora.
      p. cm.
    Previously published in 1986 with subtitle: discourses on
metapsychiatry and spiritual guidance.
    Includes bibliographical references and index.
    ISBN 0-8245-1636-2 (pbk.)
    1. Psychiatry and religion. I. Title.
RC455.4.R4H87 1996
128–dc20   96-21856
                                                     CIP

Beyond the Dream

OTHER WORKS BY THOMAS HORA

In Quest of Wholeness

Existential Metapsychiatry

Dialogues in Metapsychiatry

Forgiveness

A Hierarchy of Values

The Soundless Music of Life

Healing through Spiritual Understanding

Can Meditation Be Done?

Compassion

God in Psychiatry

Marriage and Family Life

What Does God Want?

Self-Transcendence

Right Usefulness

Commentaries on Scripture

Grateful acknowledgment is hereby given to the PAGL Foundation, Emory and Susan Ayers, Ruth and Sam Robins, Jan and Ann Linthorst, and the "Beloved Companion" for their generous support of this work.

In the multitude of dreams and many words,
there are diverse vanities: but "hear" thou God.
—ECCLESIASTES 5:7

Awake thou that sleepest, and arise from the dead,
and Christ shall give thee light.
—EPHESIANS 5:14

Contents

Somatizations – Reaction formation – Valid and invalid outlooks – Scrupulosity – Transcendence – Right thinking and positive thinking – Voodoo – Evil.

Tyrannical parents – A fundamental ethical point – Resistance – Being influential versus influencing – Coerciveness, violence, and trespassing under the guise of love – Spiritual hunger – Letting-be – An enlightened form of love – Taoism.

Moral law, spiritual law, and karmic law – Quanta of energy – Hypnotism – Being influenced – The human mockery – Sowing to the flesh and to the spirit.

Remembering – Understanding – Learning – Expressing – Authenticity of being – Intellectualism – Epistemology and semantics – Categories of thought – Experience and realization – Remembering and recollecting – Ego functions and spiritual faculties – Ambition – The phenomenal world – Distractions.

Excarnation – What is consciousness? – Transcendence – The psychotherapist and the spiritual guide – The evolution of knowledge – "Five gates of hell" – The fear of the open mind – Inspired wisdom – "Two intelligent questions" – Existential validation – What is pathology? – God is no respecter of persons – Phenomenological perceptivity – Modes of communication – Self-confirmatory ideation – Holonomic reality – Four "Ws."

Awakening – Spiritual blessedness – Bliss-consciousness
– What do you mean "spiritual"?

Abandonment – Annihilation – Irrational cravings – Existential anxiety – The divine parenthood – The longing for structure – Sick order and healthy order – Infinite structure – Formalism and ritual – "Father, why hast Thou abandoned me" – God and man inseparable.

A cultural obsession – Operationalism and hedonism – Orgasm and the supreme good – "Pleasuring" – Is sex a physical act? – We are as healthy as our thoughts are – Negative ignorance and positive ignorance.

Yielding and healing – "My cup runneth over" – Cherished ideas – Misdirected interests – Spells of depression – "The dark night of the soul" – Ego-gratifying props – The internal dialogue – To see and to be seen – Seeing and understanding – Physical problems are mental – "Mindsight" – The universal Mind.

The metaphysical is not supernatural or natural – Coming into harmony with the Fundamental Order of Existence – Natura sanans – Psychic healing – Spiritual healing – TV hypnotism.

Consciousness – "Treasures in heaven" – "Two intelligent questions" – Self-blame – Who made the serpent? – "The

sea of mental garbage" – Responsibility and culpability –
Ignorance is not sin – Sine Deo.

Working in agencies – Personal advancement as inevitable
concern – The client's welfare is secondary – What we
want and what the client wants – Real needs are spiritual – Bureaucrats and clients in adversary relationships
– "Personal helper" is a fantasy – A "beneficial presence"
can function on a transcendental level regardless of the
structure which society imposes on him.

Nothing comes into experience uninvited – Naïveté, ignorance, and innocence – The conundrum – "Wiser than
serpents" – "The secret place of the most High" – The enemy within – Right thinking – Cultural trends – Fads –
Valid values.

The right question – Is the good of God discernible as
present? – Love is not enough – Responsibility and irresponsibility – "The sound of one hand" – Enlightened
parenting – The transcendent perspective – Teaching parent, learning parent – Interest focused on spiritual values
– Indoctrination and inspiration – Marriage and the feminist ideology – "Consciousness raising" – Marriage as an
adversary relationship – Marriage as existential situation
– Marriage without interaction thinking – "Who am I sick
against?" – Separate but not separated.

The Bible record of man's evolving concept of God –
"Graven images" – The unimaginable – Love-Intelligence
– Formlessness and form – Background and foreground
– The faculty of spiritual discernment – Cause-and-effect
thinking – "Six futile questions" and "two intelligent

questions" – Definition of a beneficial presence in the world.

"Nothing comes into experience uninvited" – The holocaust – Victims and victimizers – Existentially invalid thoughts and images – Independent thinkers – Collective fantasies and ideologies of nations – The victimizer becomes a victim – Insufficient understanding of the power of thought – The Ninety-first Psalm – A blueprint for survival – Erroneous assumptions about television programs – The nightmare pill – Television transforms information into experience – From words to images – Compassion and callousness – Rising above the sea of ignorance – Spiritual luminaries.

Projective tests – Therapists and investigators – Drawing blanks – Futile questions – Intrusions into personal life – Man as an object of exploration – Resistance – "Helping people whether they like it or not" – Treating neither the disease nor the patient, but the mode of being-in-the-world – Miseducation – Recognition, regret, reorientation – The right question concerning fear – Self-confirmatory ideation – Fear a source of illness – Jesus "Fear not, believe only" – Fearlessness and courage.

Object love – I-it relationship (Buber) – True love is objectless, is not personal and not interpersonal, it is existential – God is not someone who loves, God is love – We dwell in Love and Love dwells in us.

Parental consciousness and the child – The psychologically sophisticated parent – Clinical parenting – Parents as fault-finders – The clinical eye and the loving eye –

Questions to be avoided – Blamelessness – Judging – Positive regard – Knowing the truth heals – Education of the therapist – Education as transformation – What constitutes environment? Environment is mental – The universe of Mind – Mental climate – The ideal therapist – The right understanding – Drugs – Coming into harmony with the Fundamental Order of Existence – Crime and punishment – Victimology – Yes is no, and no is yes – The four "Ws" – Safety and protection – Contagion of Crime – The healing environment of **spiritual** consciousness.

no such thing as a godless individual – The meaning of
Jesus' healing work.

also – Discipline and control – The central role of sexual pleasure seeking – Human beings and spiritual beings – Natural man cannot commune with God – PAGL – The good in consciousness – "Mind fasting" – The loss of the fear of death – The overcoming of grief.

"I want" – The Damascus experience – The victimizer as victim – Aggressiveness and passivity – Without God there is no third alternative – Sartre: "No Exit" – Should-lessness – How to deal with anger – Eric Hoffer: "Anger and Courage" – Courage and fearlessness – Liberation from the tendency toward anger – Interaction and Omni-action.

Alcoholism and addictions – Attachments to chemical substances – Epictetus – The problem of managing one's own thought processes – External remedies – The role of the serpent in the allegory of Adam and Eve – If one substance is harmful, let us find another one – Dominion and purity of consciousness – Mind fasting – "Better living through chemistry" – The character distortions of the addict.

The influences on human consciousness – The disappearance of beastliness – Six levels of cognitive integration – As thou seest so thou beest – The highest level of cognitive integration – Transcendent values – Experiential life versus spiritual consciousness – The central role of awareness – Luminosity of the beneficial presence in the world – The story of the poor fishmonger – Story of the laundryman – Story of the illegitimate child – Examples of the life on a transcendental level of cognitive integration.

Foreword to the Second Edition

Dr. Thomas Hora had a passion for seeking spiritual under-standing and sharing it with his students. Although at the moment he was not speaking about himself, the following succinctly describes what he manifested in his teaching:

> There are two issues in spiritual teaching: one is im-parting the Truth, and the other is demonstrating non-personal, nonconditional benevolence. One can then learn about the Truth and observe the Truth in action; this is effective teaching.

Thomas Hora was born on January 25, 1914, in northern Hungary. Little is known of his early life. In 1944 he married Madeleine Ernyei, a medical student who gave up her studies to become a devoted wife and companion until her passing in 1992. Dr. Hora received his medical degrees from Royal Hungarian University, Budapest, Hungary in 1942 and Charles University, Prague, Czechoslovakia in 1945. He was trained in psychiatry at Budapest General Hospital, Carlsbad City Hospi-tal in Carlsbad, Czechoslovakia, and the Postgraduate Center for Mental Health in New York.

In 1952 Dr. Hora established a private practice in New York. For the next fifteen years he was very active in professional psychiatric circles in the U.S. and Europe, delivering over forty lectures and publishing an equal number of articles. In recog-nition of his work he received the first Karen Horney Award for the Advancement of Psychoanalysis in 1958.

During this period Dr. Hora's spiritual search was in full bloom, as he studied existentialism, phenomenology, Zen, Tao-ism, Judaism, and Christianity. In addition to reading the sacred texts of the world's great religions, Dr. Hora also studied the works of such individuals as Plato, Dante, Shakespeare, Martin Heidegger, Carl Jung, James Legge, D. T. Suzuki, Mary Baker Eddy, Joel Goldsmith, and many others. Dr. Hora met with Carl Jung, Alan Watts, and a number of Zen Masters. In his search Dr. Hora gained a spiritual understanding of the teachings of Jesus, which became a cornerstone of his work.

After 1967 Dr. Hora withdrew from participation in professional societies and focused all of his time and attention on helping those who came to him with their suffering. Many who initially came to Dr. Hora driven by suffering grew in understanding and left their "patient" status behind, becoming students in search of a higher level of spiritual wisdom. Part of the foundation of his teaching is, "All problems are psychological, and all solutions are spiritual." This teaching which evolved over the course of many years came to be known as Metapsychiatry.

In describing this new body of knowledge Dr. Hora wrote:

> Metapsychiatry is a gift of God to our time.
> We have built a new road,
> which is neither religious,
> nor materially scientific,
> nor political.
> We have come to understand it
> as an epistemological method of truth realization.
>
> (Thomas Hora, *Self-Transcendence*,
> as cited by Jan Linthorst, *A Primer on Metapsychiatry*)

Dr. Hora's appeal is broad and can be considered transdenominational. Among his patients and students were Catholics, Protestants, Jews, Buddhists, and nonreligious individuals. Many who came to him were clergy or members of religious orders. He drew students from throughout the world, many of whom studied with him for fifteen to twenty years or more. Dr. Hora supervised the work of therapists and counselors. Some of his patients and students also have become counselors and teachers.

Dr. Hora's method of teaching was through Socratic dialogue and the process of cognitive dialectics separating truth from error, what is existentially valid from what is existentially invalid, and light from darkness. *Beyond the Dream* was assembled from such dialogues and discourses. Thus, each chapter stands on its own but at the same time draws on the totality of his work. The reader will find it helpful to understand that *Beyond the Dream* is a "spoken" as opposed to a "written" book, having been compiled from dialogues and not from an outlined set of ideas. The book has been carefully edited to maintain the integrity and spontaneity of Dr. Hora's responses.

Throughout his writings Dr. Hora frequently refers to the "Eleven Principles of Metapsychiatry," which are a reflection of his spiritual and existential understanding. These principles are:

1. Thou shalt have no other interests before the good of God, which is spiritual blessedness.

2. Take no thought for what should be or what should not be; seek ye first to know the good of God, which already is.

3. There is no interaction anywhere; there is only Omni-action everywhere.

4. Yes is good, but no is also good.

5. God helps those who let Him.

6. If you know what, you know how.

7. Nothing comes into experience uninvited.

8. Problems are lessons designed for our edification.

9. Reality cannot be experienced or imagined; it can, however, be realized.

10. The understanding of what really is abolishes all that seems to be.

11. Do not show your pearls to unreceptive minds, for they will demean them.

Dr. Hora continued his work to within a week of his passing on October 30, 1995. He left a legacy of many grateful students, four books, a dozen mini-books, and hundreds of tapes. Dr. Hora considered *Beyond the Dream* his most important writing in articulating the Truth.

A short time before his death, Dr. Hora spoke these words, which summarize the essence of his teaching and life-long devotion to the search for Truth:

Be grateful and remember that God is the only Lover and that God is the only Love. If we are grateful in this way then our love is nonpersonal; it is an awareness of God's Good, and this is real freedom. We are grateful for whatever good comes into our experience, what is intelligent and what is liberating. If we are conscious of being grateful, then there are no problems.

Contributing to this foreword were fellow students Heather Brodhead, Bruce Kerievsky, Michael Leach, Jan and Ann Linthorst, Ruth Robins, and Elizabeth Shane and Mitchell Shapiro. In addition, Bruce Kerievsky made a very valuable contribution to the editing process of this edition.

EMORY AND SUSAN AYERS, 1996

Introduction

Man suffers from insufficient understanding of Reality. Enlightened man views life as a dream from which he has awakened. While others around him are still involved in the dream, he himself is just a nonparticipating observer. Or, let us put it this way: enlightened man is like someone who sits in a movie and, while others around him are fully absorbed in experiencing the actions on the screen, he himself remains unaffected by the plot or by the behavior of others around him. He is just a nonparticipating observing presence. He can walk out of the cinema at any time, whereas unenlightened man gets sucked into the movie and experiences the scenes on the screen as if they were happening to him. Enlightened man is not interested in entertainment; he is unimpressed by the lure of personal experiencing.

Unenlightened life is just a movie. Everyone is dreaming the dream of life as personal selfhood. We are all dreaming that we are physical personalities interacting with one another, positively or negatively. And we are very serious about this because we do not know that we are dreaming, and so our experiences are very important to us.

The Bible says: "The natural man receiveth not the things of the Spirit of God; for they are foolishness unto him: neither can he know them, because they are spiritually discerned" (1 Corinthians 2:14). There is a great chasm between natural man and enlightened man. Natural man thinks that enlightened individuals are foolish, that they are missing out on all the fun in life, and he has some difficulty in understanding what it is all about.

The good of enlightened life is not based on experiences,

1

but on pure bliss. Bliss is blessedness, which is happiness. But the happiness of the enlightened man is not the same as that of the dreamer. The dreamer seeks happiness in excitement, in physical sensations, and frictions. Enlightened man finds happiness in beauty, harmony, peace, perfection, joy, freedom, love, creative intelligence, inspired wisdom. The Lord's Prayer says: "Give us this day our daily bread." To the enlightened man this means: The good of God is realized daily in inspired wisdom, peace, assurance, gratitude, and love.

We are making a point here about the difference between experiencing and realizing. Even a so-called "religious experience" is but a dream about becoming enlightened. Therefore, it is a form of self-deception. Reality cannot be experienced. It can, however, be realized.

On the road to understanding Love-Intelligence as the light of the Christ, we come face to face with the belief that the essence of life inheres in experiencing. The love of darkness could be interpreted in present-day understanding as the love of feeling good and the love of having pleasurable experiences. As a matter of fact, we love experiencing so much that we can even enjoy pain.

Man is attached to the dream of experiential living, pleasurable as well as painful. Life seems to be synonymous with experiencing. Experiencing means sensual, emotional, and intellectual stimulation. The darkness we are attached to is the idea of experiencing and doing. Doing is also a form of experiencing; we call it operationalism. We consider real living or being alive as consisting of activities and experiences in the world. This is the great stumbling block.

The ninth principle of Metapsychiatry states: "Reality cannot be experienced or imagined; it can, however, be realized." Many sincere seekers after the truth and the light fail to reach it because they live in the expectancy of religious and spiritual experiences. Experiencing is not a proof of life and of truth. Just because we are experiencing something does not prove that it really exists. For instance, through hypnotism man can be induced to experience whatever a hypnotist may suggest. This is a simple proof of the illusory nature of human experiences. As a matter of fact, experiences are but dreams, or illusions. They are perceptualized thoughts. The Buddhists and Hindus speak of samsara or maya, meaning illusion.

Real life cannot be experienced. Therefore, not many people are really conscious or awake, nor are they interested in being awake. Just like drug addicts — admittedly an extreme example — we too are most interested in dreaming a better dream. Drug addiction is but a socially unacceptable way of dreaming. Most of us appear to be hypnotized most of the time, even without drugs, until we wake up. When we wake up, we discover that life and being consist of Love-Intelligence.

This book deals with the convergence of Metapsychiatry and spiritual guidance.

Metapsychiatry is a scientific discipline based on a metaphysical concept of man and the universe. The healing method in Metapsychiatry is found in a special mode of communication centered around a process of hermeneutic clarification of existentially valid principles. This, in turn, brings about qualitative changes in consciousness and results in improved cognitive faculties.

The aim of Metapsychiatry is to heal man of his afflictions by elevating his consciousness to the recognition of his identity as an image and likeness of God, a spiritual being capable of transcendence.

Spiritual guidance endeavors to help man realize his own divinity and life in the context of God. Man is seen as a "place" where God's presence reveals itself as omniactive Love-Intelligence. We are led to "overcome the world" by discovering in practical ways how to be "in this world" and yet "not of it" (2 Corinthians 10:3). This level of realization is referred to in the apocalyptic passage which speaks of a "new heaven and a new earth" (Revelation 21:1).

Enlightened man has a different perception of reality. He has attained a spiritual level of cognitive integration. As Meister Eckhart put it: "God sees me with the same eye as I see God."

What Is Man?

Metapsychiatry transcends psychiatry. It asks a fundamental question, namely, What is man? It does not ask, What is wrong with man? but What *is* man? If we ask this simple question, we run into a complicated situation. There are many ways of perceiving man. Medical science simply assumes that man is a physical organism, and that his basic issues are the physiological processes taking place within the organism.

However, there is much more to man than that. Man is a psyche, an individualized consciousness, even though he may appear to be a collection of physiological systems. Thus, the very simple question, What is man? elicits complex and confusing answers. And so today there are many definitions of man, such as: man is a social animal, a socio-biological phenomenon, a molecular structure, a biochemical process, a product of interpersonal relationships, a conditioned reflex system, etc. These various assumptions about man lead to a variety of schools of thought and many forms of therapeutic methods, which are forever changing. This clearly indicates that they cannot be valid because Truth is immutable; it does not change. Whatever is mutable and transitory cannot possibly be the correct idea.

Now, we can be forgiven if we accept incorrect ideas because we don't know any better. But if we don't know that we don't know, then difficulties arise. The philosopher Heidegger compares this situation to a blind man who does not know that he is blind. Such a man is in great danger; he may

5

hurt himself. But if a blind man knows that he is blind, then he can proceed wisely and cautiously, actually begin to see in certain ways, and be safe. So then, first we have to come to know that we really don't know and then we must seek to know as much as possible. Metapsychiatry, having recognized the tragic insufficiency of knowledge about man, has been led to seek out a definition of man which has endured over the ages. This knowledge is the pearl of great price which has been neglected, skimmed over, and not taken seriously by the scientific world. It has been accepted on the basis of pure belief by the religious world, namely, that man is an "image" and "likeness" of God. Everyone is familiar with this; it is a religious cliché. Religious people believe it. Scientists disdain it, since it cannot be proven. Nevertheless, it is exactly this definition of man that Metapsychiatry takes as a basic premise for its entire structure.

In order for something to be a basic premise of a scientific system it must be understood, not only believed in; it must be actually realized, otherwise the whole structure is built on shifting sand. In order to understand the definition of man as an image and likeness of God, two things are requisite. First of all, man must be seen in the context of God. It would be impossible to understand an image and likeness of God apart from God. Therefore, all endeavors which try to study man apart from God, as a thing in itself, must be inadequate because there is no such thing as man in and of himself. Attempts to understand man as if he were a self-existent entity are based on erroneous impressions. We can study cadavers, do autopsies, we can study anatomy, physiology, and psychology; we can study group behavior, we can study man in his relationships to his fellow man, to nature, to animals, and we can bring together everything in a holistic way, but it is impossible to understand man apart from God, his Creator. Once we have considered the possibility that perhaps the biblical definition of man might be valid, we are impelled to study man in the context of God. But how can we study man in the context of God unless we already know what God is? So this definition presents us with an additional dilemma: not only don't we know what man is, but now we have to find out what God is, and do it scientifically!

For this, we must define science in broader terms. The traditional concept of science is that whatever we are studying must be accessible to quantification, measurements, and experimental validation. That limits the scientific approach a great deal to things which are tangible, which have dimensions, which have weight, etc. But science has already reached levels of understanding where we can study things which are not measurable, not quantifiable, and not accessible to sensory perception. So Metapsychiatry takes for its fundamental premise the biblical definition of man as the image and likeness of God and proceeds to ask the questions: What is God? What is Life? How can an infinite power, a creative Intelligence, have an image and a likeness? How can an invisible nonquantifiable force be *imaged* and reflected and manifested through individuals? What a dilemma! How can we reach sufficient understanding of this elusive Reality? Well this is where existentialism comes in.

Existentialism is a philosophical inquiry into the nature of existence and the context in which it manifests itself. What is existence? Existence is that which exists. Surprisingly, there are many things which seem to be but do not exist. Existence is that which exists in contrast to that which only seems to exist. Let us explore the meaning of the word "exist." The derivation of the word "exist" is a combination of the Greek and Latin: *ek —* meaning outside; *sistere* or *stare —* to stand, to stand out, to be; *ek-sistere* means to stand out, to stand apart. Existence is a quality of consciousness which is capable of observing itself, or of being aware of itself. So there is something about an existent (an individual who is capable of standing apart) who is aware of what he is doing and thinking. We are given this faculty of conscious awareness of self. This is an interesting discovery in that, under normal circumstances, there seem to be two levels upon which our lives are taking place. Animals don't seem to have this faculty at all, or only to a limited degree. But man seems to have this faculty and he can develop it even further. He can discover the "transcendent observer" within himself.

Now the question arises, What is healthy man? In Metapsychiatry we define healthy man as a "beneficial presence" in the world. In contrast to this, religion requires us to be *beneficent persons* in the world. What is the difference? One is *being;* the other is *doing.* The Chinese sage speaks of "actionless action" and "the way to do is to be." In our culture, however, we are what we do. When we emphasize being in contrast to doing, we do not say that being precludes doing because then we would be dead. But our minds are so conditioned to think in dualistic terms that whenever we say black, we think of white; whenever we say white, it is assumed it is not black. This tendency toward dualistic thinking must also be transcended. We juxtapose operationalism with existentialism. We do not imply that a beneficial presence will be passive, but the quality of his actions will be entirely different from that of the one whose view on life is primarily operational.

The word "beneficent" is derived from the Latin *bonum facere,* to do good. A beneficent person is a do-gooder, and we know that this is fraught with problems. It brings to mind St. Paul's phrase: "The good which I would I do not; but the evil which I would not, that I do" (Romans 7:19). This is a common dilemma in all areas of life. When we have an operational approach, there will always be good and bad in what we do. Take, for instance, the tremendous accomplishments in medical science. Much progress has been made in pharmacotherapy and in surgery, but how much damage is being inflicted upon the recipients of these blessings at the same time? It is a terrible tragedy that the more progress is being made, the more damage is being done. There is no way of separating the good from the evil. We speak of "side effects," but the consequences are due to the dualistic trap of operationalism.

Let us consider the meaning of a beneficial presence in the world. *Beneficence* is an activity, while *beneficial* is a quality. A person is someone who thinks of himself as self-existent, self-motivated, self-energized, self-propelled. What is the difference between a person and a presence? A "beneficial presence" is a quality of consciousness. It may be difficult to conceive of an individual who can be a great blessing to a situation just by the quality of his consciousness. Some people have the best intentions to be helpful, and yet things go sour in their presence. Sometimes we may hear someone exclaim in exasperation, Please, don't help me! This is the opposite of what we call a beneficial presence. It may be easier to understand certain concepts in juxtaposition to their opposites.

In the presence of a beneficial presence — which is a loving consciousness — things have a tendency to work together for good in an almost mysterious way.

Anyone who really wants to attain an understanding of God beyond that of a religious symbol or of a theological abstraction will be greatly helped by understanding those aspects of life which cannot be done. The great confusion in which we live stems from the assumption and erroneous impression that we can do everything and that everything entails doing something like, for instance, "making love." The other day someone said: "I realize that I don't have love. I wonder where I could get it and how I could get it." Around the issue of love there is a great deal of confusion stemming from the operational bias with which we view life. We cannot get love. We cannot make love. We cannot give love. If we try, we turn out to be inauthentic, consciously or unconsciously. At Christmas time and other holidays, families come together and the members make a supreme effort to express love toward each other. They try to do it and the result is that after these holidays people tend to run into various problems (side effects).

Love can only be *realized*. What does it mean to realize something? It means to become conscious of the reality of something. When we realize love, we discover that love really is, and that which is does not have to be produced since it already is. And when we are conscious of what really is, then that which really is becomes manifest in our experience. We say: Love expresses itself through man. We become aware of it by the quality of our presence. Such presence has a healing, harmonizing, enlightening impact on whatever situation we happen to be participating in. The right understanding of those aspects of life which cannot be done leads us to an understanding of God because they are the constituent attributes of God. Thus God becomes a Reality and we do not have to believe in God, or disbelieve in God, or intellectualize about God; God is then a tangible Reality to us, and we live and move and have our being in Him.

We may ask, What is the difference between creation and creativity? Creation is the emergence of the visible universe with all the phenomena of life. We can speak of creativity as the manifestation of inspired wisdom expressing itself through human consciousness. God is the source of all creative intelligence, and a creative individual is one who is receptive to inspired creative ideas coming from that great source and expressing itself in multifarious ways. There is an analogy here concerning what we said about love: the love of God expresses itself through man in individual ways. Similarly, the creative power of God reaches human consciousness in the form of creative ideas which man can then express. These qualities of God flow through man, who is the image and likeness of God. When we speak of an image and likeness of God — to come back to our definition of man — we are not talking about form, we are talking about the formless in the process of taking shape. Man gives expression to divine qualities in form. The Zen Master says: "Form is formlessness and formlessness is form."

I am reminded here of the Metapsychiatric definition of marriage. Conventional psychological thinking assumes that marriage is a relationship between husband and wife. Of course, when we are relating one to another there is a lot of friction, often resulting in a stalemate, and quite often there is parting. If our concept of marriage is based on conventional thinking, we are in trouble, and we know that in our culture marriages are frequently troubled. The more psychologically minded one is about marriage, the more troublesome it tends to be. Metapsychiatry conceives of marriage not as a relationship but as *joint participation* in the good of God. Of course, many people do not want this. We can say that most suffering is the result of pursuing invalid ideas of what is good. The valid idea about marriage as a joint participation in the good of God will result in harmony and blessings. We call this *existential validation*. It is a process whereby an idea can validate itself as harmony, peace, assurance, gratitude, and love.

In Metapsychiatry we are not satisfied with assumptions; we seek realizations, and in the search for realizing the nature of God we have come to understand what evil is. Realizations come about through a process of juxtaposing Reality and illusion, good and evil, what is divine and what is not, what is true and what is false. We seek to attain the realization of the true nature of God, and one of our main methods of realizing the nature of God is by continuously increasing our awareness of those aspects of life which cannot be done. Gradually we come to understand God as the harmonizing creative principle of the universe. The Bible says of God that He is of purer eyes than to behold evil ("Thou art of purer eyes than to behold evil, and canst not look on iniquity," Habakkuk 1:13), and that "God is light and in Him is no darkness at all" (1 John 1:5).

In juxtaposition to God as the principle of all good, we are led to consider the nature of evil. In juxtaposition to evil, the good of God becomes more clearly outlined in our awareness. In our pursuit of understanding Reality we have a method based on "two intelligent questions." In all our work in Metapsychiatry we ask two questions: (1) What is the meaning of what seems to be? and (2) What is what really is? With the aid of these two questions we are able to separate the real from the seeming, the good from the evil.

Phenomenology and Hermeneutics

Ice is water in crystalized form; vapor is a gas. Vapor can change into liquid and liquid into crystalline form. Gas is evanescent, intangible, with the property of expansiveness. Water is liquid and ice is solid. We see that the same substance can take on three radically different appearances. Phenomena are thoughts in visible form. It is remarkable to consider that, analogously, thoughts can undergo transmutative processes and appear either as language, or as emotion, or as behavior, or as illness, or as health.

We also speak of gaseous substances as having energy; they have the energy which we can measure through the power of the expanding pressure they exert. Similarly, thought is energy, mental energy. It has the power to manifest itself in various forms. And so it is that we speak of phenomena as thoughts having become accessible to sensory perception.

The science which studies phenomena is called "phenomenology." The philosopher Heidegger called himself not so much a philosopher as a phenomenological anthropologist, which means that he used the phenomenological method to study the nature of man. Phenomenological anthropology is the study of man as a phenomenon. Teilhard de Chardin wrote a book titled *The Phenomenon of Man*. Clearly, he considers the totality of man as a phenomenon. Thus we may say that man is a thought, having become transmuted into visible form. This may sound startling at first, but as we consider the basic nature of all phenomena we see that they have the tendency to appear and to disappear. And man, also, can be thought of as appearing on the scene and disappearing from it.

To better understand phenomenology, we propose to consider a most simple case of erythrophobia in order to demonstrate the clinical relevancy of phenomenological investigation. We aim to demonstrate that this is not just an esoteric philosophy about highly speculative theories; phenomenological perceptivity and understanding are practical issues, relevant to daily clinical work. Erythrophobia means a fear of blushing. Interestingly enough, the more fearful one is of blushing, the more prone one will be to blushing. The Bible says, "For the thing which I greatly feared is come upon me, and that which I was afraid of is come unto me" (Job 3:25).

From what has been said until now, it is possible to understand that what we are afraid of tends to become an experience. Since fear is a thought present in consciousness, it tends to express itself as a symptom. There are three main categories of thoughts which have particular clinical relevancy. These are: (1) What we cherish, (2) What we hate, and (3) What we fear. These three types of thoughts tend to have clinical consequences. The question may be asked, What is so special about these three types of thoughts? These are highly charged thoughts, just as some gases have a higher expanding energy value than others. Furthermore, the more a gas is compressed, the more expansive energy it will contain. What we cherish, what we hate, and what we fear are highly charged thoughts carrying a powerful energy level in the direction of manifesting themselves in visible form. Of course, other thoughts also have a tendency to manifest themselves clinically, but not as powerfully as these three.

Sometimes hate and fear are referred to as emotions rather than thoughts. Here we must understand that emotions are thoughts transmuted into neurovegetative reactions. The important thing to realize is that the basic stuff of life is thought, just as the basic stuff of matter is energy. Emotions are thoughts transmuted to the first stage. This differs from the psychological assumption which claims that first we feel and then we think. We believe thought to be primary. It is the fundamental energy form of existence. When God said: "Let there be light," He did not have a feeling that there should be light. He had an idea, a thought: "Let there be light: and there was light" (Genesis 1:3). The thought of God is the creative impetus which is the beginning of all that really is. "Creatio ex nihilo" means that God created the universe apparently out of nothing. Actually the universe is an idea of God, and the basic stuff of the universe is that mental energy which we call thought or idea. "Idios Cosmos" (Heraclitus) means the universe of ideas. Heraclitus also said: "Sine ratione nihil est," which means nothing can exist without thought. The universe is mental. "So God created man in his own image" (Genesis 1:27). He created us by thinking us; we are God's invention.

Similarly, man too is an inventor, with a tendency to invent many thoughts. The thoughts which man invents also seem to have creative power; alas, man is a miscreator. What we invent is often a miscreation. But we can be instruments of healthy creativity. The right kind of creativity is not an invention; it is a discovery. A discovery is the uncovering of something that God has already invented.

Let us now return to erythrophobia, which provides an elementary clinical example of phenomenology. A man thinks that he might blush in a social situation facing others, and indeed he does. If someone comes to us with the symptom of blushing, we are not going to try to find out why he is blushing, or who is to blame for it, or what he should do about it. In Metapsychiatry we understand that cause-and-effect reasoning has no therapeutic value; as a matter of fact, it tends to be therapeutically counterproductive. Furthermore, this realization has been substantiated by research in atomic physics where the study of the behavior of subatomic particles revealed that there is no such thing as cause and effect (Heisenberg uncertainty principle). What do we mean by therapeutically counterproductive? Suppose we figure out why someone is blushing. What will happen? This will not help him to stop blushing. Quite to the contrary, it will provide him with an excuse and a justification of his problem. "Why?" is a reason, and whenever we seek reasons, all we find is excuses.

Thus, if someone comes to us with the problem, say, of blushing, we are not going to try to find out why he is blushing, but we shall try to discern the meaning of his blushing. In order to find the meaning of a phenomenon, we must develop a certain faculty which we all have but which is rather dormant in most people. This faculty is called "phenomenological perceptivity"; this means discerning the patient's main mental preoccupation. This can reveal itself to us in the course of conversation, or just while being with someone for a while. Let us take, for instance, a gentleman who has such a problem. While being with him, it became clear that he was preoccupied with his baldness. Uppermost in his mind was the thought of whether women will like him, find him acceptable or not. This became clear right from the beginning. Essentially, it was a problem of vanity. Rejection by women would be intolerably embarrassing. Thus the meaning of this clinical syndrome became clear right away. In other words, the man was suffering from an invalid idea about what is important. So we see that underlying this clinical syndrome was a set of erroneous ideas. The therapeutic process would involve here clarifying to the patient, first of all, what the meaning of his blushing is, and illuminating to him the error of his reasoning. This process is called in Metapsychiatry *hermeneutics,* which means shedding light on the mental processes which underlie certain problems, thus leading the patient out of his troublesome way of reasoning to a more intelligent, mature, constructive way of seeing himself and the world. This therapeutic process is called "hermeneutic elucidation."

The question can be asked whether a patient would be willing to give up his faulty way of reasoning. It is not necessary for him to give up anything. This therapy is not operational. When a problem and its solution are sufficiently clarified, the power which brings about a change lies not in the patient, nor in the therapist, but in the realization of the truth. Through hermeneutics the patient comes to understand something; he comes to see that there are more valid ways of thinking about the situation. He may realize that whether he has hair or doesn't have hair is not an essential issue. The essential issue for each of us is to be a *beneficial presence in the world*. This points up how valuable it is for a therapist to have a valid and clear concept of mental health. Without a valid concept of mental health we would be at a loss as to what to tell this man; we would have nothing positive to offer. Since we do have a valid concept of mental health, we can help the patient realize that he can be just as beneficial a man in the world without hair as with it.

How do we know that the Metapsychiatric definition of mental health is really valid? Do we have to study all the previous theories about mental health, like, for instance, genital primacy, social adaptation, ego strength, emotional maturity, etc. in order to understand the validity of this definition? Or is there a way of understanding it independently of anything that preceded? The truth of an existential concept validates itself in individual experience. In other words, it bears good fruit. Jesus said: " ... by their fruits ye shall know them" (Matthew 7:20). We base our sense of direction on *the principle of existential validation*.

Thoughts and Feelings

There has been a controversy in the field of psychology for some time now about what is primary — thought or feeling. This controversy has not been out in the open very much because of the prevalence of authoritative writings which are in favor of the assumption that first we feel and then we think. Paracelsus said: "Nihil est in intellectu quod primum non fuerit in sensu," which means, "Nothing is in the mind that has not been first in the senses."

It is true that in human experience everything begins with sensory perception; in other words, our five senses provide us with information about what seems to be. Therefore, it is natural to come to the conclusion that first we perceive, or feel, or sense, and then we think.

What has been said until now would seemingly settle the whole controversy right at this point. However, let us not jump to premature conclusions. Things are not as simple as they appear. We must realize that there is more to human consciousness than just sensory input. If man were just under the influence of sensory perceptions, he would be nothing more than a computer. But there is much more to man. For instance, we mentioned phenomenological perception. Sensory perceptions give us information only about the material world, our apparent environment. But they cannot discern thoughts and affective states. However, phenomenological perceptivity goes beyond the five senses and makes it possible for us to be aware of qualities of thought and the mental climate which

surrounds us. Even with closed eyes we can know if someone loves us; we can be aware of a loving presence. Similarly,
we can be aware of envy, jealousy, competitiveness, tension,
hatred. There is a deeper sense of awareness which we are capable of and which computers don't have. There is, then, more
to us than just sensory information.

Going beyond phenomenology, there is a whole universe
of inspiration, inspired thought, creative intelligence, which
comes into consciousness through suprasensory channels. For
example, a teacher may be with a class of students and not
know what to talk about. But pretty soon an idea may appear
in his awareness in response to subliminally perceived needs.
We speak of ideas obtaining in consciousness. The word "obtain" has special interest for us, for it indicates a process of
receptivity. Creative ideas are received into consciousness from
a transcendent source. We speak of God as Cosmic Mind, the
infinite source of creative ideas.

Metapsychiatry goes beyond traditional psychological thinking about man as a stimulus-response organism. The oriental
religions speak of the process of opening the "third eye,"
dharma, prajna, paramita, etc., which corresponds to our concept of the process of awakening to spiritual consciousness
which makes man available to inspired wisdom, creative intelligence.

Wisdom is not intellectual. Education cannot provide man
with wisdom. A well-educated man may be well-informed, but
he is not yet a wise man. He can become a wise man only if
his consciousness is spiritualized. This makes him a different
man, a man who is tuned in on a source of higher intelligence
which is God. And the more he is tuned in on this intelligence,
the more creative, the more loving, the more harmonious and
healthy he becomes. Interestingly enough, he becomes healthier not only emotionally and mentally, but also physically, and
this is very important. Otherwise Metapsychiatry would have
no justification for its existence.

Now let us come back to the question as to what is primary — thought or feeling? As stated before, sensory percep-

tions occur as a result of external stimuli. In psychiatry they are called exteroceptive stimuli in contrast to enteroceptive or proprioceptive stimuli, which refer to internal perception. While it is true that in the human experience everything starts with sensory perceptions, it is quite different with feelings, emotions, and moods. *Feelings are byproducts of thought processes.* Feelings, emotions, and moods arise as a result of our interpretations of sensory data. For instance, let us imagine two people walking in the forest. Suddenly one of them stops, breaks out in a cold sweat, starts trembling, and points with his finger at an object in front of him, being frightened and speechless. The other man standing beside him is peaceful, unafraid, and smiling. He looks at his friend, then moves over to the object in front of them, reaches down and picks up a dried piece of wood. Now what happened here? Two people received the same sensory stimulus but one of them interpreted it as a snake, and the other as a twig. The feelings, emotions, and psychological reactions which followed were clearly manifestations of thought processes which expressed the particular way the sensory stimulus was interpreted. So we say that there is a difference between feelings, emotions, and sensory perceptions.

This process is analogous to the process of digestion. Just as bowel movements are byproducts of digestive processes, feelings and emotions are byproducts of thought processes. There are some people who become very involved with and unduly interested in their excrements. And there are many who become unduly concerned with their feelings and emotions. Individuals who are unduly concerned about their bowel movements are in danger of developing intestinal dysfunctions; individuals who are unduly preoccupied with their feelings and emotions tend to become emotionally disturbed. We can say, "Where a man's 'treasure' lies, there shall his problems be also." In order to be healthy, we must treasure spiritual values, such as love, harmony, beauty, goodness, intelligence, generosity, peace, assurance, gratitude, etc.

Let us consider what happens if in psychotherapy a patient

is led to study his feelings and emotions. The therapist is repeatedly inquiring about how the patient feels, helping him to observe the minutiae of his affective states. Such a patient is being unwittingly indoctrinated and mentally anchored in a self-concern. This is not going to be very helpful to him.

In Metapsychiatry there is a technical term for this kind of mental preoccupation; it is called "self-confirmatory ideation," which means thoughts are constantly reverting to the self, and seeking to find a certain sense of security in self-awareness. Self-confirmatory ideation is the essential basis of all pathology. This is a universal human inclination out of which proceed endless forms of problems, illnesses and suffering. Therefore, in Metapsychiatry we seek to save man from this proclivity by helping him to discover *transcendence.*

Transcendence can be defined essentially as rising above self-confirmatory ideation. In traditional psychological thinking it has been observed quite early that self-confirmatory ideation is not conducive to health. Freud called it narcissistic thinking. Narcissism is, of course, one of the most blatant forms of self-confirmatory ideation. Consequently, the assumption was that the remedy would be to help the patient to become concerned with others instead of with himself. The idea was to guide the patient to establish meaningful relationships with others. However, this is just another pitfall and exercise in futility, for another is just another self. Self-confirmatory ideation is interest in self, in one's own self. In meaningful relationships we become additionally interested in the self of another. The result is a compounding of self-confirmatory ideation. We can only be unselfish for selfish reasons. To be selfish or to be unselfish is the same.

Orthodox psychoanalysis focuses attention on the self and calls it the study of intrapsychic processes. Reformed psychoanalysis focuses attention on interpersonal relationships, which is an extension of the interest in the self and is still mired in futile preoccupations with the mystery of the self. So the extent of this reasoning is shallow, primitive, and horizontal.

Horizontal thinking means thinking in terms of self and other, or self and society, or self and environment. The existential psychotherapist Binswanger speaks of *Eigenwelt, Mitwelt,* and *Umwelt,* which mean the world of self, the world of relationships with others, and the world of relationships with the environment. But this is still horizontal thinking. As long as our thinking is horizontal, we have not attained a realization of the Transcendent.

In transcendence we rise and expand our conscious awareness into the full-dimensional mode of thinking, and the context of our reasoning includes God, Love-Intelligence, the Source of all energy, wisdom, love, power, freedom, and creativity. Once we attain a transcendent perspective on reality, everything changes, just as when we climb up on a mountain, the view is entirely different than it was in the valley. As man attains the realization of his full potential, the various concepts which previously were considered very scientific and important lose their validity, and life is seen entirely differently. For instance, the concepts of interpersonal relationships and marital relationships disappear, and in their place there emerges a discovery of *joint participation* in the good of God, which makes harmonious coexistence possible.

Thought as Energy

Thought is fundamental to life. Essentially, thought is energy which has the tendency to transmute itself into phenomena. Invalid thoughts will transmute themselves into invalid phenomena, which means that invalid thoughts are harmful, while valid thoughts are health promoting. It is not a mystery that it is not a desirable condition of mind to entertain unloving thoughts. As we grow in the understanding of this basic principle of the transmutation of thought energy, we will become very careful about what we are thinking. We may develop a discipline of mind where we do not indulge ourselves any more in negative and existentially invalid thought processes.

What are fantasies? Fantasies are pictorial thought processes. As we said previously, thoughts constitute mental energy, and this mental energy, like all energies, has the quality of transmutability into other forms of energy. The first transmutation of thought energy tends to be image making. Thought is at first conceptual, second pictorial, and third behavioral or somatic.

For example, let us suppose someone envies another for owning a beautiful automobile, and suppose he allows himself the luxury of indulging in thoughts of envy. There develops a certain cathexis, which means an emotional charge in connection with that envy. Then, pretty soon, he may find himself fantasizing about something happening to that automobile, an accident, or it being stolen or damaged through some malicious mischief. Already the idea of envy begins to transmute itself into pictorial form. He is already producing a movie in his mind. This is called imagination, which is synonymous with fantasizing. Imagination is image making in consciousness.

There is a movement here from concept to image. This may progress into behavior if there is a desire to act out the fantasies. This is the third stage of transmutation of energy from idea to action, which is behavior. Behavior can be verbal or physical. But suppose one is too civilized to act out his fantasies and does not permit himself this form of energy transmutation, in which case he may have to find another form of transmutation. Instead of physical action, this energy is then channeled into the body. It becomes transmuted into a physical symptom. This is called somatization. Every time this individual may see the automobile, he may get a migraine headache, or his blood pressure may go up, and he may hate the car or the owner. So the original thought has now become psychosomatic pathology.

Let us repeat then: first there is the idea, then the concept, then the image, then behavior, then somatization. After that follows the rationalization of the somatization, which means trying to cope with it by explaining it away, or developing a defense mechanism of denial and "reaction formation." For instance, "I don't hate the owner of this car: I am not interested in this car; as a matter of fact, I love him." There is an attempt to transmute the original energy from envy to love. This mechanism is frequently encountered also in homosexuality, lesbianism, and other forms of carnal interaction.

To cope with existentially invalid thoughts in this manner is very burdensome, complicated, and makes life miserable. Therefore, we must learn the discipline of thinking and seeing life in the context of existentially valid ideas. If our outlook on life is existentially valid, then we are not subject anymore to these troublesome ideas; we do not envy, we are not jealous, we are not competitive, hostile, afraid, irrationally ambitious. None of these things moves us anymore. We are imbued with the right perspective, which is the spiritual outlook on life. We are involved with spiritual values. The thoughts which obtain in our consciousness are determined by the perspective which we have on life.

There are five invalid perspectives on life which are prolific sources of existentially troublesome thinking, and an endless variety of problems flow from them. As will be seen later, these are the "five gates of hell," namely: sensualism, emotionalism, intellectualism, materialism, and personalism. A perspective on life based on any one of these five categories of thought is a source of many difficulties.

Sometimes we encounter a certain category of thought which is referred to as religious scruples. Scrupulosity is viewed in psychiatry as obsessive-compulsive neurosis. The trouble with religious prohibitions and intimidations is that people are not given a chance to understand the dynamism of the transmutations of mental energy. Dogmatic religion says: "Thou shalt not...." If we forbid someone to think certain thoughts, like for instance, "thou shalt not covet," which means you should not envy, this may result in an intrapsychic conflict where the religious man tries to suppress his covetous thoughts. He is prohibited from entertaining certain thoughts; consequently he develops defense mechanisms against these thoughts. Obsessive ideas and compulsive symbolic acts are ways of attempting to repress the forbidden thoughts. This is the meaning of scrupulosity.

Arbitrary prohibitions without understanding lead to complications. Religion, which Jesus hoped would liberate man, can actually enslave him, and instead of healing him can make him sick. Consequently, some people have a fear of religion and an aversion to the Bible. This, of course, is tragic because Jesus was the greatest healer who ever lived and his teachings can really set us free, provided they are understood in an existentially valid way based on sound epistemology.

The right understanding of Jesus' teachings is not repressive but liberating because they do not say what we should think or should not think; they tell us what really is. "The law was given by Moses, but grace and truth came by Jesus Christ" (John 1:17). Jesus reveals to us what is existentially valid; he turns us away from the five invalid perspectives on life and gives us a new perspective, the spiritual perspective, in the context of which all thoughts which obtain in consciousness are health promoting, harmonizing, and existentially valid.

Now then, if our thoughts transcend the "five gates of hell," it stands to reason that when these thoughts transmute themselves, the result will be peace, harmony, assurance, healing, freedom, love, intelligence, creativity, harmony, and joy. And this is health.

There is another thought form which in psychoanalysis is referred to as "free association." It consists of revealing the random thoughts coming to mind in connection with some dream, or childhood experience, etc. The thoughts which obtain in consciousness at any moment are determined by the perspective within which we view life. Therefore, if our perspective on life is any one of the previously mentioned five invalid categories, then the thoughts which occur to us in the course of free association will also be determined by that particular context. Therefore, the issue is not so much the thoughts which come up in the course of free association but the context which gives rise to these thoughts.

Suppose someone had a dream of having a pleasurable encounter with Gina Lollobrigida. It stands to reason then that all his thoughts in the course of free association will have the character of sensualism, because Gina Lollobrigida, as portrayed in her movies, is a symbol of sensualism. So we can say that free association is not really free, but is circumscribed by the context in which our perspective is focused at a particular time.

In order for therapy to be effective and valid, we must help our patients to transcend the "five gates of hell" and find that perspective which is the fountainhead of existentially valid thoughts. These, in turn, through the process of transmutation of energy, manifest themselves as healing. And that is how health comes into being. The Bible puts it very simply: "As he [man] thinketh in his heart, so is he" (Proverbs 23:7).

To be healthy, happy, effective, and successful we need to learn to think right. Right thinking must not be confused with positive thinking. For while right thinking is always positive, positive thinking is not always right. Right thinking is existentially valid thinking.

Other phenomena worthy of consideration are witchcraft, voodoo, black magic, hypnotism, cursing, and so on. Since all thoughts—valid and invalid ones—seem to represent energy, they can transmute themselves and create phenomena. For instance, voodoo is perhaps the best known system where, in the context of religious superstition, certain destructive thoughts are suggested to individuals, or expressed about individuals either in their presence or their absence. These thoughts often manifest themselves in some tragedy concerning those individuals. There have been cases reported in medical literature where certain individuals, upon whom a voodoo curse had been pinned, actually died, in spite of efforts of physicians in a hospital trying to save them. They just died and no one could explain it medically, so powerful is a voodoo curse upon those who believe in it.

Voodoo, cursing, witchcraft, and hypnotism each have power and impact on people as long as they believe in it, or on people who disbelieve it. If we believe that a curse has power, we are vulnerable. But if we disbelieve it, we are vulnerable as well. To believe or to disbelieve is the same. In both instances we are involved in struggling against a power. When we disbelieve in something, we are fighting against believing in it; therefore we are honoring it as a power. There are two interesting relevant lines in the Bible which say: "But I say unto you, that ye resist not evil" (Matthew 5:39)... "but overcome evil with good" (Romans 12:21), which means if we are resisting evil, we are honoring it as a power. But if we understand that only the good of God is real and has power, then we do not get involved with evil either in a positive or a negative way.

Shouldlessness

The habit of thinking in terms of what should be or what should not be tends to make us willful and tyrannical. Many a tyrannical parent is an involuntary victim of this semantic trap. However, we need not be victims of habits of thought. With a little attention and discipline we can abandon such arbitrary and coercive language and attain "shouldlessness." Shouldlessness is a most attractive and desirable quality of mind. In the Beatitudes Jesus speaks about it as meekness: "Blessed are the meek: for they shall inherit the earth" (Matthew 5:5). We can consider shouldlessness as synonymous with meekness.

Interestingly enough, when we become shouldless, our lives become simple and efficient (*fuss-less*). For instance, there is a case of a young mother who had a great deal of trouble with her four-year-old child at feeding time. The child would refuse to feed herself and would demand to be fed. The mother kept insisting that a four-year-old child *should* be able to feed herself. Consequently, every meal became a "battle royal" with a great deal of fuss. The mother did not realize that she had a tyrannical approach to the whole process of feeding. Only when she heard herself say, "You should feed yourself," did she awaken to the realization that what is needed is a "shouldless" mentality.

Tyrannical words produce tyrannical attitudes and these in turn provoke tyrannical and rebellious reactions. The life of a tyrannical individual is very difficult because he encounters many types of resistance. The word "should" tends to trigger negative reactions.

Absolute shouldlessness can only be attained when the following principle is understood: "Yes is good, but no is also good" (the fourth principle of Metapsychiatry). Whenever this principle is first mentioned, there are always some misinterpretations voiced. For instance, some may say this principle is fatalistic philosophy, meaning that man is a victim of circumstances. The second misinterpretation believes this principle to recommend Pollyannaism, which is a form of self-deception. And the third misinterpretation calls it a principle of nihilism, meaning that nothing matters. None of these, however, constitutes the right understanding, for this principle refers to a cognitive realization of the nondual nature of Divine Reality, where everything is harmonious, intelligent, and "very good." Whenever we understandingly affirm this principle, we have placed our problems into the hands of God, and from then on, things tend to work out in a most favorable way, for God is the harmonizing power of the universe and is omniactive Mind.

Contrary to the human dimension of experience, yes and no in Divine Reality carry no value judgment. In human terms we assume that "yes" is good, meaning positive, and "no," being negative, must therefore be bad. But in the context of Divine Reality nothing is ever bad: Therefore, even "no" has a positive connotation.

The Metapsychiatric therapist does not speak about what should be or what should not be. Metapsychiatry is concerned with developing the faculty to discern what is. The habit of thinking in terms of what should be or what should not be constitutes a "mind-set" which clouds the ability to see what is. It is therefore advisable to dispense with the habit of thinking in these terms. For instance, we don't say that horizontal thinking shouldn't be. We say that it interferes with the faculty of perception.

A fundamental ethical point in Metapsychiatry is the respect for people's right to be wrong. It is important that patients be given the freedom to be wrong. It is not the therapist's task to influence his patient. Someone asked, But what do you do if the patient does not want to change? Patients have a right not to want to change.

Patients seek help believing that they are unhappy or sick and hoping to find a way to be happier and healthier. Let us take for example a middle-aged man who went to see a therapist because he was getting increasingly less capable of enjoying his homosexual marriage. He was becoming impotent. He was hoping to have his potency restored. He believed that it was wrong to be impotent. The therapist refrained from thinking about what should be or what should not be, and instead sought to understand the meaning of the problem. He knew well that whatever change may occur in the patient's life will not be brought about by what the therapist wants, nor by what the patient wants. Change occurs under the impact of the truth realized in consciousness.

The therapist invited the patient to try to understand the meaning of his impotency. In the course of exploring the meaning of this phenomenon, it was discovered that the patient had recently become interested in spiritual studies. He had taken an intensive course in Transcendental Meditation. He also became interested in the study of comparative religions. As a result of this, he was awakening to new realizations about what God is, what man is, what life is, and what health is from a spiritual standpoint. As a result of his progress in spiritual understanding, it was becoming more and more difficult for him to continue in his previous lifestyle. This manifested itself as a growing inability to sustain his homosexual involvement. Consequently, it dawned on him that he was not getting sicker but healthier, that his impotency was actually a good sign, that it was not something to fear but to accept. The right understanding of spiritual values is a power active in his consciousness to bring about a transformation of his mode of being-in-the-world.

As we see, the therapist did not have to impose his own ideas on the patient, nor did he have to accept the patient's

ideas about what should be or what shouldn't be. The power
to bring about change lies in the understanding of what is,
which, in this case, was the emergence of spiritual consciousness in the patient.

According to Jesus, it is the knowledge of the truth that
makes man free. This fact eliminates one of the great psychoanalytic stumbling-blocks, namely, the concept of resistance.
Resistance always requires two people: one who wants something, and the other who does not want it. Since the therapist
has no personal wants, there is no one to resist. In Metapsychiatry there are no interpersonal relationships. As for
intrapsychic conflicts, they are considered to be collisions of
two or more forms of ignorance. When two forms of ignorance
collide, we can speak of an "implosion" of nothingness. Since
truth is irresistible and omnipotent, it abolishes all forms of
ignorance, just as light abolishes darkness.

As mentioned above, the Metapsychiatric therapist does not
influence his patient; nevertheless, he is influential. The therapist is influential by virtue of the quality of his being and
by his ability to shed light on what is. Metapsychiatric therapy is a hermeneutic process. The Metapsychiatrist is neither
a "should" thinker, nor an influencer, nor a "why?" asker. He
is an elucidator, a clarifier. To ask "why?" would imply that
there is a cause. For instance, had the therapist asked why this
patient was getting impotent, he would have had to blame it
on Transcendental Meditation. But since he was exploring the
meaning of this impotency, he wound up giving credit to the
increasing spirituality in the patient's consciousness.

Cause-and-effect thinking is a narrow-minded way of looking at life, and Metapsychiatry seeks to transcend it. Here
there are mainly two questions asked: (1) What is the meaning of what seems to be? and (2) What is what really is? To
illustrate, let us come to the gentleman with the impotency
problem. If we ask, What is the meaning of his problem?
we see that the meaning of his problem is an erroneous
mode of being-in-the-world. "Mode of being-in-the-world" is
an existential term. Everyone has a specific mode of being-in-

the-world which can be, more or less, in harmony with the Fundamental Order of Existence. Our patient had a specific form of misdirected mode of being-in-the-world, manifesting itself in a homosexual life-style, centered around the idea that the good life can be found specifically in the practice of sodomy.

Thus, the first question helps to understand a patient's mode of being-in-the-world. Following that, we ask the second question, But what is what really is? This question refers to the issue of what constitutes a healthy mode of being-in-the-world. The answer to it is that man, as an image and likeness of God, is a spiritual being and participates in existence as a beneficial presence in the world. When this is brought home to a patient, his mode of being-in-the-world undergoes a confrontation with what really is. What seems to be collides here with what really is. Regardless of the patient's initial reaction at this point, he will never be able to shake off the power of the truth which was planted in his consciousness, somewhat as a seed. The seed will germinate and, sooner or later, bear fruit.

If potency is expressing itself in coerciveness, violence, and trespassing under the guise of love, it is a sickness. Sickness drives man to seek therapy. When a man seeks spiritual understanding, he is being drawn to the Christ. There is a spiritual hunger in man, no matter how depraved he seems to be, or how deeply immersed in perversion and ignorance he may be. Everyone is drawn to the Christ-idea because it is the light of the world.

Jesus said: "Take my yoke upon you, and learn of me. . . . For my yoke is easy, and my burden is light" (Matthew 11:29, 30). The yoke which Jesus described as easy and the burden which is light could be understood in our terms as "letting-be." "Letting-be" is an existential term. It originated in Taoism. Letting-be, translated into existential philosophical conceptualization, actually means reverent, loving responsiveness to that which is from moment to moment. It is a highly constructive, supremely spiritual attitude toward all life forms, not unlike Albert Schweitzer's reverence for life. Essentially, it is a Christ-like stance of the Metapsychiatric therapist. Letting-be is a most enlightened form of love, but it must not be confused with leaving alone, which is neglect.

The Law of Karma

We tend to assume that everything written in the Bible is spiritual, and everything religious is spiritual. Nothing is further from the truth. For instance, the Ten Commandments are not really spiritual laws but moral principles. The law of karma is an epistemic law because it refers to thought processes. For instance: "Whatsoever a man soweth, that shall he also reap" (Galatians 6:7), is an epistemic law. The word "karma" is a Sanskrit word referring to actions and the consequences of actions. Epistemology is the study of the nature of knowledge, i.e., mental action, or processes of the mind. The Bible speaks in many instances of the significance of mental processes. For instance: "For as he thinketh in his heart, so is he" (Proverbs 23:7).

We have been able to realize a law which says: "Nothing comes into experience uninvited." This, too, can be called an epistemic law. Thoughts entertained in consciousness express themselves either in words or actions, and they have a tendency to attract corresponding experiences. Therefore, this can also be called the *law of correspondence.*

Thoughts, indeed, seem to carry quanta of energy; and whenever we have a thought, we can express it either verbally, or emotionally, or through action, behavior, or activity. Whenever we send out a thought, it tends to return to us in some form. Thought then is energy which can manifest itself in a variety of forms. If we don't send out a thought, it can expand its energy internally in a beneficial or harmful way. These phenomena can be called the epistemic law of mental energy.

33

Unenlightened man is at the mercy of these mental processes. In proportion to our ignorance, we are vulnerable to our own thoughts and to the thoughts of others. Jesus strongly emphasized the importance of thoughts. He said, for instance: "Take no thought, saying, What shall we eat? or, What shall we drink? or, Wherewithal shall we be clothed? For after all these things do the Gentiles [the ignorant] seek" (Matthew 6:31–32).

Most religious systems encourage their devotees to work within the karmic law in such a way as to produce positive results. For instance: "As ye would that men should do to you, do ye also to them likewise" (Luke 6:31). This can help us understand the difference between religion and enlightenment. Most of what religion consists of is the effort at utilizing moral and karmic laws in a positive way. Prayer thus becomes an endeavor to escape the consequences of having violated the moral law. It is therefore a mistake to confuse religiosity with spirituality.

Life on the level of the karmic, or epistemic law is very difficult. It consists mostly of interaction experiences, that is, what one individual does to another, and their consequences. When it comes to spiritual understanding, we rise above this level; we realize that all this is just relative ignorance. It is life as it *seems* to be. On the level of personal interaction and the karmic law, life is not really what it seems to be; it is just one thought relating itself to another thought. It is as if two and two is five were talking to two and two is six. This would not really be mathematics. It would only seem so. Moreover, it is very troublesome. It reminds us of one of the problems of trying to manage a friendly relationship. It involves much effort and is not easily sustained.

As long as we see life in these terms it is a constant struggle to be nice, to be good, friendly, just, honest, helpful, generous, and to be liked and avoid being disliked. This is spoken of as getting along with people and managing our affairs with the least amount of conflict. Furthermore, on this level of understanding we are also very vulnerable to hypnotism.

There are many forms of hypnotism. Whatever is a new

trend in the culture, or among friends and relatives, or whatever is suggested in the broadcast media exerts a great influence. The question arises: How can we protect ourselves from being influenced? We cannot stick our heads into the sand. However, the apostle Paul shows us the way of protection when he says: "The law of the Spirit of life in Christ Jesus has made me free from the law of sin and death" (Romans 8:2). What does that mean? It means that when we understand spiritual law, when we become spiritually enlightened, when we catch a glimpse of omniactive Truth as the sole Reality of the entire universe, then we are lifted up to a higher level of awareness and discover that God is the only power, the only Presence, the only Life, the only Mind there is, and this Mind is not susceptible to hypnotism, to intimidation, seduction, and provocation, to praise, pampering, persecution, or to self-confirmatory ideation. We discover life above the level of personal interaction. Suddenly, we understand what Paul meant when he said: "None of these things moves me" (Acts 20:24). We cease to be carnally minded and we become spiritually minded. When we are spiritually minded, God is our mind and we gain immunity from the tribulations of this world, which means there is a way to rise above the inanities of this world. However, it must be pointed out that if we are to rise above the tribulations of this world, we must lose interest not only in its pains but also in its pleasures.

From the perspective of spiritual enlightenment, the karmic law is revealed to us as no law at all but as a mockery of law. Everything in the human dimension of consciousness is transitory, including human existence. It appears and disappears. But in Divine Reality nothing can disappear. Life is immortal, life cannot die. Spiritual laws convey the nature of Spiritual Reality.

Spiritual laws must be realized in individual consciousness to the point that one's outlook on life changes drastically. Spiritual law and Spiritual Reality are identical. When we say, "There is no interaction anywhere; there is only Omniaction everywhere," we are referring to two laws. We are making two statements: one about human appearance — life; and one about the nature of Divine Reality — Spiritual law. We must come to discover in individual experience that it is really true. And the more clearly we can see that this is so, the higher we have risen on the Mount of Revelation.

Spiritual law cannot be violated; it is inviolable. But we can be ignorant of it and suffer the consequences. Even a most hardened sinner is ultimately just an ignorant individual. In proportion that we come to understand spiritual law, in that proportion it will become impossible for us to ignore it. So we are lifted gradually from the quagmire of human mockeries.

Everything on the level of personal mind is a mockery of the Divine Mind because the Divine is nondual. In Divine Reality there is no good and evil; there is only good. And there is no such spiritual law that would work ill. Whereas karmic law is two-sided, it can bring evil as well as good into experience. Therefore, it is not really a law, it just seems to be. The serpent spoke to Eve in the garden of Eden. He said: If you eat of this fruit, "ye shall not surely die. For God does know that in the day ye eat thereof, then your eyes shall be opened, and ye shall be as gods, knowing good and evil" (Genesis 3:4–5). This was the first mockery of God because God knows no evil; evil is unknown to God. God is good, period.

The Sermon on the Mount as well as many other passages in the Bible show us the way out of the karmic law and are pointing in the direction of spiritual law. For instance, "Be not deceived; God is not mocked. . . . For he that soweth to his flesh shall of the flesh reap corruption; but he that soweth to the Spirit shall of the Spirit reap life everlasting" (Galatians 6:7–8). Sowing to the flesh means entertaining carnal thoughts and being preoccupied with the pleasures and pains, the glories and disasters of the body. On the other hand, sowing to the spirit means turning our thoughts with increasing appreciation to Spiritual Reality and spiritual values. This results in increasing harmony, health, freedom, love, longevity.

What Can Be Done and What Cannot Be Done

A Viennese psychoanalyst remarked once that writing things down is the first step toward forgetting. The Metapsychiatric principle of learning is as follows: What we understand we do not have to remember, and what we remember we usually don't bother to understand. This is an epistemological principle. Epistemology — the study of the nature of knowledge — is an important part of Metapsychiatry because only what we really know has an impact on our mode of being-in-the-world, not what we just know about.

The process of understanding is a fascinating study because understanding is something that we cannot do. Here again, we are facing the fact that there are vitally important things in life, which, however, cannot be done. How does one partake in something which one cannot do? We all realize that to understand the truth is very important, and yet it is something that we cannot actively bring about. We can volitionally express ideas, behavior, affection, emotions. If we are trying to express love, for instance, at will, then it will be artificial. We may deceive ourselves or we may deceive our loved ones. Let us take a flower, for example. A flower expresses beauty, but this kind of expression is entirely different from what we express volitionally. Similarly, beauty, harmony, integrity, love, joy, peace, assurance, wisdom, freedom, health are all qualities that express themselves through man. If we wanted to express these qualities volitionally, actively, we would become inauthentic. Existentialism emphasizes the importance of authenticity of being. The human experience is fraught with conscious and unconscious falsehoods because we do not differentiate clearly between what is genuine and what is a "put on." Authenticity of being is important for health and for fulfillment in life, but it requires commitment, attention, and understanding. We have to become perceptive of what is genuine and what is false, what just seems to be and what really is. There are many things in life that seem to be but are not really.

Let us come back to the issue of understanding. Here again, authenticity and radical sincerity are required because we can easily fool ourselves that we know something while we only know about it. This is also called intellectualism. Intellectualism is fundamentally fraudulent. Every intellectual statement is a "lie and the father of it," because when we make an intellectual statement, we pretend that we know something and actually it is not true; we only know about it. The essence of intellectuality is fraud. Jesus must have known this clearly when he spoke about "a liar and the father of it" (John 8:44). But how does understanding, genuine knowing, come about? Let us ask, Is it possible to understand that two and two is five? No, it is not possible to understand what is not true. It is only possible to believe it. We can understand, i.e., realize only what is true. Again, we are here confronted with an epistemological principle, namely, that it is not possible to understand what is not true. Only truth can be understood.

Some people believe that they can understand what they have experienced. But suppose we experience something that isn't true? Where are we then? Therefore, experiencing is not reliable as a road to understanding. Experience is an organismic reaction to some situation, a reaction through emotions, sensations, intellect; the totality of the organism reacts to certain factors. These things are not reliable; we cannot judge truth on the basis of experience.

In Metapsychiatry there is a great deal of stress laid on epistemology and semantics. Therefore we say, Truth and Reality cannot be experienced; they can, however, be realized.

To come back to the issue of understanding, there are several prerequisites for understanding to occur. One of them is not to try to remember what is being said; the second is not to agree with what is being said, nor disagree; the third is not to believe what is being said, nor to disbelieve it; the fourth is not to try to trust someone, nor to distrust him. What happens when these four categories of thought are eliminated from our way of facing an issue? The open mind is attained and it is only under the condition of open-minded receptivity that understanding can come about. "Except ye become as little children, ye shall in no wise understand the kingdom of heaven." The primary requisite for understanding to happen is the open-minded confrontation of that which reveals itself from moment to moment.

Now in what way does remembering, believing, agreeing, trusting, disbelieving, disagreeing, mistrusting — all these mental attitudes — interfere with understanding? All these mental attitudes are willed; we can will ourselves to believe, to disbelieve, to agree, to disagree, to trust, to distrust, or to remember. These are ego functions. The ego interferes with that receptivity which makes grace possible. Understanding is nothing else but grace. It is by the grace of God that this cognitive event occurs in consciousness which we call understanding or realization. "As many as received him, to them gave he power to become the sons of God," said Jesus (John 1:12). We may ask, What about the rest of the people? The rest of the people were trying to figure him out, and trying to decide whether to believe him or to disbelieve him, to agree with him or to disagree with him, or to label him as, say, a Rogerian or Jungian, etc., to diagnose him and thus "put him in his place."

Receptivity is not an ego function; it takes place in the absence of the ego. The open mind is open when the obstacles are not there. The natural way is the open mind. The closed mind is a product of experience and education. Education helps us to develop a closed mind.

Realization is a synonym for understanding. If we want to define realization we can say that realization happens when a certain aspect of truth becomes real to us. The truth has its own power of self-validation. We can realize, for example, that two and two is not five but four through the fact that it works and brings harmony into our computations. Truth imparts harmony. Truth heals, liberates. Falsehood creates problems. "Ye shall know the truth, and the truth shall make you free" (John 8:32). And this applies to our checkbooks, our marriages, to our jobs as well. Whenever we are "standing under the light of truth," we are healed and liberated from our problems.

What is understanding? It is "standing under the light of the truth." Ideally, education means *e-ducere*, which means to lead out of darkness into the light.

Truth cannot be spoken of directly because it would be a defilement of it. If we speak of the truth directly, it is not the truth. For instance, if we say, God is Love, that is not the truth; it is only a statement about the truth. Therefore, all spiritual guides throughout history have had to resort to parables, riddles, analogies, and mythology in order to lead individual minds toward the realization of the truth. The Zen koans also belong among these aids to realizing the truth. A Zen Master gave this koan to a student: "Things are not what they seem to be; neither are they otherwise." St. Paul said something similar when he said: "Things which are seen were not made of things which do appear" (Hebrews 11:3).

Experiences are organismic reactions to certain stimuli. Grace is spiritual awareness. Understanding and realization are not organismic; they are spiritual. There is another dimension to knowing which is not organismic, which is not in the brain but in the being of man, in consciousness, spiritual consciousness. It is a transcendent realization. The worlds of psychiatry, psychology, and theology are confusing the two things; they are confusing realization with experiences. When someone says, I have an experience of grace, he is revealing the prevalent confusion existing in the world of psychology and religion, because grace cannot be experienced. It can only be realized as a blessing. Realization is the awareness of what is real, and this awareness is not an experience. A great deal of confusion is generated in religious literature which speaks of "religious experiences." This is a self-confirmatory term. There is no such thing as a religious experience.

Experiences and spiritual realizations are two entirely different things; there is a radical separation between the two. Until we understand this difference, we shall not understand ourselves as spiritual beings and God will remain just a concept. As mentioned before, experiences are organismic reactions to stimuli coming either from the outside or from within and they can be sensory, emotional, or intellectual. We experience our thoughts, our fantasies, our dreams, our imaginations, all the mental and organismic processes in the body and outside the body — all these can be experienced.

Sometimes a spiritual event in consciousness is misinterpreted as an experience. This is happening to those people who have genuine so-called "religious experiences." They do not realize that they are not having an experience; they are having a transforming realization, a spiritual awakening. A spiritual realization comes to consciousness very peacefully, like the white dove which settled on Jesus after he was baptized. It comes peacefully, without fireworks. It descends imperceptibly and it transforms our entire outlook on reality, on life. Our character is healed and we become a "new man."

These things cannot be discussed or argued about or debated. We can only enter into dialogue about it, which means to jointly participate in the search for truth. Dialogue is entirely different from conversation, chattering, debating, discussing, or contending. What we are engaged in here is a joint participation in the process of hermeneutic clarification of the truth.

It seems appropriate to say a few words about remembering. What is remembering? It is a brain function; it is a human effort at storing information and retrieving it. Therefore, it interferes with understanding. Accepting-rejecting, believing-disbelieving, agreeing-disagreeing, trusting-mistrusting, and remembering-forgetting are all ego functions; therefore they interfere with understanding. Is there a spiritual equivalent to remembering? Yes there is. It is called recollection. We call back some knowledge. We rely on the spiritual faculty of *recall*. While remembering is an ego function, recall is a spiritual faculty of calling on the "Great Computer" to retrieve the information which is needed at a particular moment. It is generally believed that the faculty of remembering is diminishing with age; what about the faculty of recall? This faculty, being spiritual, improves with the passage of time through an improved understanding of Spiritual Reality.

If we are studying to be spiritual guides, it is necessary that we understand the spiritual faculties of man. After all, a spiritual guide needs to awaken in other people their spiritual faculties. And how can we be spiritual guides unless we understand clearly the difference between ego functions and spiritual faculties?

If we are eager to transcend our egos, then there is no dualism. There is only God and there is only the glorious liberty of the children of God. There are no entanglements with the yoke of psychological bondage. Spiritual guidance transcends psychology, psychiatry, and all other "ologies." This is the road and we are free to take it or to depart from it, should we find it difficult. But it is possible to overcome the world, if we are interested. Jesus said: "In the world ye shall have tribulation: but be of good cheer; I have overcome the world" (John 16:33). If we are followers of Jesus, we have to be committed and not drag our feet, so to speak; those who wish to drag their feet take courses in psychotherapy, not in spiritual guidance.

If you want to benefit from what is said and not suffer unduly from the shock of unusual information, don't try to remember. Just let it do its work. It is not necessary to exert a mental effort to understand anything. As a matter of fact, the harder you try to understand what is being said and to remember it, the less likely it is that understanding will occur. Just relax and let what you hear do its own work. All that is needed is to cultivate an interest; God's only requirement of us is to be sincerely interested. Actually, there is nothing else we can do in the area of spiritual growth. If we are ambitious in this area, we shall be like the gardener who is trying to pry open a rosebud. We have to be patient and maintain a sincere interest. Otherwise we shall not be able to become enlightened. A teacher can point in a certain direction, explain and clear the way in the desert, and if one is sincerely interested in understanding, it will come by the grace of God. This type of education is entirely different from other forms of education. Conventional education requires an effort and hard work. In spiritual education effort and hard work are a hindrance. What is needed is sincerity and interest because they are the basis of receptivity. God's grace is flooding the whole universe all the time, but there is not enough receptivity to it in human consciousness. Therefore the blessings are scarce. God is not stingy with His love and with His power, but we are distracted. One of the main distractions of ambitious people is effort.

Let us explore what ambition is. It is again an ego function. What does the word "ambition" mean? What is ambivalence? It means being of two minds about something. In ambition we have the word "ambi," meaning double, and "ition," which stands for *eo, ire, ii, itum,* which means moving in two directions at the same time. Thus the word "ambition" reveals that ambitious people are caught up in the dualism of human intending. One cannot be successful without being a failure at the same time, and that is ambition. Ambitious people are successful and failing at the same time. That is the tragedy of the human dualistic mode of being-in-the-world. So instead of ambition we aspire for understanding. We cultivate an interest in Spiritual Reality, and by the grace of God it comes to us like a white dove, descending on consciousness. There is a story about the nuclear physicist Oppenheimer, who was observed staring out of a window for a long time, and when asked what he was doing, he replied, "Don't you see? I am working!"

We must also understand that receptivity is not a passive state. Our dualistic inclinations assume that we are either ambitious — which is an active state — or we are not ambitious, which is a passive state, and receptivity therefore may be misinterpreted as passivity. But if receptivity is neither active nor passive, what is it? Receptivity is attentiveness and responsiveness. When we are floating on water, for example, are we passive or active? Floating is neither active nor passive; it is attentive. What are we attentive to when we are floating? We are attentive to an invisible power called buoyancy. This is an analogy for wakeful receptivity. The search for enlightenment is neither ambitious nor lazy; it is reverent, loving, grateful, attentive, and responsive to that which reveals itself from moment to moment. This is an existentially valid position which we need to learn. The world is a distraction from Reality and is constantly working against our receptivity to God. The world is "every high thing that exalteth itself against the knowledge of God" (2 Corinthians 10:5). At this point we are trying to understand the existentially valid attitude which facilitates the unfoldment of understanding, and whatever interferes with this is distraction. Anything external, internal, worldly, cosmic, operational — whatever interferes with that basic, reverent, loving, receptive orientation — we call the world, the world of distraction. What we are seeking is conscious grace, which is enlightenment.

An interesting thing happens when we come to realize God to a sufficient degree. Distractions come to our attention, but they do not come into our experience. If a distraction comes into experience, we get disturbed by it; but there can be distractions that do not distract and therefore are not distractions. They are just phenomena. We speak of this world as the phenomenal world. What does the word "phenomenon" mean? The word "phenomenon" is derived from the Greek and is composed of two root words: *phaos,* which means light, and *apophansis,* which means statement. Another explanation of the word "phenomenon" is *phainein, phainomenon,* which means light. So phenomena are appearances and the phenomenal world is the world of appearances. A great tool of existential psychotherapy is phenomenological analysis, which we shall discuss later. Suffice it to say at this time that all distractions are phenomena. They are things that seem to be. They are appearances but not realities. We can say that they are thoughts appearing as form.

"Prepare Ye the Way..."

I have been asked about the meaning of excarnation. The meaning of excarnation is implied in the Bible first in the ascension, then in the scene on the Mount of Transfiguration, and by the following statement: "Whilst we are at home in the body, we are absent from the Lord....We are confident, I say, and willing rather to be absent from the body, and to be present with the Lord" (2 Corinthians 5:6, 8).

The Bible also states that "the Kingdom of God is within you." Let us explore what "within" means and clarify it. We are so used to thinking organismically and psychologically that we assume that within means inside the body. Even if we don't admit it, that's how we think. This seems to be the natural way, but actually it does not make sense. Where is the Kingdom of God located? In the lungs? In the nervous system? In the brain? Where within you? Someone suggested that it is in the heart; what does the heart symbolize? In Metapsychiatry we speak of consciousness rather than of heart, and so within means in consciousness. Where is consciousness? Neurophysiology would locate consciousness in the brain, but we know that the brain does not really have consciousness; it is just a relay system. Therefore consciousness cannot be localized. Consciousness is not in the organism; the organism is in consciousness. Awareness is what religions call soul, and it is a synonym for consciousness. Soul is the faculty of awareness.

In Metapsychiatry we speak of consciousness. Consciousness is a unique faculty of man, enabling him to be aware of himself in a transcendent manner. This is the divine element in us. To fully appreciate it is very important, because until we have learned to appreciate the Divine in us, we are undeveloped and we live below the level of our potentialities. Heidegger speaks of being-in-the-world as transcendence. The more perfectly we realize being-in-the-world as transcendence, the more perfect spiritual guides we become.

It is important to differentiate between being a psychotherapist and being a spiritual guide. The perspective of a spiritual guide is spiritually transcendent; the perspective of a psychotherapist is dependent upon what school of thought he adheres to. Psychotherapeutic systems can be intrapsychic, interpersonal, social, interactional, mythological, bio-energetic, etc.

It is interesting to consider the development of knowledge in general, because there is a parallelism in this field. If we take, for instance, the development of astronomical knowledge, we see that first there was the flat earth viewpoint, which is called the geocentric viewpoint. This indicates a primitive and narrow mental horizon. The geocentric viewpoint assumed that the earth was the center of the universe. In psychotherapy the intrapsychic viewpoint assumed that everything can be known about man by looking inside of him, into his body and into his psyche. The idea was that studying the dynamics of the psyche would help us to understand man. This viewpoint is just as primitive as was the geocentric viewpoint in astronomy. After Kepler, Galileo, and Copernicus, we gained a broader perspective in astronomy and we attained the heliocentric perspective, which meant that the sun was the center of the universe, a center around which the planets revolved. After the heliocentric perspective, we attained a galactic knowledge. We have realized that the sun is one of an infinite number of stars which make up a galaxy. From the galactic viewpoint we have attained an intergalactic viewpoint. Here we suddenly see that there are many galaxies in the universe. The intergalactic viewpoint led to a cosmic consciousness. Every schoolchild today is already free to develop a cosmic consciousness. This is a tremendous step forward. Today we are able to conceive of an infinite expanding universe. Some astronomers have advanced from cosmic consciousness to a cataclysmic consciousness. This is based on the discovery of black holes in the universe and the matter-antimatter phenomena which indicate the possibility of cataclysmic events taking place in the universe. There are exploding galaxies and black holes which swallow up planets, and then there is the issue of matter-antimatter collisions. Wherever matter comes into contact with antimatter, it disappears. It turns into nothing.

Analogously, in the area of the knowledge of man we have the intrapsychic, i.e., anthropocentric viewpoint, then the interpersonal, then the socio-dynamic viewpoint, then the interactional viewpoint, the transactional viewpoint, the mythological viewpoint, then the existential viewpoint, indicating an ever widening context of perception. The existential viewpoint is a largely expanded viewpoint, going beyond the socio-dynamic perspective. In the socio-dynamic viewpoint society is the context, which can be socio-economic, socio-political, cultural, etc., but in any case it sees man in a much broader context than the original psychotherapies. The existential context sees man in the context of existence. What is the context of existence? In this viewpoint we speak of modes of being-in-the-world. Therefore the context of our study of man in existentialism is his mode of being-in-the-world. How does man express his essential potentialities within the context of the world around him, which includes everything that preceded but goes beyond it? Here the world itself becomes a manifestation of existence.

Metapsychiatry goes one better to existentialism. The context of Metapsychiatry is Spirit, God, infinite omniactive Love-Intelligence. Here man is not only in the world but also beyond the world — that's what Heidegger means by being-in-the-world as transcendence — we are "in the world but not of it." So of all the various schools of thought concerning man, Metapsychiatry approximates or speaks to the issue of spiritual guidance in a most relevant manner.

What school of thought corresponds to that cataclysmic viewpoint in terms of the study of man? The last book of the Bible is called Revelation, but its other name is Apocalypse, which means cataclysm. This corresponds to the cataclysmic viewpoint in astronomy. St. John's description (vision) of the "new heaven and a new earth; for the first heaven and the first earth were passed away" (Revelation 21:1) indicates a total spiritualization of consciousness. There exists here a remarkable parallelism, and interestingly enough, there is a similar parallelism in atomic research as well, but going in the other direction. In physics the movement of knowledge goes from matter to molecules to subatomic particles to high energy physics, where there are no more particles, there is just pure energy. This reveals the true nature of Reality as pure energy (spirit=energy) and the disappearance of the phenomenal world. This, too, is an apocalyptic, cataclysmic realization.

Let us now ask again, In what way is it more helpful to be a spiritual guide than to be a psychotherapist? I am sure all of you know the proverbial story of the four blind men trying to describe an elephant. If we have a spiritual perspective, then we can see the whole elephant and only then can we know what an elephant is. If we only see part of an elephant and try to put together all this information, we will never really know what elephant is. Therefore, the broader our perspective on man, the more perfect our understanding will be. We can see then that to be a spiritual guide is far beyond any type of psychotherapy.

Something happens to us when our perspective expands. The Bible refers to this by stating: "As he [man] thinketh in his heart, so is he" (Proverbs 23:7). The broader our perspective on Reality, the more understanding, the more compassionate, the more inspired, the more perceptive, and the more capable we are to benefit people on all levels, even if they are in the stage of believing in a flat earth. Even then we have the intuitive wisdom of communicating with them in a beneficial way. But if we don't have that perspective, we are as the psychiatrist who has certain preconceived limitations within his specialty from which he cannot get out. He is boxed in, so to speak, in a particular knowledge in which he was trained.

No matter what wonderful contributions to psychotherapy were made by individuals in that field, it does not mean that they have already attained ultimate knowledge. The danger is that we can get attached to a particular frame of reference. There seems to be a fear in many to go beyond these viewpoints. They are afraid to expand their mental horizons. We may ask, What is this fear? This fear is an indication that we are cherishing what we already know and leaning on it for a false sense of security. The trouble with this kind of subjectivity is that it misinterprets reality and generates a great deal of anxiety. We cannot rely for information on feelings.

In this connection it may be helpful to consider the "five gates of hell." The "five gates of hell" are (1) sensualism, (2) emotionalism, (3) intellectualism, (4) personalism, (5) materialism.

What is sensualism? It is a mode of being-in-the-world where the primary preoccupation is with sensory awareness: pleasure and pain. It judges reality purely by sensory awareness. This is a very troublesome condition, for it leads to all sorts of disorders: disorders of the senses, of the skin, sexual problems, etc.

Emotionalism is a mode of being-in-the-world which is primarily preoccupied with emotional experiences and seeks to cognize reality on the basis of feelings. Emotionalists try to use their feelings as sources of information concerning what is and what is not real. Feelings provide misinformation, but they seem to us very valid. We are convinced that things are really the way they feel, which of course is a mistake. We cannot rely on feelings to provide us with valid information. Furthermore, people who become emotionally based have a tendency to develop anxiety neuroses and a wide variety of emotional disturbances.

The third gate of hell is intellectualism. Intellectualism is knowing about things and placing great importance on being known as knowing. Intellectualists are living filing cabinets and they like to display their contents. So the sensualist leans on his sensory perceptions, the emotional man uses his feelings as a source of information, and the intellectual tries to figure things out in his head. He is on a continuous "head trip." Various difficulties stem from intellectualism, such as contentiousness, headaches, high blood pressure, and various other somatizations.

The fourth gate of hell is personalism. Personalism is thinking about what others are thinking about what we are thinking. It can be very painful and disturbing when one is caught up in such ruminations. Personalists have difficulties with people, conflicts with friends, family, etc.

The fifth gate of hell is materialism. Materialists are involved in accumulating material objects and possessions.

The process of obtaining an open mind can be very frustrating and painful and even anxiety provoking. Besides the "five gates of hell" which have specific pathogenicity, there are three more factors which we must become aware of, namely, what we cherish, what we hate, and what we fear. The gates of hell comprise the things we are inclined to cherish: a sensualist will cherish his sensory perceptivity; an emotionalist will cherish his feelings; an intellectualist will cherish his knowledge; a personalist will cherish his relationships; and a materialist will cherish his possessions. So, then, the underlying common denominator in these modes is that we are inclined to cherish that which is familiar and that which other people cherish, because if two people cherish the same thing, they have something in common and it makes them feel good. It gives them the impression that they are on the right track. This is the basis of group formations, school loyalties, and loyalties to various ideologies. Anything that would threaten to deprive us of what we cherish, or invalidate what we cherish, will provoke fear and resentment. The more we are inclined to cherish any one of these "five gates" — or all of them — the more vulnerable and insecure we shall be in life, and the more we shall be given to anxiety reaction, resentfulness, frustration, and even hatred. Therefore, the Zen Master says: "Above all cherish nothing." In our language this saying translates as "Cherish only God," because "nothing" is a Buddhist God. In other words, God is no thing, and the Buddha nature is love, beauty, intelligence, harmony, peace, serenity, assurance, joy, health, freedom, perfect being. The Buddha nature is a synonym for the Christ consciousness. Thus, the gate of Paradise is to cherish nothing. "Thou shalt have no other gods before me" (Exodus 20:3) and "Thou shalt love the Lord thy God with all thy heart, and with all thy soul and with all thy mind" (Matthew 22:37).

The Bible says: "Prepare ye the way of the Lord; make straight in the desert a highway for our God" (Isaiah 40:3). What does that mean? We cannot produce grace, but we can study and meditate, and listen to some teachings which show us how to get rid of the obstacles to grace. And that is what we are engaged in here. Our aim is to prepare the way of the Lord, make straight a highway in the desert. Every mountain of selfishness must be brought low, and every valley of sin shall be exalted; the rough places must be made plain, and the crooked straight, so that we may become receptive to grace and inspired wisdom. "Every valley shall be exalted, and every mountain and hill shall be made low; and the crooked shall be made straight, and the rough places plain" (Isaiah 40:4). This is what we call being spiritually integrated and enlightened. We have an open and receptive consciousness where Divine Intelligence has the possibility of reaching us.

Righteous judgment requires inspired wisdom. Every moment of the day and night God is pouring out His love and wisdom to anyone who is receptive enough to hear it. Jesus was struggling with people who had various kinds of impediments to receiving the word of God, or who were hampered in their spiritual perceptivity. For instance, at one point he said: "For this people's heart is waxed gross, and their ears are dull of hearing, and their eyes they have closed; lest at any time they should see with their eyes, and hear with their ears, and should understand with their hearts, and should be converted, and I should heal them" (Matthew 13:15). This points to an epistemological problem. The knowledge of God requires us to purify our consciousness of all the things which we have been miseducated to cherish, because as long as we cherish certain things which we are accustomed to, we cannot receive, and we cannot perceive spiritually. Under such circumstances we do not know what is really going on; we only know what someone else is saying about what is going on.

In view of the fact that Metapsychiatry relies heavily on the Bible, especially the teachings of Jesus, the question frequently arises about the relationship between Metapsychiatry and religion. Is Metapsychiatry a new religion? Or, if it is not a religion, does it in any way interfere with traditional religious practices?

Essentially the question boils down to this: What does it mean to be religious and what does it mean to be spiritually enlightened? It is said that religions are more often than not involved with moralism, formalism, even ethnicity. For instance, a Polish Roman Catholic may find it difficult to be accepted in certain Catholic churches which are predominantly, say, Irish; or blacks may feel unwelcome in a prevalently white Protestant congregation, etc.

Unfortunately, religions in the past have tended to divide people and to foster intolerance, fear, guilt, and other forms of conflict. In contrast to this, spiritual enlightenment — which is the goal of Metapsychiatry — is concerned with existentially valid universal principles to enable man to love his neighbor as himself and be transcendentally compassionate to all.

However, the most fundamental difference can be found in the basic questions which constitute the point of departure between religion and Metapsychiatry. All formal religions start with one implicit question, namely, What should we do to please God? Metapsychiatry starts with radically different questions, namely, What is God? or, What is what really is? and, How is it possible to know what really is?

The religious question results in operationalism; the Metapsychiatric question leads to existentialism. Operationalism is concerned with mastery, influencing, and inevitably with manipulation, bribery, and fear. Existentialism is concerned with understanding what is in order to live in harmony with the Fundamental Order of Existence.

In the history of religions and civilization there have emerged from time to time certain exceptionally gifted individuals who hit upon the right questions and found right answers. These individuals appeared to have exceptional powers and wisdom, and they tried to convey their knowledge to the world, but the world always found it hard to hear the message and to learn to ask the right questions. Jesus is known to have exclaimed — perhaps somewhat despairingly — "Having eyes, see ye not? and having ears, hear ye not?" (Mark 8:18). And again: "And this is the condemnation, that light is come into the world, and men loved darkness rather than light, because their deeds were evil" (John 3:19). It is possible to surmise that the word "deeds" refers to operationalism.

Enlightened man actualizes within himself the principle which Jesus formulated the following way: "I can of mine own self do nothing" (John 5:30); "But the Father that dwelleth in me [omniactive Mind], he doeth the works" (John 14:10). Omniactive Mind expresses itself through man in specific types of necessary and useful activities from moment to moment. Therefore, man who is involved with mental busyness is disregarding the impulses of omniactive Mind.

In Metapsychiatry we do not worry much about Western or Eastern thought. The question we are concerned with is, "Is it existentially valid or not?" Here we have *the principle of existential validation.* This is a very useful idea which unifies all cultures by transcending them, and makes it possible to evaluate them in a pragmatic way. The values which come to us from various parts of the world, from various cultures, times, and ages, can be known as to their validity.

The principle of existential validation comes to us from Jesus Christ. Jesus formulated this principle of existential validation the following way: "Ye shall know them by their fruits" (Matthew 7:16). What does that mean? Any idea, or system of values, or religious system, anything that impinges on individual existence, can validate itself or disqualify itself by its consequences for the health and fulfillment of the individual. That which is existentially valid is subject to existential validation. If it is life enhancing, health promoting, increasing the capacity for love, wisdom, and beneficence of the individual, if it makes it possible for an individual to realize his inner potential, if it brings man into greater harmony with the Fundamental Order of Existence, it is valid. If it has a disruptive, pathogenic effect, it is not valid. This principle of existential validation liberates us from sectarianism and cultural isolation. It makes it possible to know what to consider seriously and appreciate and what can be dismissed out of hand. "Ye shall know them by their fruits." If this marvelous principle were more universally understood, there would be no more intolerance or prejudice, xenophobia, fear, religious hostilities, or political strife. It would be a unifying principle.

In Metapsychiatry, where the primary objective is the health and the fulfillment of the individual, the principle of existential validation is very important. The art of the healing dialogue is based on clarification of certain values which individuals have consciously or unconsciously espoused and which have resulted in a misdirected mode of being-in-the-world. If we grow up in a certain culture, we tend to accept unwittingly certain values which may be socially and culturally acceptable but which are existentially invalid. The result is that we wind up with a misdirected mode of being-in-the-world.

In Metapsychiatry pathology and sickness are considered manifestations of misdirected modes of being-in-the-world. Consequently, we do not treat diagnostic categories, neither do we treat personalities, nor do we treat diagnostic categories along traditional psychiatric lines (like schizophrenia, neurosis, manic-depressive states), and, furthermore, we do not diagnose people in a traditional way. What we treat is modes of being-in-the-world.

Let us be clear about the fact that there is no such thing as a person. Person is just a concept. "God is no respecter of persons," says the Bible (Acts 10:34). Man is not a person. He is an individual consciousness and this consciousness can be imbued with certain ideas. If these ideas are existentially valid, they manifest themselves in health, harmony, freedom, and fulfillment. If the ideas which fill an individual's consciousness are invalid, he will find suffering and various forms of disturbed and frustrated ways of being-in-the-world. The healing dialogue is based on a method which is called hermeneutic clarification of the underlying value system which governs the thinking and the activities of an individual. We have already mentioned ambition, for instance, as an invalid value. If we subject ambition to an existential analysis, we discover that ambition, while socially approved and accepted, is existentially invalid because it really creates a conflict within individuals. It is moving in two directions at the same time, forward and backward. The same applies to the idea of personal success; it is not possible to pursue success without, at the same time, courting failure. So the success-hunting individual has a misdirected mode of being-in-the-world.

Every one of us is like a sponge which has absorbed certain ideas about what is good, what is desirable, and what is important; and it is these ideas which determine our mode of being-in-the-world. The question now is, How can we discern the ideas which govern an individual's mode of being-in-the-world? This is accomplished through a method which is called phenomenological analysis. *Phenomenological analysis* requires us to be trained in phenomenological perceptivity. Everyone has the faculty of phenomenological perceptivity, but it needs to be developed through training. The basic requirement for this faculty is the open mind. The father of phenomenology is Edmund Husserl, the German philosopher, who called this feat of the mind époché, which translated from the French means "bracketing." It refers to the need to put everything that we already know into brackets and put it up on a shelf, so to speak, so as to be able to confront whatever reveals itself in a nonjudgmental open-minded way. Once we have learned to confront situations and individuals in that manner in an interview situation, we will find that suddenly things reveal themselves and we have a clear picture of what makes an individual "tick" — what values, what objectives, what ambitions, what wants, what desires, what misconceptions, what mis-education, what ideas, govern his mode of being-in-the-world. Jesus spoke of the need for this kind of open mind when he said: "Except ye [be converted, and] become as little children, ye shall not enter into the kingdom of heaven" (Matthew 18:3), which means in order to be receptive to inspired wisdom and to realize spiritual values and Spiritual Reality, this capacity for the open-minded confrontation of that which reveals itself from moment to moment is an absolute requirement.

Self-confirmatory ideation is a mental process whereby we are constantly seeking to reassure ourselves that we exist. It can take physical form, it can take emotional form, or it can take intellectual form. The essence of personalism reveals this universal tendency toward self-confirmatory ideation (ideation means persistent thinking about something). When we are involved in personism or personalism we ruminate over our thoughts about what other people may be thinking about what we are thinking. The essence of personalism is self-confirmatory ideation and it can result in paranoia.

Some people do not like the term "self-confirmatory ideation," and they prefer to talk about egotism instead, but actually this is not just simple egotism. The basis for self-confirmatory ideation is the dread of nonbeing. Everyone is scared of nothingness, of nonbeing, of annihilation, of being nothing, of dying, of being ignored. This is a universal fear and is called "existential anxiety." It is this existential anxiety which we try to combat through a process of self-confirmatory ideation. And the more scared we are, the more intense the desire to confirm ourselves in one form or another; there are a million ways in which we can reassure ourselves that we really exist, and so it is an almost inseparable aspect of the human condition. Of course, it can be healed.

How can existential anxiety be healed? How can we be liberated from this dread of nonbeing? Salvation, liberation, resurrection, healing, enlightenment have a common objective, namely, to help us to be unafraid and to live with a sense of assurance that we are not alone, that we are not separated, that we are not what we seem to be, but that "neither are we otherwise." It is possible to know ourselves in a larger context. In proportion that we come to realize this existential fact, in that proportion the "dread of nothingness," as Heidegger calls it, will be mitigated, or diminished, and the compulsive urge for self-confirmatory ideation will leave us, and it will be possible to live in PAGL, which is peace, assurance, gratitude, and love.

A more advanced understanding, based on existential research, has abandoned the concept of "person" and sees man as an individual consciousness. Personhood implies self-existence, whereas an individual consciousness is an aspect of the divine consciousness. We can have great appreciation of each other as individual manifestations of divine consciousness. This may appear strange to some people because all the great knowledgeable people in the field of theology and psychology speak of personhood. But, of course, there is progress going on and progress in understanding often requires us to revise our ways of conceptualizing. Great progress is being made in understanding the brain, for instance, and the nature of reality. A group of scientists (Bohm, Pribram) has developed a new way of looking at reality which is quite revolutionary. They have developed a holographic paradigm of reality. Holography is a form of photography which uses laser beams to project three-dimensional pictures into space; the projected image seems real and seems to be there in three dimensions, while it is only illusion. The idea is that the human brain is a hologram and what we see is not really what is. The material world is but a holographic projection and the brain functions as a lens which transmutes certain frequencies of vibration coming from the Infinite Source and projects them as material forms. These scientists' claim is that there is no such thing as solid matter anywhere, that this is a phenomenal world, and everything that seems to have form and shape and solidity and texture is just a holographic image. The brain interprets reality and the universe as material and finite.

When the question was asked, How is it possible that we all see the same thing? the point was made that our brains are conditioned by the culture and our common assumptions. Thus we have very similar lenses and we interpret what we see in a similar way, with only subtle differences. It is said that mystics were able to perceive reality not through their brains, and they could see what ordinary people cannot see, because most of us rely on our brains to interpret what we see. The mystic can apparently transcend this holographic instrument and discern reality in a nonfocused manner. ESP, psychokinesis, seeing at a distance, and other phenomena are also explained by this research. Time and space are explained as results of the brain's way of interpreting reality; that is, there is no such thing as time and space. For instance, if someone through ESP becomes aware of something happening, say, in California, the explanation is that California is simply not there but here; if there is no space, then there is no such thing as "there," and there is no such thing as "was." There is only "is," because there is no time.

Thus we go beyond the concept of personhood and endeavor to see one another as individual divine consciousnesses, and that is just another way of saying that man is the image and likeness of God. The only reality about us is consciousness. It is becoming more and more evident that consciousness survives the body. Therefore, the more clearly we shall understand ourselves as consciousness, the less afraid we shall be of dying. The less we understand this, the more we are pushed by fear into self-confirmatory ideation and out of that push come all sorts of problems.

We have to clarify the issue of consciousness. There is consciousness and there is the content of consciousness. One can be conscious of garbage. One can be conscious of two and two being five. We can be conscious of many invalid thoughts. An unenlightened consciousness may have many mistaken and misguided ideas filling it and distracting it from what really is.

The fantastic things which Jesus was demonstrating, such as walking through closed doors, walking on water, transporting himself instantaneously from one place to another, all illustrate his understanding that there is no "there," only "here"; that there is neither time nor space. Solidity of matter, distance of space, or duration of time — these were of no consequence to him.

So far we have spoken of the "five gates of hell" and of self-confirmatory ideation, and now we may consider the four "Ws." They are: (1) Who am I? (2) What am I? (3) Where am I? (4) What is my purpose in life? As can be seen, this is a meditation in our "closet," the secret compartment of our consciousness. The answer to the first "W" is: I am an image and likeness of God, a manifestation of Love-Intelligence. Omniactive Love-Intelligence is an existential name for God. God is also omnipresent, omnipotent, omniscient. The second, What am I? is answered by: I am a divine consciousness. Where am I? I live and move and have my being in omniactive Divine Mind. The fourth "W," What is my purpose in life? is answered: My purpose is to be a beneficial presence in the world. Students of Metapsychiatry meditate on the four "Ws" daily. People sometimes ask what the distinction is between the first and the second "W." The first refers to identity; the second refers to substance.

What is the value of meditating on the four "Ws"? It establishes us in the awareness of the right context. To see ourselves and others in the right context is very important. For instance, the question was asked, How do you encourage your children or praise them without indoctrinating them in self-confirmatory thinking? If, for instance, a child brings home from school good marks and the parent wants to praise him, how does he praise him without making the child proud or egotistical, vain or self-confirmatory? If a parent criticizes a child, he is teaching him to be self-confirmatory in a negative way. If he praises the child, he is doing the same thing because then the child will be self-confirmatory in a positive way; if he tells the child he is great, it is the same as if he tells him he is no good; in all cases the result is self-confirmatory thinking. And we know that self-confirmatory ideation is the basis of all problems in life. It was said before that the four "Ws" help us to see ourselves and others in the right context. Unless parents are able to see the child in the context of God, as an expression of Divine Love-Intelligence, no matter how they phrase their words, it will lead to self-confirmatory thinking in the child. But if they have the right viewpoint on the child, then implicitly it will be communicated to the child that God is manifesting Himself in the good work. Clearly, it is not a matter of handling things; it is a matter of seeing and knowing something. When things don't work out, we know that it was a manifestation of ignorance. The child made a mistake. He was not sufficiently aware of who he is and where he is and what he is. Therefore he made a mistake. So we do not blame him. We blame ignorance. And when we praise him, we do not praise him. We praise the Lord for making it possible for the child to do well. The context of parental seeing and thinking is crucial in being able to praise and criticize without ill effects. Without that, no matter what technique and what words we use, they will always be personalized anyway. And that is how meditation on the four "Ws" can help us.

It is a fact that the outside world (outside of the home) sees the child as a little person, an autonomous entity entirely apart from God — who may not even exist, or perhaps exists only as a symbol — but isn't such a child, whose parents are able to see him in the right context, greatly blessed?

In spiritual guidance it is important not to judge and not to blame under any circumstance. The moment we are judging and blaming, we have disqualified ourselves from the possibility of being helpful; therefore, we observe but we do not judge. In judging we approve and disapprove. In observing we clarify. Only clarification is helpful. Blaming leads to self-confirmatory ideation. Sometimes an individual whom we have loaded with guilt and blame may seem to have reformed, but while his behavior may have changed, his thinking processes have possibly become more self-confirmatory. So it is possible to help someone outwardly, while aggravating his condition inwardly. The basic problem is the tendency to self-confirmatory ideation. This must be guarded against.

The Curtain of Time

The concept of self-confirmatory ideation is particularly important to spiritual guides. Among religiously inclined individuals it is not unusual to come across some who can quote the Bible from beginning to end and seem very religious, and yet their interest in spiritual life is not authentic. I am reminded of a young man, a patient in a mental hospital who was a convert to Christianity, who to all appearances was very sincerely interested in God, but was not able to live right. He was frequently getting into trouble with his family and others, and was irritating people. Occasionally he would hallucinate. His was a case of pathological religiosity. Sometimes it is difficult to know whether an individual is sincerely religious, spiritually minded, or mentally disturbed. One thing is crucial in recognizing pathology, namely, the presence of the element of self-confirmatory ideation. When an individual — no matter how theologically sophisticated — is exploiting his knowledge for his own self-aggrandizement and is referring to himself overtly or covertly, crudely or in subtle ways, he is bearing witness to himself under the guise of bearing witness to God or to the truth. Here we can know that we are faced with a serious problem. The differential diagnostic point in such situations is the element of self-confirmatory ideation.

Health requires self-transcendence. The healthy, spiritually minded individual loses himself in Christ, while in pathological religiosity there is no self-transcendence. If we understand this important differential diagnostic sign, we will also know how to help such individuals. In Metapsychiatry there are no special techniques, only principles. One of the principles is: "If you know what, you know how." If we can discern the problem and if we understand the process of being healthy, of being truly spiritually minded, we will know how to approach such an individual in a helpful way.

The most essential requirement for a spiritual guide is the attainment of such integration that the very quality of his presence is beneficial. Beyond this we have to know that the main feature of healthy spirituality is self-transcendence. In addition to this, there is another important element. It is described in the Bible that Jesus was accused by his listeners of bearing witness of himself. "Thou bearest record of thyself; thy record is not true" (John 8:13). The Bible clearly states that if someone bears witness to himself, his spirituality is not authentic. Jesus' reply to this accusation bears on our work in spiritual guidance. He said: "Though I bear record of myself, yet my record is true; for I know whence I come and whither I go; but ye cannot tell whence I came, and whither I go" (John 8:14). We see here the importance of the four "Ws," the realization of which must take place in a patient, or any other individual, as to who he is, what he is, where he is, and what his purpose in life is. If there is a basic understanding of our identity, of our substance, of our location, and of the quality of our presence, then self-confirmatory ideation will cease to be a problem.

It may take a certain amount of creative intelligence to be able to communicate this to an individual, but that cannot be taught. It comes through inspiration based on purity of motive in the healer. Purity of motive makes it possible to be inspired moment to moment in conveying these ideas in such a manner that it may become meaningful to the individual in distress.

In spiritual guidance we do not resort to techniques based on preconceived notions as is done in psychoanalysis or various forms of psychotherapy. We rely on inspired wisdom. Inspired wisdom is creative intelligence obtaining in receptive consciousness from moment to moment under conditions of PAGL (which is peace, assurance, gratitude, and love). Inspired wisdom makes it possible to communicate meaningfully with individuals who are in need of guidance. It is a spiritual method of responding to people in need, and it can be learned by all who have given up relying on feelings, the known, on what we think or what someone else has thought, what is in vogue, or what is official, etc. Inspired wisdom comes when there is a willingness to rely on God unconditionally. It is the open mind.

Heidegger speaks of the *Gelassenheit zu den Dingen*, which means it is all right to have everything, to have technology, to have possessions, to have information, to have filing cabinets, to know about everything as long as one is not clinging to these things. We are not advocating ignorance but freedom. The issue is open-minded receptivity to Divine Intelligence.

Let us return to the concept of self-confirmatory ideation as a diagnostic criterion for pathological religiosity and also for all forms of pathology that we can run into in life. One of the forms of self-confirmatory ideation which is frequently encountered in academic circles is the cherishing of what one already knows. It is very difficult not to lean on what we already know. There is nothing wrong with knowing, but we must be alert to the tendency to lean on the known for a sense of security. Such a sense of security is acquired at a great price; if we lean on what we already know and cling to it, we cannot learn anything new, and certainly we are not open to God, to inspiration. Our lives become less and less creative and more and more routinized. Among psychiatrists and psychotherapists we can distinguish two kinds: the artisans and the artists. Even in spiritual guidance one can imagine that some individuals might tend to become artisans. We certainly know that some clergymen are just artisans who perfunctorily perform certain services. Their sermons are boring. They seldom come up with an original idea. Their lives are uncreative. To live and work creatively it is necessary to lean on God, and that requires courage. It is somewhat like trying to float on emptiness. But once we have learned this, it is easier. Life then becomes most interesting. We are never bored — and more than that — we are not boring. Sometimes we seek parameters for functioning. We want to lean on parameters. This hampers creativity and inspiration because we then have preconceived ideas as to what should be. We may rationalize that an individual isn't yet ready for this, that he must first be psychotherapeutized along Adlerian or Sullivanian lines, etc., and that perhaps afterward he could be guided toward the spiritual path.

There is, of course, a great tendency to think that in order to be a spiritual guide one must first be a psychotherapist. But the glorious thing about spiritual guidance is that it transcends all psychotherapy; a spiritual guide does not have to be a psychotherapist. A spiritual guide has to be a divinely inspired *understander* and *clarifier* of an individual's mode of being-in-the-world. Someone may say, If you want to run, you have to first learn to walk, but in spiritual guidance we want to "fly." The Zen Master Suzuki was once asked, "How does it feel to be an enlightened man?" Suzuki replied, "Oh, just like an ordinary man, except about two inches above ground."

If we take as an example the ability to float, we see that in floating one leans completely on buoyancy, and so it is with God; when we lean on God, we lean on seemingly nothing. Some people get the hang of it right away and they can float. The analogy about floating approximates what it is to let go of all the cherished idols we cling to, and learn to face life with nothing but God.

The issue of time is another problem which is very interesting to consider. It is called the issue of temporality. Temporality is closely associated with character. There are three categories of character disorder from which we are inclined to suffer. One is pride, another is ambition, and the third is vanity. If we inquire into the temporality of these character disorders, we find that pride is always related to the past. Ambition is oriented toward the future, and vanity is in the present. People who live in the past are inclined toward pride; people who look forward to the future have a tendency to become ambitious, and people who live in the present like to look into the mirror. Associated with these three categories of character problem is the flip side of each. The flip side of pride is shame; the flip side of ambition is fear, while vanity's flip side is embarrassment. Were we to tell someone, "Your problem is that you are proud," will he be able to stop being proud? Not likely. None of these character problems responds to a direct attack. Therefore, such an approach is not helpful. In psychotherapy these problems become horrendous because they are unyielding. In Metapsychiatry we can talk about such a problem without condemning it or without demanding of the patient that he stop being proud or ambitious. We don't say, "You shouldn't be proud" or "You shouldn't be ambitious" or "You shouldn't be vain." We can say instead, "I discern that your suffering has something to do with certain ways of relating to time." Or, "It seems that you are living in the past," or, "You are thinking too much about the past and about yourself in the past," or "You are future oriented," or "Your problem seems to be connected with temporality." We do not say, "You shouldn't live in the past, or in the future." We try to clarify these problems in terms of how they are connected with thinking about time.

Our definition of mental health speaks of being a beneficial presence; a presence is not the same as living in the present. There is a very helpful passage in the Bible, in the book of Ecclesiastes, which says: "That which hath been is now; and that which is to be hath already been; and God requireth that which is past" (Ecclesiastes 3:15). This passage describes the problem of being time-bound. Unenlightened man is stuck in the dimension of time, but Reality is timeless. Therefore, if we are time-bound, we cannot be in touch with Reality. The only way to be healed of pride, ambition, and vanity is to abolish time. How do we abolish time? By learning to appreciate timelessness. In creative, inspired living, whenever God is speaking to us, at that instant when inspiration reaches consciousness, the temporo-spatial coordinates of experience are suspended. By learning to appreciate timelessness we become liberated from the imprisoning effect of time and are healed of these three common forms of character disorder.

God is not in the past and God is not in the future and God is not in the present. Where is God? We have to have some verbal expression for that dimension of Reality where God can be found: It is eternity, *the timeless now.* It is good to understand the difference between the present and the timeless now. The present, the past, and the future are time frames, and God cannot be framed. Therefore, we need a certain concept which is extratemporal, and that is the timeless now which is synonymous with eternity. Eternity is timeless.

This, of course, is of great practical value whenever we are disturbed by something that has happened in the past. Most people have had some unpleasant, regrettable, painful, disturbing experiences that happened in the past and that they fear never being able to get over. The right understanding of timelessness and of God's omnipresence makes it possible to pray effectively for the healing of the past.

Recently, a very disturbed gentleman came for help. He had given a speech in a certain organization where he was a guest. He got carried away, and what he was saying to the people in that audience was very disturbing to them. As he spoke, he lost control of himself; he did a lot of bragging and made some provocative statements. Afterward he was crestfallen; he received letters accusing him of having caused people suffering by what he said. He didn't know what to do. We considered the possibility of healing the past through prayer. We considered the fact that God is not in a time frame but in the timeless now, and that what is needed is to catch a glimpse of God's presence and to know that in the presence of God all things are healed. Therefore, we proceeded to lift the "curtain of time" and peek, so to speak, underneath this curtain and behold the healing presence of Divine Love. We further considered what the curtain of time was made of. This curtain of time, i.e., the existential structure of time, is made of dreams, fantasies, and imagination. The past is a dream, the future is a fantasy, and the present is imagination. A Zen Master put it this way: "The past is gone, the future is not yet, and the present eludes us."

As long as we live in time, we do not perceive Reality. We see our own thoughts about Reality. By peeking under the curtain of time we seek to behold Reality, the presence of the healing power of Divine Love. Such perception can relieve us of the burden of past mistakes. How is that possible? It is the realization that we do not have the power to cause unalterable wrong, because God is the only power and the only intelligence, and what was is, and that which is, is not under our control but under God's control. Therefore what is needed is a healing to take place in the consciousness of the individual who is disturbed by what was. As he gains peace in the awareness of God's presence, the past is erased and is healed. An interesting thing happened in the aforementioned case; after we had peeked under the curtain of time, this individual became peaceful and grateful in the knowledge that God can heal the past. The next day he received a telephone call from the man in charge of the organization where he gave his talk, and found that things had changed. His talk was, in fact, appreciated and no ill effect remained from what he said. Thus we had confirming evidence of the fact that it is possible to heal the past by contacting God in the timeless now. This is a very comforting realization. We do not have to suffer for past mistakes. All we need is to understand the three "Rs" of Metapsychiatry.

The three "Rs" of Metapsychiatry are as follows: recognition, regret, and reorientation.

When we have a problem we need to recognize its meaning. Then we need to regret it, because problems usually ensue from mistakes or insufficient understanding. Let us clarify what we mean by meaning. Meaning must not be confused with cause. As we said earlier, we transcend cause-and-effect thinking. Meaning is the mental equivalent of a problem, of a phenomenon. Phenomena are externalizations of thought processes. Therefore, if we seek to understand the meaning of a problem, we seek to discover the underlying thinking processes which have expressed themselves as a problem. Thought processes have a tendency to become phenomena and become perceptually accessible. By recognition we mean coming to understand the meaning of a problem. In other words, we have to see that we made a mistake, that we were mistaken and in what way we were mistaken. In the above case, the man got carried away with himself and spoke on a level which was both self-confirmatory and above the heads of the audience. That created the disturbance. He came to recognize the meaning of that problem and he regretted it sincerely. Then he sought reorientation by peeking under the curtain of time and realizing that God is the only power and the only presence and the only intelligence and has the power to heal the past, the future, the present, and everything. In that realization he found his peace and that peace was the healing, which then was confirmed by the telephone call. It is possible to heal the past because the past is a dream, the future a fantasy, and the present imagination.

We spoke earlier about phenomenological perceptivity. It is a method described and explained by Edmund Husserl whereby an open-minded confrontation with that which reveals itself can make it possible for a spiritual guide to discern the meaning of a problem and shed light on it for the patient, thus helping him to understand it. This kind of shedding light we call *hermeneutic elucidation*. It helps the individual to attain the first R, namely, recognition. Recognition entails knowing the meaning of the suffering — not "why" we are suffering — but what the meaning of it is, i.e., its mental equivalent. The next step is regret, which would correspond to repentance, followed by the reorientation process where the mistaken mental thought processes are corrected through a confrontation with Divine Reality. In that correction the outlook of the individual is spiritualized and healing takes place.

Recently a man was complaining about a hernia. As we were talking about this and his other problems, it became clear that he had a mode of being-in-the-world in which he was exerting much effort to get people to feel sorry for him. He was in the habit of exerting himself to get his family, his friends, and even business associates and strangers to feel sorry for him. This was a method of self-confirmatory manipulation. It became clear that his hernia was an expression of that effort over some years. This was clarified to him. He could see it. He recognized it. But he did not regret it. He then had surgery performed. The hernia was repaired. He enjoyed the experience, praised the surgeon, and spoke of the wonderful care he received in the hospital. The whole experience was right down his alley, since people were solicitous of him. After the operation he seemed happy, but he hadn't stopped exerting himself to get people to feel sorry for him. This mode of operating continued. A short time afterward his hernia returned. He could see that this was his way of confirming himself. He could see that he was doing it. But he had not realized that there is a more intelligent way to live. He was not ready to take step No. 2. He did not regret it. What needs to be healed, then, is this idea which is in his mind, that the successful way to live is to have the power to get people to feel sorry for him.

Contrary to conventional thinking in the field, this is not a psychosomatic case; psychosomatic implies that the body can get hurt by the mind. But this is an obsolete concept. There is no such thing any more as psychosomatic medicine. There is only phenomenology. Mind and body are one, and what we see in the world is the manifestation of certain ways of thinking. Thought is the basic stuff of life. Thought is a unit of mental energy which can manifest itself as speech, as activity, as behavior, or as symptom. The hernia in the above case needed to be repaired surgically and it will probably have to be done again, but all that work will be of no help unless this individual's thinking is redeemed; so the issue is the mode of being-in-the-world. It is the basic ethic of psychotherapy, and particularly of spiritual guidance, that we cannot heal anyone unless he has reached the point of sincerely desiring to be healed, and it would be a trespass to try to heal anyone against his will.

The first of the eleven Metapsychiatric principles is as follows: "Thou shalt have no other interests before the good of God, which is spiritual blessedness." The issue of interestedness is crucial. We have to reach a point where we are more interested in living in harmony with God, which we call omniactive Love-Intelligence, than anything else. Perhaps that is what Kierkegaard meant by "willing one thing." Purity of heart means purity of interest, wholehearted interest in spiritual good. What is spiritual good? It is PAGL (peace, assurance, gratitude, and love). The interesting thing about PAGL is that it is also a criterion which can help us to know whether we are on the right track on any issue in life, or whether we are just deceiving ourselves. If there is no awareness of PAGL, chances are we are just deceiving ourselves, which is very easy to do. PAGL is a sort of landmark, or a sign, which can help us to know whether or not we are on the right track. And when we are praying about any problem we may face, if we reach the point which we call the "PAGL point," then we know that the problem is healed. If we meditate and reach PAGL point in our meditation, we can stop. There is a sense of assurance that whatever we are facing has been healed.

Psychoanalysis does not have the awareness of the dimension of the spirit. What it is working with are purely humanistic concepts. It is an attempt to change the past by altering the present. But the present is still a time frame. It is not really possible to change the past by altering the present. It is possible to be healed only if we succeed in abolishing the past ("And God requireth that which is past," Ecclesiastes 3:15).

We are also trying to understand the possibilities beyond what has been experienced until now. What were considered limited possibilities are gradually receding. We are continually expanding the horizons of limitation and pushing into areas which have not yet been realized. It is better to be idealistic than realistic. Had the Wright brothers been realistic, there would be no aviation today.

Let us ask again, What is spiritual guidance? At the outset of these lectures it was stated that spiritual guidance is not an activity. It is a quality of consciousness which is receptive to inspired wisdom and which is responsive to manifest needs. If we are going to teach spiritual guidance, then the primary issue is learning the open-minded receptivity to creative Intelligence which meets every moment's requirement. The open mind is the central issue in spiritual guidance.

Conventional psychological thinking knows only sensations, emotions, and intellect as basic factors. It presumes that if one is intellectual then one supposedly has to learn to feel. If one is emotional, one has to learn to think. If one is sensual, one has to sort of distribute these three human experiences evenly so that one may become an integrated human person, with one's feelings, sensations, and intellectual thinking ability in balance. And this supposedly makes for a healthy person. This is the avowed purpose of psychotherapist manipulation of man, namely, to bring about a balance. But we cannot mix psychology with spirituality, just as we cannot mix oil with water. What is needed is to understand what spirituality really is. When we confuse our feeling responses to situations and issues with intuition, we just don't know what we are talking about. The way we feel about something is not the same as having intuitive understanding of something. Intuition is a colloquial word for inspiration. Intuition based on feelings is not intuition. It is subjectivity. Furthermore, it is totally unreliable and is inseparable from judgment. But true inspiration, spiritual insight, is on a different level of consciousness.

In Metapsychiatry we distinguish two sources of thought: one is the "sea of mental garbage," from where all invalid thoughts, which we are constantly being flooded by, come. We can surmise that Teilhard de Chardin would call this the "noosphere." The other source of thought is the "infinite ocean of Love-Intelligence," from where all intelligent, valid, constructive, helpful, and creative ideas come. The dividing line between the human and the spiritual modes of awareness we call the firmament. If we are going to be spiritual guides, we cannot mix up the two; we cannot practice psychotherapy one minute and spiritual guidance the next minute. Those who

wish to practice psychotherapy are entitled to study psychotherapy, but those who are interested in spiritual growth and
realization must be helped to rise above the firmament so that
they may have a Divine perspective on Reality rather than a
human one.

Above the firmament, in the "ocean of Love-Intelligence,"
man does not become callous, unfeeling, and intellectual;
man becomes intelligent, infinitely compassionate, spiritually
loving, serenely dignified, peaceful, assured, grateful, and harmonious. He lives in a different dimension of consciousness
which transcends all psychology (including Jungian psychology), psychotherapy, psychoanalysis, and other human systems. And that is what Metapsychiatry understands to be
spiritual guidance. There is a difference and a radical separation between psychology and spiritual consciousness. Anyone
who mixes the two just does not understand what the difference really is, and a great deal of confusion follows this kind
of mixing.

The vast majority of people want to make a go of life below the firmament, and they try to manipulate and conduct
things in the "sea of mental garbage." There are a great many
pleasures in the "sea of mental garbage," and there is a great
deal of suffering and confusion there as well. As the Bible
says: "Wide is the gate, and broad is the way, that leadeth to
destruction, and many there be which go in thereat: Because
strait is the gate, and narrow is the way, which leadeth unto
life, and few there be that find it" (Matthew 7:13–14). And we
may add: "Few there are who are interested in finding it." But
it is not our job to make people interested. That is God's job. If
we are going to be spiritual guides, this is what it is all about:
"the straight and the narrow." We must be prepared to face
the fact that there will be a great many people who will not
want to have any part of the narrow way. We must understand
that this is not a matter of liking, disliking, or arguing about
it. It is something to contemplate. Is it possible to debate or argue about the merits of two and two being four? It can only
be considered by everyone and contemplated. If we are sin-

cerely seeking God, we must eventually commit ourselves to this. This is spiritual guidance. Everything else is just messing around in the "sea of mental garbage."

As mentioned before, the basic issue in training for spiritual guidance is learning the open-minded confrontation of that which reveals itself from moment to moment, which is entirely different from training for psychotherapy or the legal profession or philosophy or any academic subject.

Metapsychiatry is offering the tools necessary for a spiritual guide in the form of the three "Rs." It also explains what recognition requires of a spiritual guide: it requires recognizing an individual's mode of being-in-the-world through phenomenological perceptivity. So a spiritual guide needs to discern a patient's or a client's mode of being-in-the-world and the meaning of his presenting problem, so that he can hermeneutically clarify it. He then explains that regret of the mistake on the part of the client and his reorientation are requisite for a healing to take place. The healing is always one of the "signs following," as the Bible states. When consciousness is elevated above the firmament, human problems are healed. This is not psychotherapy. It is phenomenology. Training in phenomenological perceptivity rests on the attainment of the open mind.

It may be helpful at this point to clarify the difference between intellectualism and intelligence. To put it into simple language, *intellectualism* is a desire to be known as knowing. This was designated previously as one of the gates of hell. *Intelligence,* on the other hand, is the ability to utilize, express, and communicate ideas in a clear and concise form.

We might mention here that spiritual consciousness is not very popular or highly valued when it comes to individuals being committed to it. It may be popular to profess it, to talk about it, to read about it in books, but not to commit oneself to it. There are two ways we can become committed to spiritual life: one is through suffering, the other is through wisdom. It is, of course, difficult to become totally committed to the spiritual life through wisdom alone. Even Jesus is described in the Bible as having been "in all points tempted like as we are" (Hebrews 4:15).

At times it happens that individuals come to us ostensibly for psychotherapy while actually seeking to find God. Therefore, we have to tune in on the wavelength upon which an individual is starting out with us, and gradually clarify the difference through the process of hermeneutic elucidation.

The eighth principle in Metapsychiatry states: "Problems are lessons designed for our edification." This is a very important principle because it helps us not to be afraid of problems, but actually welcome them as opportunities for growth. Every time a problem is understood in its meaning and is clarified and appropriately regretted, it leads to reorientation and we ascend a rung on the ladder of consciousness.

A young wife and mother reported the following: "It came to my attention recently that I go around all the time cherishing a completely fictitious concept of my husband, and I am interpreting everything that is going on in the home in the light of an idea which has no relation whatsoever to his view of himself. When I saw this, I became increasingly embarrassed about my hateful point of view of him. I seem to be locked in a dream, my own dream, which I am projecting onto other individuals to the detriment of the entire family, including myself. I have suffered for many years from the idea that I am being hated. Now the question which preoccupies me is, how could I get out of my dream?"

The way to be healed of such problems is by realizing that our dreams are not ours. The dreams which we are dreaming are not our dreams. They are just suggestions and fantasies which have taken hold in our consciousness; they happen to be there but they are not ours. Only what God gives us can be ours and God does not give us hateful dreams or unloving ideas. Unless we recognize that these things are no part of our true being, we can never be helped. If there really were a hateful individual, he would be beyond hope. Hateful thoughts do not belong to the man God created. He is a pure consciousness of Love-Intelligence. Just because certain factors are messing up our life experience, it does not mean that they are ours, that they belong to us, or that we are such individuals. These thoughts must be separated from us in order that we may be healed.

Some garbage thoughts are being transmitted from generation to generation and are at times cherished like heirlooms. Still, they are no part of our true being, even if we got them from our parents or grandparents. This is good to know, because if we were to blame ourselves, there would be no way to be healed. When we blame ourselves we claim ownership and are secretly proud of our disastrous heritage. So the dreams we are dreaming are not our dreams. The prejudices which we feel and express are not our prejudices, they are just prejudices. If we walk in the streets of New York City and our faces get dirty from the soot and smog, that does not mean that we are dirty people. It only means that we happen to have dirt on our faces. The dirt is no part of our true being. Our insanities are no part of our true being either. That realization is very helpful when it comes to healing and liberation. We disavow these ideas and we endeavor to behold our pristine purity as expressions of Divine Love-Intelligence.

The Bible says: "The Spirit itself beareth witness with our spirit, that we are the children of God: And if children, then heirs; heirs of God and joint-heirs with Christ" (Romans 8:16–17). The wave bears witness to the ocean and the ocean to the wave. The wave is the ocean and the ocean is the wave. And so the son of man is the son of God and God expresses himself through the son of man, and man is the manifestation of God. The only way that God can be known is through man expressing the qualities of God. That's what we really are.

Garbage thoughts and dreams are no part of our being, just as pollution is no part of the sea. All the garbage in the sea may be moving with the waves, but pollution is not the sea. It is not even part of the sea. It does not belong to the sea. The sea is pure and always was pure. The garbage is entirely separate from the sea. But the wave and the sea are one as man and

God are one. The purity, the perfection, and the love of God constitute the real individual.

Whenever something needs to be healed, this separation must be clearly realized. The moment this is clearly realized, the healing can take place.

Sometimes people get panicky about "their own" thoughts. But if they realize that what seems to be their own thoughts are not really their own thoughts, they do not have to get panicky. Only God's thoughts constitute the real man.

There are certain aspects of mental pollution which create in us experiences. For instance, hate is exciting; interaction is entertaining; intimidation can be overwhelming, etc. When we understand the illusory nature of these experiences, they can be successfully transcended, especially interaction, which seems to be the most ubiquitous element in human experience. Interaction seems particularly desirable when we feel alone, isolated, neglected, ignored, or unloved. These conditions conjure up a dread of nothingness, which then leads to a desire to stir up some interaction.

I know a couple who had a very stormy marriage. For many years they had frequent fights. In exploring the problem, we found that the wife was terrified of solitude and quietness. She could not stand being in the house because it was too quiet. This gave us the clue as to what the problem was. It was the dread of nothingness, and the marital squabbles were but a form of entertainment and reassurance that they are really there as individual beings.

On the spiritual path we are studying to realize the glory of our "nothingness." Unenlightened man clamors for confirmation of his personal somethingness. Heidegger made the dread of nothingness the central theme of his philosophy. ("Nothingness, in contrast to all that seems to be, is the veil of being.") When we realize the true nature of being, we come to understand that nothingness is not dreadful but supremely comforting, because nothingness is allness, for that is what really is. It is not nothing but the divine essence of everyone.

At this point true compassion can emerge as love based on

understanding that the garbage is not part of real being. Compassion, then, requires the presence of enlightened love. It is clear then that compassion cannot be turned on at will. Real compassion requires some understanding of what is man and what is not man. Here it is helpful to distinguish between compassion, empathy, and sympathy. The compassionate man says, "I love you because I understand you." The empathizing man says, "I know how you feel." The sympathizing man says, "I feel for you."

Human sentiments like empathy and sympathy have little to do with Reality and are devoid of healing power. They have a temporary soothing effect, but they do not heal. Quite to the contrary, they tend to make a reality of the problem. True compassion heals because it is based on understanding of the truth of man as an expression of divine consciousness where nothing enters "that defileth...or maketh a lie" (Revelation 21:27).

Time and Timelessness

Metapsychiatry is timeless. What do we mean by that? In Metapsychiatry we are not working in the dimension of time. Metapsychiatry is ahistorical, acausal, and nonteleological. This means we are not interested in the history of the patient; we are not interested in why he is sick and who is to blame for it; we are not interested in the purpose for which he is sick.

Temporality has a lot to do with character, and we have described certain problems associated with it, as well as their flip sides: pride and shame; vanity and embarrassment; ambition and fear. It is now becoming clearer that these characterological factors have their own temporality: pride and shame are in the past, vanity and embarrassment are always in the present, and ambition and fear are of the future. So we have here six characterological factors which have their own specific temporality. If we abolish the temporality, we abolish the problem. If there is no past, we cannot be proud or ashamed. If there is no present, we cannot be vain or embarrassed. If there is no future, it makes no sense to be ambitious or even afraid.

Suppose someone said, But ambition is important; couldn't I retain at least a little ambition? But the question is, Is it possible to be ambitious and be free of fear? Certainly not. If we want to be free of fear, we must sacrifice ambition. We cannot make a deal with the devil. There is no possibility of living a fearless life as long as we are ambitious. The moment we are future oriented, there is fear.

So let us face the fact that if we don't want to be ashamed and prideful, we must give up the past; if we want to be free of fear and ambition, we must give up the future; if we want to be healed of vanity and embarrassment, we must give up the present. Where does this leave us? After we have given up the past, the future, and the present, we find ourselves in the dimension of timelessness.

What do we find in the realm of timelessness? In the realm of timelessness we discover God. Time is just something that seems to be, viewed from the narrow perspective of human experience. In Reality there is no such thing as time. In the dimension of timelessness we discover inspiration, which is the dynamic of enlightened living.

Reality cannot be experienced. All the previously cited characterological factors can be experienced, but Reality is timeless. It cannot be experienced; it can only be realized. Contrary to the prevailing statements of mystics in the literature that Reality can be experienced but cannot be described, we can say unequivocally that anyone who claims to have experienced Reality is either a fraud or else that person is deceiving himself.

What is the difference between experiencing something and realizing something? Experiences are mediated by the neuro-vegetative nervous system, whereas realizations take place in consciousness. If Reality is timeless, then none of the temporalities belong in the realm of the real. They are purely experiential. Therefore, they only seem to be. And the more involved we get in the experience of time, the more we live in unreality.

Since Metapsychiatry is ahistorical, acausal, and non-teleological, it is firmly anchored in Reality. Someone may ask, Is faith necessary for this realization? No, all we need is understanding. If we thought about faith, we would be talking about religion; but we are talking about science. Neither faith, nor believing, nor accepting is required. We are simply working in the direction of understanding Reality. This Reality happens to coincide with many biblical statements, especially the teachings of Jesus, understood existentially, but this does not mean that we are talking about religion. We are talking about life lived in absolute Reality.

Psychotherapy can be effective only to the extent that it helps the patient to realize more and more of what is real and what is not real. Unfortunately, sometimes we try to achieve the impossible. For instance, a patient may be suffering from anxieties, fears, and phobias, and we try to cure him of his fears, never noticing the fact that ambition is also a problem. It is like trying to give the patient a coin which has only one side. There is no such thing as a one-sided coin. So this kind of psychotherapist fantasy is just that. If the aim of psychotherapy is to help the patient attain better contact with Reality, then he needs to be guided out of temporality into the realization of the timeless. In the realm of the timeless there is no fear, no anxiety, there are no neuroses, no psychoses, no depressions, there are no problems. Everything is perfect and healthy and loving and harmonious and supremely intelligent.

When we speak of the aim of psychotherapy, the impression is unavoidable that we are talking about the future of the patient, and thus we seem to be contradicting ourselves. However, this is not so. We have to understand the difference between "now" as an aspect of the present, and "moment by moment" as an aspect of the timeless. The word "aim" is unavoidable because our language itself is time-bound. The realization of the difference between now as a time frame and moment by moment as an aspect of the dynamism of the timeless is very helpful.

Similarly, the word "hope" seems to point toward the future. Hope, however, is a religious concept. Enlightenment reveals the good of God which already is and manifests itself moment by moment in timelessness. Therefore, we "hope to dispense with hope" and replace it with the grace of actual realization.

When someone comes to us asking for help with a problem, it is important to have a clear idea of what would be helpful. To bring this understanding to the patient is the aim, but this aim is not in terms of the future, but moment by moment. The therapeutic process, which is conducted in the realm of the timeless, is not now. It is moment by moment. The timeless is not static. It is dynamic, but not in the terms in which we are accustomed to thinking. It is not really possible to understand something tomorrow or yesterday. If we explore the amazing event which takes place in consciousness in a moment of understanding or inspiration, we realize absolute timelessness. The famous French phenomenologist-psychiatrist Eugene Minkowski wrote a book entitled *Le Temps Vécu*, in which he speaks of the transcendence of the temporo-spatial coordinates of experience, which takes place in the moment of inspiration and understanding.

Actually, real life is not happening in time. It transcends the experience of time and space. If we have ever become aware of the moment when we understood something, we must have realized the extratemporal nature of that event. In psychoanalytic literature this is sometimes referred to as the "aha experience."

It is interesting that in the English language we speak about making extemporaneous comments. Usually we mean to say that our comments are not premeditated and prepared ahead of time. But if we consider the word "extemporaneous," we see that it hints at the fact that unpremeditated speech has a quality of transcending time. Extemporaneous means outside of time. Indeed, the gift of making extemporaneous comments hinges on our receptivity to inspired wisdom, reaching our consciousness from the realm of the timeless, which is the realm of Love-Intelligence.

All realizations of Reality are extratemporal. The Metapsychiatric therapeutic session, while it is restricted to a segment of time — say thirty minutes — is essentially timeless in its process. The entrance into the realm of the timeless abolishes all problems: fear, tension, guilt, shame, pride, ambition, vanity, obsessions, and compulsions; emotional hang-ups disappear in proportion to the extent that the timeless Reality of true existence is glimpsed. Every little glimpse has a powerful therapeutic impact. It is like beholding God. In proportion to the degree that God becomes real to us — and not only in terms of a religious denomination but existentially — in that proportion we are lifted out of the quagmire of human temporality.

"He That Hath an Ear ..."

In most forms of teaching, the basic style consists of debating and also, to some extent, contending, especially if there are pharisaical tendencies in the students. In the Metapsychiatric area of seeking spiritual understanding, however, only dialogue can be fruitful. This means that opinions have no place in this kind of learning. The Zen Master strongly recommended, "Above all, cherish no opinions." In order to be able to participate in a dialogic process, we must be willing to abandon, or put aside, opinions. What are opinions? They are cherished ideas, personalized ideas. As long as we cherish opinions we cannot participate in a dialogic process, because we have an investment in affirming our opinions.

If we cherish opinions we are inclined to contend. Therefore, opinions have to be set aside — at least temporarily. The Zen Master also says: "The wise man has no opinions whatsoever about anything." We may ask, What does a wise man have? A wise man has a thirst for understanding. He does not claim personal knowledge. At the drop of a hat he is ready to alter his thoughts. There is an amusing story about an American newsman who traveled all the way to the Himalayas to see a famous wise man, living on a mountaintop. When he finally arrived, he said: "Great and exalted Master, please tell me what is the secret of life?" The wise man thought very deeply for a long time and then he said: "The secret of life is like that river." The reporter exclaimed, "Is that all?" And the wise man said, "You mean it isn't?" ...

The thing to keep in mind is that in order for dialogue to take place — and by the way, this is essential in the healing process as well — the focus of attention must be on the increasing realization of whatever aspect of the truth is necessary to be known at a particular time.

Let us recall the three "Rs" of Metapsychiatry: recognition, regret, and reorientation. These three factors can become clear only under conditions of dialogue. The Bible character Daniel was a great spiritual guide, as can be seen from his therapeutic sessions with King Nebuchadnezzar. Nebuchadnezzar had dreams and visions which troubled him greatly, and there was no one who could understand or interpret them, until finally Daniel was called in. Nebuchadnezzar, who was a man in an existential crisis and was very fearful, asked Daniel to interpret his dreams to him. Nebuchadnezzar was faced with the necessity of recognizing the meanings of his dreams. But even though he asked for it, he was not willing to accept them because they were too horrible to face. We may look at this situation from our own standpoint as spiritual guides, called upon to help someone.

King Nebuchadnezzar suffered from delusions of grandeur. He had an exalted image of himself. He had fantasies about his own greatness. He thought himself to be the king of the whole world and that his kingdom, power, and fame reached to heaven, and from one end of the world to the other. Daniel saw through this and said to him, in a sense: "Beware, because you are going to become psychotic if you continue in this way of thinking, and you will go through a period of depression where you will be like an animal of the fields, knowing nothing but complete degradation. And this depression will last until you come to recognize that God alone is mighty and you are His servant" (see Daniel 4). Daniel was trying to help him recognize the problem — which was self-confirmatory ideation of psychotic proportions — and was trying to get him to the point of regret where he would recognize his mistake and abandon his self-exaltation. Daniel was also prescribing the reorientation process which would be necessary in order to be healed. Had Nebuchadnezzar listened to Daniel he could have been spared seven years of total desolation. It took the king seven years to come to recognize his mistaken mode of being-in-the-world, to regret it, and to reorient himself. When he reformed by acknowledging God as superior to himself he regained his sanity.

Here the Bible provides us with a beautiful model of a spiritual guide endeavoring to heal and to prevent a tragedy from occurring, failing in the short run but succeeding in the long run, because Nebuchadnezzar remembered that the God of Daniel is supreme, and after seven years of psychotic depression he finally was willing to see that point; only then was he healed. His thinking about himself and about reality was reformed, or reoriented. So Daniel is a marvelous model of a therapeutic spiritual guide, and also of an individual who could be in the midst of malicious intrigues and hostility from the courtiers around him, and even beastliness, and yet remain unscathed. The whole empire around him was collapsing from malice and moral decay, yet he remained unscathed (see Daniel 6). Daniel is truly a paradigm of spiritual uprightness.

Let us come back now to the issue of dialogue. In dialogue we put aside all other considerations except the search for understanding whatever is existentially valid. For instance, Nebuchadnezzar had an existentially invalid fantasy about himself, an exalted self-confirmatory idea. In his own eyes he was the strongest, the smartest, the most powerful man in the world, and it was hard for him to listen to the interpretation offered by Daniel. In order to be able to participate in a dialogue, we must be interested in one thing, as Kierkegaard says: "Purity of heart is wanting one thing." If we can put aside all other motivations, all other thoughts and opinions and just seek to understand as much as possible of the truth which is existentially valid, then we can participate in a dialogic process. In a dialogic process there is a place for asking questions and seeking clarification, but there is no place for debating, because the truth cannot be debated; one cannot arrive at existential truths through a process of debating. Debate has its place in a courtroom and politics but not when it comes to existential hermeneutics.

A dialogue can be very easily aborted. The moment a dialogic explanation hits upon an opinion, a resistance phenomenon occurs and at that point dialogue stops. There is nothing we can do in such a situation except wait until the other individual becomes ready for dialogue. When we understand an eternal truth, there is a sense of peace, assurance, gratitude, and love (PAGL). When we harbor opinions, we are "uptight." This understanding makes it easy to differentiate between truth and opinions. As far as others are concerned, we respect people's right to be uptight, to cherish opinions. There is nothing we can do about it, and even if we could, it would be wrong to try. It would be trespassing. If someone therefore insists upon clinging to an opinion, that is his privilege and we have no right to try to rob him of it. But when we harbor opinions, we tend to run into existential crises. Thereby we can be sure that opinions are not the truth, because truth is liberating and opinions are enslaving. The freedom Jesus speaks about is not sociological or economic or psychological. It is spiritual freedom, which we call PAGL. It is also accompanied by wisdom, joy, harmony; these are the spiritual qualities which we become aware of and which heal us every time we get a glimpse of the truth which is beyond opinions, which is existential.

Jesus said: "To this end was I born, and for this cause came I into the world, that I should bear witness unto the truth" (John 18:37). A spiritual guide who is a beneficial presence in the world bears witness to the truth, both by the quality of his presence and by voicing the truth to those who have ears to hear. "He that hath an ear let him hear" (Revelation 2:7, 11, 17, 29). It is not something that we can force on people. We have to wait until they ask. Unsolicited solicitude is trespass. Jesus never healed anyone who didn't ask him to. He was not offering unsolicited solicitude. He respected people's right to be wrong or to be sick or to disbelieve. He was constantly bearing witness to the truth through the quality of his presence and through his words, but he was not pushing it on anyone. When he returned home to Nazareth, he was not able to heal the sick because there was no receptivity. He said, in fact: "Nemo propheta in sua patria" (No man is a prophet in his own country). And so he left. He did not force his healing ability on anyone.

I am reminded of a poster I once saw. The caption went as follows: "The truth will make you free, but first it will make you mad!" Praying for someone who is not receptive is also a trespass. When we pray we try to behold in our mind's eye man in the context of God. We are required to love our neighbor as ourself, and since we pray for ourself at all times, we also endeavor to pray for our neighbor. But this is a blessing, not intercessory prayer.

A very helpful way to pray for ourselves is by meditating on the following statement: "I am a *place* where God's presence reveals itself as omniactive Love-Intelligence." And if someone asks that we pray for him or we want to bless someone in a specific way, we can endeavor to behold him in a similar way as a place where God's presence reveals itself as omniactive Love-Intelligence. If we pray for ourself this way and if we pray for others this way, then we are loving our neighbor as we love ourself. This way we can pray even for people who call themselves atheists, not in order to influence them but in order to fulfill the commandment, because influencing is a sin. It is a trespass. To be influential is right. A beneficial presence in the world, a witness to the truth, is influential, but he does not influence.

The question was asked, What is the meaning and the benefit of thinking of ourselves as a place? It leaves the ego out of our thought. The existentialists speak of man as *clairiére de l'existence*. Heidegger speaks of man as *Lichtung des Daseins*, which means that man is a place where existence manifests itself. We think of ourself as a transparency, or a place, or a consciousness, or a presence. In all these conceptualizations of prayer the ego is put aside, and that is important. If our prayers contain a thought of what should be, it is a trespass; if it is an acknowledgment of what already is, then it is prayer. The prayer of beholding endeavors to see spiritually in the mind's eye what really is beneath what seems to be. Someone may be a very aggressive, cruel, and objectionable character, but beneath that we know that he is a child of God. The important differentiation is that there must be no thought of what should be. We seek to behold what really is.

The second principle of Metapsychiatry states: "Take no thought for what should be or what should not be; seek ye first to know the good of God, which already is." In our prayers we seek to behold (not visualize, fantasize, or imagine, which is qualitatively different), or see in consciousness, what really is in spite of what seems to be. That is true prayer in which there is no influencing, no trespassing, because the objective is to know the truth. The meaning and purpose of life is to come to know Reality.

Matter is being discovered more and more as just a holographic appearance of vibrations and therefore as not what it seems to be. With holography it is possible to project images in space, which look very substantial, but actually they are just coherent light projected through a special photographic plate. The latest scientific research claims that the brain is this kind of holographic plate through which vibrations are being projected into space which makes the universe appear in the form of material substance. But actually matter is not substantial, and the basic stuff of life is just vibration.

As to emotions, they are just thoughts organismically interpreted. The basic stuff of life — even beyond vibrations — is thought. We tend to see everything in the context of our organism, but that does not mean that our organism is what it seems to be. Joy and love are not emotions. They are spiritual qualities which we can be aware of by the grace of God; they are attributes of God.

We seek to understand ourselves ever so deeply in the context of God's creation. In various periods there were and are new theories put forward. The latest one is that the visible universe is a holographic image of God. Divine ideas flow into His universe and are interpreted by the brain through a process of holographic projection, which makes ideas appear as solid stuff. But the solid stuff is not really solid. We are trying to understand this. There is no man alive — not even Karl Pribram and David Bohm who are in the forefront of this research — who can fully understand what is being discovered. But one thing is becoming clear, namely, there is no such thing as solid stuff anywhere, contrary to our sensory perceptions.

Since God is the source of all intelligence, life, love, wisdom, and truth, if we are going to petition God, there is only one thing we can sensibly petition for, namely, we can plead for understanding. We all pray all the time, even the avowed atheists. Man is unavoidably, inescapably, a prayerful creature but many pray to the wrong god, and that is a tragedy.

What happens if someone seeks spiritual guidance believing that that's what he really wants and, while sitting with him, it becomes clear that this is not what he really wants? What can the spiritual guide do in such a case? The spiritual guide has to discern the discrepancy in the motivation and find a way of meaningfully communicating it and clarifying it to the individual so that he could become aware of this dichotomy of motivation within himself. Once the individual becomes aware of divergent motivations, he has the freedom to say, "Well that's what I really want," or, "That's not what I really want," or he can say, "All right, I will give this up and choose the other." The more clearly we can help someone to see his conflicting or divergent motivations and his self-deceptions, the more helpful we shall be to him, but this requires the ability of discernment. There is a very interesting Taoist saying relevant to this issue: "If the right man does the wrong thing, then the wrong thing will work the right way; but if the wrong man does the right thing, then the right thing will work the wrong way." Motivation makes the difference; the right man is the one who has existentially valid motivations. And so if someone comes to us for spiritual guidance, we can help him to see that as long as he has wrong motivations he is not being the

right man, and things will keep going awry in his life even if
he behaves in a Christian way.

Thought is a basic unit of mental energy. Thought is energy. There are two kinds of thoughts: valid thoughts and
invalid thoughts. The principle of existential validation helps
us differentiate between the two. If a thought or a series of
thoughts are life-enhancing, health-promoting, healing, loving, and clarifying, they are existentially valid and they are
energy which blesses us and heals us. Invalid thoughts, while
they may appear rational and logical within a certain context
of reasoning, have the opposite effect.

Everything intellectual is an abstraction, but if the abstraction is valid, it can be helpful. Let us take, for instance, the
very useful intellectual abstraction "God is love," which is
not the truth but a statement about the truth. Anything that
appears in the form of a thought is, in a way, an abstraction of Reality because Reality is beyond thought. Thoughts
can help us to discern Reality, but thoughts themselves are
not the Reality. The Zen Master says: "The finger is not the
moon." Once, when I told my dog, "Look, there is your food,"
he began licking my finger. And that is, in a sense, what we
do, too.

The more clearly the truth is established in our consciousness, the more protection we have from invalid thoughts. If
we are unenlightened about what is valid and what is not
valid, then we are at the mercy of all sorts of invalid ideas
invading our consciousness and showing up in various forms,
in problems which can be physical, mental, emotional, social,
economic, behavioral, or any other type.

Mind fasting is a Taoist concept which corresponds to the
statement Jesus made when asked by his disciples why they
could not heal the epileptic boy: "This kind goeth not out but
by prayer and fasting" (Matthew 17:21). Jesus did not refer to
abstaining from food. He referred to abstaining from certain
ways of thinking. He placed great emphasis on the power of
thought. At one occasion he said: If you only think about committing adultery, you have already committed it. ("Whosoever

looketh on a woman to lust after her hath committed adultery with her already in his heart," Matthew 5:28.) So the entertainment of invalid thoughts is harmful to us and has a tendency to transmute itself into problems. Energy, according to the second law of thermodynamics, has a tendency to transmute itself into other forms. As mentioned before, the basic stuff of life is thought and thought appears to be energy. It behaves as energy because it has the tendency to transmute itself into emotions, feelings, sensations, symptoms, behavior, speech, and various other phenomena of daily living. A phenomenon is a thought in visible form. When thought energy transmutes itself and appears in visible form, then we speak of phenomena.

"Bracketing" helps us to participate in a dialogue and in discerning the meaning of phenomena, because it provides us with an open mind. Mind fasting is an integral aspect of the healing process. For instance, if we have critical thoughts about someone and we begin to feel very uneasy about it, then in order to see that individual in the context of God, we must abstain from critical thoughts about him. This is mind fasting. It is the abstaining from entertaining existentially invalid thoughts and prayerfully endeavoring to acknowledge what is existentially valid. Thereby we heal ourselves of the burden of malice, hostility, antagonism, and all sorts of unpleasant thoughts which can easily transmute themselves into a stomach ulcer, or a headache, or into allergies, etc. Mind fasting is a very helpful and important mental hygiene principle. The closer we are to the truth of being, and the clearer we understand ourselves as spiritual beings, the more perceptive we are of invalid thoughts. It is somewhat like when we have learned to appreciate taking showers every morning and being clean, the more intolerable it is for us to be dirty. We are stewards of consciousness. It is our task to maintain the purity of our consciousness. The more we appreciate PAGL, the more intolerable it is to think and talk in critical ways about anyone.

Attitudes are congealed thoughts. Congealed emotions are emotional disturbances where the emotions rule our lives, such as when someone is chronically angry and hateful and gets high blood pressure or something else from it.

The question was asked about the difference between bracketing and the Buddhist concept of self-emptying. Bracketing is, as mentioned before, the seeking of open-minded confrontation of whatever reveals itself from moment to moment. The Buddhist form of self-emptying is a method of mind fasting sought in meditation where all calculative thinking ceases and one is completely receptive to inspiration: where there is no more cogitation taking place, *ideas obtain.*

Let us clarify the meaning of ideas obtaining in consciousness. It is insight into God as a source of all creative, intelligent and valid ideas. Right knowledge comes to all who are willing to be receptive in this open-minded way where ideas can obtain in consciousness.

Information and Transformation

The central focus in Metapsychiatry is God, but not the God of the traditional religions. In religions God is a symbol of reality. In Metapsychiatry we seek to develop the faculty of direct contact, not with the symbol of reality, but with Reality itself, the "God beyond God" (Tillich).

Reality and absolute truth are synonymous. Jesus explained how healing occurs by saying: "Ye shall know the truth and the truth shall make you free" (John 8:32). Not the symbol of truth. The symbol of truth cannot make us free, but the knowledge of the truth itself can make us free, that is, it can heal us. In this sense we are radically different from religious teachings and denominations. Our endeavor is to help our patients to come into contact with this Reality. This may sound very difficult and, indeed, it is not easy, but it can be realized.

An important thing to know is the difference between information and transformation. It is common knowledge that no amount of reading of books — or even the Bible — will have any therapeutic effect. One can become very educated and well-informed, but there will not be the slightest therapeutic effect. Healing will not occur through reading books. Neither will it happen through listening to lectures and sermons. Reading books and listening to lectures is gathering information. Information in and of itself has no therapeutic value.

What is needed is transformation. There is a relevant passage in the Bible: "Be not conformed to this world: but be ye transformed by the renewing of your mind, that ye may prove what is that good, and acceptable, and perfect will of God" (Romans 12:2). In this passage the secret of transformation in contrast to information is revealed.

To move from information to transformation, we are required to do something. Goethe said something relevant to this issue, namely: "Whatever we have inherited, we must reacquire." Information is something that we receive from books and lectures. But in order for this information to become existentially integrated, it must be proven in individual understanding. The information we receive must be put into practice through participation in existence as a beneficial presence in the world. For instance, it is not enough to know that God is love. We must also be loving. It is not enough to know that God is truth. We must also be forthright and honest in our daily life. It is not enough to know that God is beauty, harmony, joy, freedom, intelligence, and goodness. We must also live that way. Information is passive gathering of data. Transformation requires participation.

In therapy we are not only providing information. We seek to help our patient attain transformation. In order to help him attain transformation, we must gain a clear understanding of his mode of being-in-the-world. For instance, there is a case of a young man who keeps getting fired from his jobs and repeatedly rejected by his friends, both male and female. The harder he tries to ingratiate himself with people and establish close relationships with his employers, friends, or relatives, the more he gets rebuffed. In Metapsychiatry we refer to this as a misdirected mode of being-in-the-world. This is a broader concept than the concept of "repetition compulsion" introduced by Freud.

Psychoanalysis seeks to explain repetition compulsion on the basis of childhood experiences. Psychoanalysis asks: "What's wrong with this man? Why is he behaving this way? And who is to blame for it?" In Metapsychiatry we do not ask these questions. We ask, What is he doing? What is his mode of being-in-the-world? What is the meaning of this mode of being-in-the-world? And what is the healing remedy? So we do not blame anyone — not his parents, society, not even the patient. But we see that this problem is based on an erroneous assumption about what is important in life. The patient assumes that the important thing in life is to have good personal relationships, and in order to have good personal relationships, he has to be clever and manipulative and make a pest of himself. As a result of such behavior, he suffers repeated rejections which, in turn, have a devastating effect on him.

So what is needed here is for the patient to become aware of his mode of being-in-the-world and of his erroneous assumptions about how to live in an intelligent way. Then he needs to come to understand what constitutes a truly intelligent mode of being-in-the-world. The model of the intelligent mode of being-in-the-world for us is Christ Jesus, whose main qualities can be summed up in two outstanding features, forthrightness and love.

Our patient, however, was neither forthright nor loving, but calculative, scheming, manipulative, and obsequious. By acquainting him with the qualities of the Christly mode of being-in-the-world, we are providing him with information about an existentially valid way of living. He may agree with us and accept this information, even gratefully and eagerly, but chances are he will try to use forthrightness and love as a technique for more successful interpersonal manipulation. He may not commit himself to the Christly way until he has suffered much more. Suffering may eventually compel him to a point of commitment to the right values, and only then will a healing occur. The Bible says: "Commit thy way unto the Lord; trust also in him; and he shall bring it to pass" (Psalm 37:5).

The psychoanalytic theory behind transformation is based on the concept of the corrective emotional experience. The idea is that man has certain bottled-up emotions from childhood on, and through free association, dream interpretation, and transference analysis within the context of the relationship between the therapist and the patient, a corrective emotional experience can take place in the patient. This, in turn, will have a therapeutic effect on him. For instance, coming back to this patient, the idea would be that he would begin to "butter up" the therapist and try to establish a close, interpersonal, emotionally charged relationship with him and make a pest of himself. If the therapist, in spite of all this, persisted in being patient, kind, and accepting, this would give the patient a corrective emotional experience, which would hopefully lead to understanding.

Now let us ask, What is the difference between a corrective emotional experience and a real healing? We have seen that emotion is not enough, because it is just information. No matter how powerful the corrective emotional experience may be, it is essentially still just information occurring on an affective level. The patient discovers what is wrong in a more meaningful way. So now he knows what is wrong. Knowing what is wrong will not heal him. Jesus did not say, "Ye shall know what's wrong, and you will be healed." That is not enough. It is the integration of the truth in an existentially meaningful way that brings about a healing.

What is the difference between an emotional experience and existential integration? Emotions and feelings are not reliable indicators of Reality; they are purely subjective and subject to misinterpretation. Existential integration is of an entirely different order. Existential integration takes place when the truth validates itself by transforming our mode of being-in-the-world. A healthy individual has a harmonious and fulfilling mode of being-in-the-world, fulfilling in the sense of being able to express his inherent potentialities in a most beneficial way in his daily life.

Far from being just metaphysical and theoretical, Metapsychiatry provides us with a most practical and useful way of being in this world as a beneficial presence. The interesting thing to contemplate is that Metapsychiatry starts out with a metaphysical assumption about man and the universe and winds up being supremely practical in daily life. This indicates that its metaphysical assumptions about man and the universe are thus validated. If they were just mystical nonsense, they could not possibly have practical consequences of a beneficial, life-enhancing nature.

The Teacher and the Teaching

What is the important thing about a lamp? The important thing about a lamp is the light it sheds. The important thing about Jesus was the Christ. The important thing about a teacher is the teaching. The human tendency, however, is to get hung up on the concrete rather than on the abstract. We get attached to personalities, and we have a tendency to see life in terms of interpersonal relationships.

This is what happened to psychotherapy. Psychotherapy has fallen victim to myopia, or shortsightedness, which is a universal human frailty. It is a tendency to cling to the concrete, the tangible, or the material, and lose sight of the essential which is spiritual. A lamp is good for nothing if it does not shed light. A teacher is good for nothing unless he has something valid to teach. It is the teaching that is important, not the teacher. It is the Christ that is important, not Jesus. Jesus was a man who expressed the Christ, who manifested the light of truth and love and perfection and reality to the world. He even said: "I am the light of the world: he that followeth me shall not walk in darkness, but shall have the light of life" (John 8:12).

And so in psychotherapy we have to be careful to see beyond personality, because no amount of "improving" of personality can be therapeutically valid. There are politicians, psychopaths, and all sorts of con artists in the world who have beautiful personalities. They are very clever, very smooth, very articulate and appealing, and yet that has nothing to do with health. A beautiful personality can be a terrible disease. So if psychotherapy is conceived of as the restructuring of personality, it is like trying to polish up a lamp to make it look nice in the living room, without ever considering whether it will give light.

Man is a manifestation of Love-Intelligence. Everyone has the potential of being what he really is. But if psychotherapy focuses attention on improving the personality, then it is dealing with make-up. Psychologists speak of personality make-up. Personality is just make-up. If psychotherapy is to be authentic and helpful, it must deal with the essence of man. Essentially, we are spiritual beings. We are not personalities. We just seem to be.

There are no creative personalities. There is only creative intelligence, and some people have awakened within themselves a higher degree of receptivity to certain aspects of that creative intelligence. They are called artists. But we can aim at higher levels of awareness where it is not only in a circumscribed area of activity that we are receptive but in the totality of being. An enlightened man is an existential artist; his life is a work of art. Everything about him expresses beauty, harmony, originality, joy, and love. He is a substantial being. He is authentic. In existentialism this is a very favored term. Authenticity of being means becoming manifestly what we really are potentially.

In ordinary life there is a lot of copying going on. What do we mean by copying? People copy each other. They imitate each other. In psychology it is called identification. If something appeals to us about someone, we try to copy him. This gives rise to fashion, fads, and trends which keep changing. The basis of this idea is that man is what he appears to be, and that all one has to do is to improve one's appearance. This kind of shallow reasoning gives rise to admiration and envy. Admiration is nothing but disguised envy.

Children learn to live in accordance with the values of significant adults around them. If adults around them believe in emulating others, admiring certain models and envying them and trying to copy them, then naturally, children will grow up trying to live that way. This is called adaptation. The child adapts himself to the world according to the basic assumptions which govern the thinking of his parents. We could say that children are extensions of parental consciousness.

Admiration, envy, identification, imitation, copying, pretending, stealing, lying, make-believe — these are universal tendencies of unenlightened man, who is judging by appearances. Jesus said: "Judge not according to the appearance, but judge righteous judgment" (John 7:24). What did he mean by righteous judgment? Righteous judgment means judging according to what really is.

It is interesting that unenlightened man wants to be like everyone else and, at the same time, he would also like to be unique, which is very difficult to accomplish. Sometimes these two tendencies become separated, and there are some who are mainly concerned with being like others. These are called conformists. But then there are people who sense that there is something wrong with monkeying others, and they discover a great idea — nonconformity. This reveals the human tendency toward dualistic thinking. If "yes" is bad, then "no" must be good. So if the establishment is governed by rules of conformity, then the nonconformists conform to the rules of the nonconformists, and we see the same process going on in both camps, which means that to be a conformist or a nonconformist is the same. Always there is fear of being in or out of step with the herd.

This process is going on in all walks of life: the social, scientific, political, cultural, religious, and psychotherapeutic spheres of life. The conformists condemn the nonconformists, and the nonconformists have contempt for the conformists. This is the mockery of human existence. It is also tragic. Shakespeare said: "To thine own self be true." How can man be true to his own self if he is forever trying to copy others? It is possible to overcome this mode of being-in-the-world. Jesus once said that the difference between him and other people was that he knew where he came from and he knew where he was going. ("I know whence I came, and whither I go," John 8:14.) What Jesus was pointing out to us was that authenticity of being and liberation from the mockery of ordinary unenlightened life requires us to become acquainted with the truth of our being. We are required to discover what it means to be an image and likeness of God, what it really means when we say that we are spiritual beings. It means that God is our mind, that all intelligent ideas, all vitality, all energy, all love, all happiness, all joy and beauty, all the spiritual qualities which constitute true being, are manifestations of God's self-revealing activity. And while we are all expressions of these qualities of infinite Mind, everyone is unique and different from everyone else. This surprising idea points to the infinity of creative Mind. We are all manifestations of the same God, and we all manifest the same God in individually unique ways.

So here we have the authenticity of being established as a fundamental aspect of Reality which says: "You don't have to envy anyone or anything; you are the most perfect and unique individuality that you can possibly desire to be. There is no need to copy anyone, or to try to be like someone else. It is foolishness. You just become aware of what you really are, and you will find excellence, perfection, beauty and intelligence. There is nothing more to be desired." Spiritually we are unique individualities created by Divine Mind. Once we become aware of this, then what Jesus said about perfection does not sound so absurd to us anymore. He said: "Be ye therefore perfect, even as your Father which is in heaven is perfect" (Matthew 5:48). The right understanding of the truth of being gives man a great sense of assurance and peace, and makes it possible for him to be loving and satisfied.

Beyond Nothingness

Most of the time we think of love in the context of inter-action between individuals. We want to get love and to give love. If we think in these terms and see love as coming to us from someone, we feel good, secure, and unafraid. We have the illusion of security. But when this is not forthcoming and instead something else is coming forth — as for instance criti-cism or rejection — we get frightened and hurt. We can become resentful. This often takes the form of a headache or some other symptom. Therefore, it is important to understand love in a broader context.

The third Metapsychiatric principle says: "There is no interaction anywhere; there is only Omniaction everywhere." When we say that there is no interaction anywhere, we mean that a great deal of suffering comes from expecting love from others and building our lives on that idea. If we are living in that context or with such a mind-set, then we are vulnera-ble, insecure, and easily disturbed. But if we understand love as the essence of God expressing itself through us freely as goodness, intelligence, generosity, and assurance, then love is a spiritual sea, the medium in which "we live, and move, and have our being" (Acts 17:28).

No one can deprive us of the happiness and assurance of knowing that we are living expressions of Divine Love. It relieves us of the curse of conceptualizing the good in inter-actional terms. Problems are basically psychological, which means interpersonal. Solutions are spiritual, which means omniactional. There is nothing wrong with Reality. It is just that we do not see it clearly. We need to expand our vision.

It is interesting to consider what happens to an individual whose perspective on love and on life is expanded into infinity. If such an individual comes into contact with someone whose vision is interactional, this contact is entirely different from the usual contacts between people. Interaction between unenlightened people could be characterized somewhat along the lines of Zen symbolism as the sound of two hands clapping. But the former situation represents what the Zen Masters have so mysteriously designated as the "sound of one hand." This means that instead of clashing personalities, there is transcendence.

Now the question could be asked, What is so attractive about conflict and friction and clashing of personalities? In asking several people about it, the unanimous answer was that it either feels good or it feels bad. But the important aspect of it seems to be that it "feels," which means that it is a self-confirmatory experience. Thus it seems that we want to feel that we exist, and we are afraid to become aware that perchance we don't.

Loneliness and abandonment is something we all dread. We are afraid of nonbeing. Truly, this fear would be justified if it were possible to "not be." But it is not possible to not be. Thus we secretly live in fear that something might happen which is an impossibility.

The fear of nonbeing is a universal human experience which needs to be individually confronted. Furthermore, we have to come to see how this fear drives us to seek escape from loneliness, or from being ignored, or being insignificant, abandoned, etc. Loneliness is often experienced as excruciatingly painful and frightening. We have to come to understand that what we are afraid of is an impossibility. In order for an individual to cease being, God would have to be destroyed. Therefore, our being is absolutely secure. We are inseparable from God. God is our being. Therefore, nonbeing is an impossibility.

The fear of nonbeing underlies all the self-confirmatory

schemes to which we are inclined to resort. Dreams and fantasies constitute self-confirmatory ideation, which functions as a mental defense against the emerging sense of nothingness, or, as the Buddhists call it, "sunyata" (emptiness). The healing remedy is, of course, as follows: The more we learn to become conscious of God's being and our oneness with God, the more peaceful and assured we will become about our existence.

It is clear to anyone that it is impossible to isolate a wave from the sea. Similarly, man can never be separated from his creative principle, God. Jesus said: "I am not alone, because the Father is with me" (John 16:32). The realization of this truth will relieve us of existential anxiety and make it possible to endure solitude. When nothingness has been understood as a purely subjective experience, not an actual reality, we become capable of beholding Reality.

Beholding is seeing with the inward eye, the eye of God within us. Meister Eckhart said: "I see God with the same eye as God sees me." It makes no difference whether the individual we are beholding is in the next room or thousands of miles away, because in Divine Reality there is no distance; there is neither time nor space.

We see that we are emanations of Divine Mind and so is everyone else, and when this is clearly established in consciousness, we behold ourselves and others in the context of Divine Reality, which is infinite, timeless, spaceless, and completely perfect.

In the prayer of beholding we do not beseech God to make someone well; we endeavor to realize that he is well because he is God's spiritual manifestation. At most, we ask God to help us to see that the perfection of his creation is already an established fact, that we are joint participants in the good of God. Our work is nothing else than a constant endeavor to improve and increase this realization. The more clearly we can see this, the more our lives will correspond to what really is. "Open thou mine eyes, that I may behold wondrous things out of thy law" (Psalm 119:18).

The possibilities of the prayer of beholding are limitless, and with it comes a release from self-confirmatory ideations which are but manifold compulsive defense mechanisms designed to ward off the fear of nothingness, or nonbeing.

Another aspect of this process is the attainment of enlightened decisiveness. Decisiveness is a very desirable quality. However, there are healthy ways to be decisive and unhealthy ways to be decisive. Unhealthy decisiveness is based on willfulness, or superstition, or a gambling instinct of taking chances, or being reckless, which is imprudent to say the least. Healthy decisiveness is based on prudence, flowing out of reflection and inspired wisdom.

Recently, while driving on the road, a couple had the following experience. While the husband was driving, the wife noticed that the gasoline indicator gauge had not moved from its center position for a long time. She suddenly turned to her husband and said: "Let's get off at the next exit and find a gasoline station." As they turned off the road, the car began to sputter and slow down, coming to a halt at the nearest gasoline pump. The gas tank was empty.

This example illustrates the nature of enlightened decisiveness, which requires the ability to hear and to obey. The ability to hear is attained through a willingness to forgo daydreaming, fantasizing, and calculative thinking. The ability to obey requires "shouldlessness" and an understanding of God as omniactive Mind, the source of all wisdom and love.

The word "obedience" tends to elicit negative reactions, because of the connotation of human tyranny and childhood coercive experiences. But the obedience we are talking about here refers to the willingness to listen to and to be governed by impartations of Divine Mind, coming to us moment by moment. "And thine ears shall hear a word behind thee, saying, 'This is the way, walk ye in it, when ye turn to the right hand, and when ye turn to the left'" (Isaiah 30:21).

In order to enhance our receptivity to inspired wisdom, it is desirable to start out the day by prayer and meditation. This must be continued until PAGL is reached. PAGL — meaning peace, assurance, gratitude, and love — is the Metapsychiatric equivalent of an enlightened, i.e., spiritualized, consciousness. With that state of consciousness we can look forward to the day with confidence.

The human consciousness could be compared to a delicate musical instrument which must be kept in perfect tune if right musicianship is the aim. And if at any point it gets out of tune, one must stop all activity and retune the instrument. If in the course of the day we find ourselves disturbed, or out of sorts, or insecure, it is best to withdraw into prayer and meditation until PAGL is reestablished. Jesus recommended that we be "sober and vigilant, watch and pray" (1 Peter 4:7; 5:8).

A young lady reported the following: "My work consists of key punch operation, and all I know is how to put information into the terminal. I don't understand the rest of the process at all. On several occasions I heard some inner voice speaking to me and urging me to ask about the correctness of the data before me. At first, I didn't think much of it, but as it occurred repeatedly I started paying closer attention to it. It was like having an invisible supervisor talking to me. Later on, I started to hear this voice in consciousness in other areas of my life. And again, I was reluctant to pay attention to it. But later on I realized that this is a familiar experience and I began paying attention to it all the time, and thus I have come to know what inspired wisdom really is. I listen, I pay attention, I obey, and it helps me in every situation."

Inspired wisdom is often referred to as intuition. This is but a conventional term for inspiration. However, most people tend to disregard it, preferring to rely more on calculative, rationalistic reasoning. Intuitive insights and inspired wisdom are often in conflict with rational reasoning. Intuitive, inspired wisdom tends to override superficial logic and calculative thinking. If we are obedient and know how to hear, we can make decisions which seemingly make no sense at all, yet prove to be supremely intelligent and ingenious.

Of course, we are not talking about "hunches" and so-called "gut feelings" and "brain storms," which tend to be just subjective emotional preferences. We are talking about being in conscious awareness of infinite Mind's promptings in the context of PAGL.

The fifth principle of Metapsychiatry states: "God helps those who let Him." This principle can be utilized consciously whenever choices and decisions confront us. To let God help us means to suspend all calculative thinking, anxiousness, and worried mental agonizing about what should be or what should not be. We need the courage which dares to "not know" in order to discern what God knows. The Oriental sages tell us that "knowing can come only from not knowing." Therefore, willingness to not know can make us receptive to inspired wisdom.

To many this may seem like foolish passivity, or even irresponsible "do nothingness." But, in fact, this is not negligence, or apathy, or passivity, or aggressiveness. It is "alert reverent responsiveness" which forms the basis of enlightened, creative, and intelligent decisiveness.

Transubstantiation

The process of understanding spiritual guidance, or enlightenment for that matter, can be compared to climbing out of a valley. In the valley everything looks natural and things seem to make a lot of sense. As we begin climbing out of the valley and up the mountainside, things begin to appear in a different light. With every step we take upward, new vistas open up and things which we saw before reveal themselves as not at all what we thought them to be while in the valley. We gain a different perspective and we are able to encompass things in a broader context.

It is interesting to consider that medical science has traditionally moved from the wider context to the narrower. The microscope has helped us to narrow down our focus on reality to ever smaller areas. Similarly, in the field of psychiatry medical science has also tried to move from the wider to the narrower perspectives, exploring ever smaller details of the brain, hoping to find answers by learning about microscopic elements of the structure of the brain. Research has moved from the anatomical structures to the histological structures, then to the molecular structures, and the chemical structures, and finally the electro-physiological structures of the brain.

Our studies of matter move from the macroscopic to the microscopic, and beyond the microscopic into the atomic configurations. Thus scientific research, including physics, has a tendency to move from the larger to the smaller, from the wider to the narrower perspectives. In physics we have come to the point of studying the behavior of subatomic particles, which are way beyond microscopic and molecular dimensions. Physicists tell us of an area where matter disappears into waves. And the substance of these waves is pure energy. But what energy is, is not clear.

These waves supposedly behave in peculiar ways. They seem to be unpredictable and subject to influences coming from the observer in some mysterious ways, so that the observed is determined by the observer. A further fascinating aspect of these waves is that they can intermittently appear as particles — meaning materially substantial — or as waves — meaning materially insubstantial. Thus matter disappears into a mysterious something called energy.

There is a story about the definition of a specialist: A specialist is someone who learns more and more about less and less, till finally he comes to know everything about nothing. So then psychology, medicine, and physics, by moving from the larger to the smaller, are like the proverbial Cheshire cat, which gradually disappeared until there was nothing left but the smile.

In Metapsychiatry, while we do not spurn research into ever smaller elements of matter, we are moving in the opposite direction, namely, from the smaller to the larger, from the narrower to the wider horizon, from the finite to the infinite, out of the valley, up the mountain, to the limitless vistas at the summit. The aim here is ascension. In ascending into ever wider perspectives, the hope is of attaining the viewpoint of infinity. We wish to see life *sub specie eternitatis*. We seek to behold Reality in the context of infinite Mind.

So no matter what psychotherapeutic school we may be studying, we are all studying the same phenomena, except from different levels of perception. When we descend into the narrowest spheres, matter disappears into a mysterious undefinable something called energy. When we move up the mountain to ever higher perspectives, the same thing happens — matter disappears into an undefinable substance called

Spirit, God, Mind, Love-Intelligence. At the end we come to the same place.

If we study the students of matter, we find that those who have advanced the furthest in their understanding of physics have become philosophers (Schroedinger, Heisenberg, Einstein, von Braun, and others). Their philosophy has the character of metaphysics. They have moved from physics to metaphysics just as we are moving from psychiatry to Metapsychiatry. In whichever direction we move, when we come to the end of our journey, we all meet. We meet in Spiritual Reality where everything becomes very clear in its own particular way.

For those of us who are still in the process of the journey it is of great value to know that the higher we rise on the upward path, the healthier we become and the less problematic life becomes. In contrast to that, the narrower the outlook on reality, the more troubled life seems to be. How is that possible?

In Metapsychiatry, we have succeeded in identifying five areas of narrow-mindedness which are endless sources of suffering: (1) sensualism, (2) emotionalism, (3) intellectualism, (4) personalism, and (5) materialism.

All these are going on in the valley. But as we rise out of the valley higher and higher, we begin to see man not in parts but as a totality, an integrated whole, a functioning manifestation of Love-Intelligence. Then we are *in* Love and *in* Intelligence. In the valley people think that love is an emotion and that intelligence is intellect. But as we rise out of the valley we see that love and intelligence are something else. They are not intrapsychic processes. They are not in man; man is in them. Love and intelligence do not come from inside us; we live and move and have our being in Love-Intelligence, somewhat like fish in the sea. We do not produce love or intelligence; intelligence and love govern us. We begin to see ourselves in a broader context, and that is of vital importance.

Psychoanalysis, moving from the wider to the narrower, has focused attention on intrapsychic processes and seeks to understand man by penetrating, so to speak, *into him*. The more we study what is inside, the more we find that there is nothing there. In the meanwhile we discover psychodynamics, parental relationships, introjection, primal scene problems, defense mechanisms of the ego, and all sorts of other things, not unlike the atomic physicists who find electrons and protons and mesons and quarks and seemingly endless other things until they come to the end and discover that there is really nothing but energy.

Real energy is found on the top of the mountain to be spirit, as we mentioned before. So, as we move out of the inwardness of things into beholding the context in which life manifests itself, we begin to see ourselves in a different light. Perception depends on context. The Bible says: "In him [God] we live, and move, and have our being" (Acts 17:28). God is the context in which life occurs. Therefore, in order to understand life and all things in the universe, it is necessary to view things in the context of infinite Mind, Love-Intelligence.

Here the universe reveals itself as perfectly harmonious and all things within it are beautiful, good, and meaningful. There comes upon us an awareness of peace, assurance, gratitude, and love, and problems just vanish. Each individual becomes a beneficial presence in the world. Without doing anything, by the mere fact of his perspective on Reality, his presence becomes a focal point of harmony and healing in the world. And that is the Christ consciousness. In this perspective all psychotherapeutic schools lose their significance and are seen as just transitory phases of the human struggle for understanding.

It is helpful to know that no matter what we are involved with in the valley, it is just a transitory phase in our journey, and it will disappear as we rise higher on the ascending path. It is also interesting to consider that when Jesus ascended, his physical body dissolved. In other words, matter became spirit — just as the subatomic particles disappear into waves and the waves turn into energy. So in ascension the substance of matter disappears. It dematerializes itself. We can rightfully think in terms of incarnation progressing to excarnation.

When Jesus was born, the Bible says: "Spiritus caro factus est," which means spirit became flesh (matter), and when he ascended, matter disappeared into spirit. We could take this as an indication of scientific progress. Science is already reaching the point of *transubstantiation* of matter. Physical science is reaching that point by narrowing its perspective to its ultimate. Metapsychiatry seeks to reach that point through broadening its perspective into infinity.

Jesus said, "He that followeth me shall not walk in darkness, but shall have the light of life" (John 8:12). The journey which Jesus took was from the valley to the pinnacle, and we are trying to follow in his footsteps. Every step of the way we find very worthwhile because as we climb higher, things get better and more beautiful. Our burdens fall away. Of course, while climbing up the mountain there is a great deal of downward drag to be overcome, and we may ask what this downward drag is. It is the collective thinking of the people in the valley.

Many well-meaning people would like to be loving but find it difficult. We hear them ask, Why can't I love? What's wrong with me that I cannot love? The sixth principle of Metapsychiatry states: "If you know what, you know how." For instance, if we know what a car is, we will know how to maintain it in running order. Similarly, we must first find out what love is and really understand it. Then we shall know how to love.

We have defined love as the ability to express the good of God. Love is the very substance of life. Love and intelligence constitute the substance of Reality and we are the manifestations of this substance. So we are not really made of flesh and blood (as we seem to be), but we are made of love and intelligence.

When Jesus gave his disciples bread and wine, he said: "Take, eat; this is my body." And he took the cup, saying: "Drink ye all of it: For this is my blood of the new testament . . . " (Matthew 26:26–28). In the history of Christianity many wars were fought over the meaning of this statement, individuals were tortured and burned at the stake, and all sorts of theological disputations and conflicts were fought. Even today this still remains a controversial issue in some circles. But if we understand substance to be spiritual love and intelligence, then the "flesh and blood" of every divine creation is spirit, and the problem of transubstantiation becomes insubstantial. Jesus was saying, in fact, that "by accepting and partaking of my teaching you will wake up to realize that you are made of the same stuff as I am, because everyone is an image and likeness of God." We are emanations of Divine Love-Intelligence. The realization of this truth makes it possible to be spontaneously and naturally loving and to lose all sense of prejudice against our fellow man.

The Bible explains: "It is the spirit that quickeneth; the flesh profiteth nothing" (John 6:63). We understand this to mean that Love-Intelligence is life-giving energy. Flesh and blood as matter are but their symbolic manifestations in the phenomenal world. As spiritual beings we are made of the same stuff as God. In Metapsychiatry we speak of God as Love-Intelligence. Love-Intelligence is indestructible, omnipotent, omniscient, omnipresent, and omniactive. We live and move and have our being in Him, or Her, or It.

Communion is only possible between identical substances. Water cannot commune with oil; spirit can only commune with spirit, light with light, love with love.

Sometimes we are asked whether the appearance of flesh and blood has a purpose. To this we can answer that the purpose of the appearance of flesh and blood — and matter in general — is analogous to darkness. The purpose of darkness is to make it possible for us to be conscious of light. Jesus said: "This is the condemnation [problem], that light is come into the world, and men loved darkness rather than light, because their deeds were evil" (John 3:19). Suffering stems from attachment to darkness (materialism and operationalism). We cherish the idea of material (experiential) living. This is the dream from which the Christ is seeking to awaken us.

On the road to understanding Love-Intelligence as the light of the Christ, we come face to face with the belief that the essence of life inheres in experiencing. The love of darkness could be interpreted in present-day understanding as the love of feeling good and the love of having pleasurable experiences. As a matter of fact, we love experiencing so much that we even enjoy pain.

What man is attached to is the dream of experiential living, painful or pleasurable. Life seems to be synonymous with experiencing. Experiencing means sensual, emotional, and intellectual stimulation. So the darkness we are attached to is the idea of experiencing and doing. Doing is also a form of experiencing. We call it operationalism. So what we consider real living, or being alive, is to have experiences and to operate in the world. This attachment is the great stumbling block.

The ninth principle of Metapsychiatry states: "Reality cannot be experienced or imagined; it can, however, be realized." Many sincere seekers after the truth and the light fail to reach it because they live in the expectancy of religious and spiritual experiences. Experiencing is not a proof of life and of the truth. Just because we are experiencing something does not prove that it really exists. For instance, through hypnotism man can be induced to experience whatever a hypnotist may suggest. This is a simple proof of the illusory nature of human experiences. As a matter of fact, experiences are but dreams, illusions, and perceptualized thoughts. The Buddhists and Hindus speak of it as samsara or maya, meaning illusion.

Real life cannot be experienced. Therefore, not many people are really conscious or awake, nor are they interested in being awake. Drug addicts, for instance, are only interested in dreaming a better dream. Drug addiction is but a socially unacceptable way of dreaming. Most of us appear to be hypnotized most of the time, even without drugs, until we wake up. When we wake up, we discover that life and being consist of Love-Intelligence.

The question now remains, Is there a way of facilitating the process of awakening? Yes, there is one thing we can practice besides prayer, study, and meditation. We can learn to lose interest in our experiences. For instance, it is quite impossible to stop smoking, because if we were to stop smoking, we would be just dreaming the experience of nonsmoking, which is a dream of deprivation. However, it is possible to lose interest in smoking, because smoking is just an experience, i.e., a dream. It is possible to lose interest in excitement, in contending; it is possible to gradually disassociate ourselves from our experiences and reach a point where events come to our attention but not into our experience.

The seventh principle of Metapsychiatry states: "Nothing comes into experience uninvited." When we are advanced on the spiritual path, we reach a point where we have stopped inviting experiences. Events come to our attention only and we respond to them dispassionately with intelligence and love. For instance, someone I know was stung by a bee and the place began to swell up and become red and clearly very painful. But this individual observed the process without fear, quite dispassionately, and didn't say, "I got stung by a bee." Instead, she thought to herself, "This is an event of a bee sting, and tissue reaction seems to be taking place. It seems to be happening, but right now I am interested in looking after my friends and my other activities. I am an expression of Divine Love-Intelligence. That is my life." Quickly she forgot about the pain and the entire incident. The symptoms promptly disappeared without a trace.

This example must not be interpreted as recommending carelessness and negligence. It illustrates the power inherent in a right understanding of man's true substance as Love-Intelligence, which, in turn, gives man dominion over his fears and entrapment in the hypnotism of his experiences.

We are learning to transcend experiential life and to lose our attachment to darkness and operationalism. The aim is to discern the light of the Christ, Reality, true Life, which is the true substance called Love-Intelligence.

When we come to know ourselves as Love-Intelligence rather than flesh and blood, then we are enlightened, liberated, and saved. This is bliss-consciousness.

Willfulness

A young woman reports the following: "I have a situation at my place of work where one of my colleagues, a man, doesn't seem to do any work at all, and this is driving me insane. I am working very hard, nonstop, and he is just loafing on the job and is getting away with it. It disturbs me no end. I tried to talk to myself and tell myself that it is none of my business; nevertheless, I suffer a great deal from this situation. I keep thinking that he should work just as I do."

This is a good example illustrating the fact that what we are suffering from is not what other people do or don't do, but what we are thinking about them. Our tormentors are not people but our thoughts. However, God gave us dominion over our thoughts. What does that mean? It means that we have the power to turn our attention to more valid thoughts. Or, to put it in another way, a certain shift has to take place in what we cherish, what we hate, or what we fear. Someone put it this way: "It seems to me that what is asked of us is 'capitulation.'"

This, of course, is correct because healing can occur only if we are willing to capitulate before the will of God. The most marvelous and liberating capitulation is this: "Father, thy will be done." This is an acknowledgment of Reality. The moment we acknowledge Reality, we are lifted out of the insanity of "should" thinking into the sanity of conscious awareness of what really is. Reality is the fact that God is the only power, the only Mind, the only Operator, the harmonizing principle of the universe, and that of our own selves we can do nothing, and we can control nothing.

By capitulating to God we regain our sanity because we get in touch with Reality. "Should" thoughts are insane thoughts because there is no such thing as personal power, personal mind, personal control and will. As long as we are thinking "should" thoughts, we are existentially insane (which is not a psychiatric category). Contact with Reality brings healing, not only to ourselves but to the situation in which we happen to be, as well.

Yielding or capitulating to the will of God sometimes feels like dying. "Whosoever will save his life shall lose it: and whosoever will lose his life for my sake shall find it" (Matthew 16:25).

One of the significant methods leading to surrender is a linguistic method, namely, we seek to eliminate from our vocabulary and thinking process the word "should." This method is very helpful if sincerely applied. Then there is the method of learning to be interested in spiritual good rather than in personal power and control.

With the help of these and other steps we come closer and closer to a realization of a life in God under the governing presence of omniactive Mind, Love-Intelligence. Gradually, our willfulness and stubborn resistance and rigidity disappear, and more and more we become mindful of a higher intelligence working in our affairs. Finally, we reach a point where not for an instant do we lose sight of the fact that God is our life, and Divine Mind governs all our thoughts, decisions, choices, motivations, actions, responses, and expressions. We thus become spontaneous people instead of rigid, tyrannical, and self-righteous individuals. Our entire mode of being-in-the-world becomes spiritualized and there is a complete and radical transformation in the way we are thinking, speaking, seeing, acting, and responding.

Among the many new trends which come and go with great rapidity in our culture is the trend of "assertiveness training" which, interestingly enough, follows right on the heels of another trend called "relaxation response." These arise from the seeming fact that life appears to be humanly controlled and dualistic. People don't seem to understand that to be assertive or to be timid is the same thing. Assertiveness is self-confirmatory and so is timidity. As the French say, "Plus ça change, plus c'est la même chose." The more things seem to change, the more they remain the same.

Unenlightened life is anchored in the self-confirmatory world of ideation. What we are about is liberation from the self-confirmatory idea of life because the self-confirmatory idea of life is self-destructive and is the source of all suffering and confusion. "Be not conformed to this world: but be ye transformed by the renewing of your mind, that ye may prove what is that good, and acceptable, and perfect, will of God" (Romans 12:2).

All self-confirmatory ideation is seductive, provocative, and intimidating. If we live in the belief of personal power, then we live in dread of powerlessness. The question may be asked, Does it take personal power to surrender to the will of God? Two things are required: exhaustion or wisdom.

A schoolteacher reported the following: "I work in a nursery school and there is currently an epidemic of colds among the children and teachers. Oddly enough, this is quite a frequent occurrence. The whole school tends to come down with something from time to time. Since I am working in this school, I would like to know how not to get a cold. This seems to me to be a very difficult situation because in looking at these children, one has the impression that sickness is their normal condition of life. They are neglected children. Some of them are even so-called 'abused' children. Most of them come from disturbed families. I would like to know how to be helpful to them and protect myself at the same time."

There are mainly two ways to get sick: by wanting to or by not wanting to. At this point we must ask, What is the meaning of epidemics? Epidemics reveal a universal preoccupation with one's physical selfhood. There is a universal natural inclination in everyone toward self-confirmatory thinking. And whenever someone comes up with a new way of doing it, everybody jumps on the bandwagon and then we have an epidemic. Every time a new type of disease is publicized, it starts a trend.

Some years ago, when appendectomy was perfected as a surgical procedure and publicized in the papers, there was an epidemic of appendicitis all over Europe. Then there was a time when doctors discovered the technique of tonsillectomy, and there followed an epidemic of tonsillectomies. The world seems to be eagerly waiting for new forms of self-confirmatory experience.

However, those on the spiritual path know that there is divine permission and power to refuse to indulge in self-confirmatory ideation. Thus one can be spared the suffering so common among people. One must be willing to be interested in the good of God more than in physical experiences. The Bible says: "We are confident, I say, and willing rather to be absent from the body, and to be present with the Lord" (2 Corinthians 5:8).

The prevalence of self-confirmatory thinking centers on the body; we want to feel that we have a body. It is interesting to consider the legal term "habeas corpus," which means that you have a body and are therefore a legal entity. Consequently the law respects your right to physical integrity. But we say: "You just seem to have a body, and the sooner you realize that you are a spiritual entity rather than a physical person, the sooner you will be free of this pervasive desire for self-confirmatory experiences."

The understanding of man's spiritual nature is not easily arrived at, yet it is possible. And when that realization is attained, the inclination to illness and grief is greatly diminished.

There is a story in the Bible of a rich young man who came to Jesus and said, "I am very interested in spiritual enlightenment; I would like to be your disciple. What must I do?" Jesus said to him, "Go home and give away everything that you have." He couldn't do it because he cherished his material possessions. As long as we cherish material possessions — which includes the body — it is impossible to attain spiritual consciousness, because whatever we cherish is our reality. If we are materialistically inclined, we cherish the physical presence of our loved ones, and that is called possessiveness. Possessiveness is a particularly stubborn form of materialism which makes it impossible to see that what is really valuable is not matter but spirit.

When we look at a statue of the Buddha, we see that it is made of a piece of metal or clay worth a few cents, but what the face is expressing and communicating is priceless. It cannot be bought for money. And the value of that sculpture is not in the brass but in the expression which it communicates. That is spirit in juxtaposition to matter.

When we love one another we love the spiritual qualities which we manifest rather than blue eyes, brown hair, organs, etc. We have to outgrow the primitive form of love which focuses on the tangible, and we have to cultivate an appreciation of spiritual qualities in one another to a point where these become of primary value. In proportion that we have learned to appreciate spiritual qualities, our interest in the material substance of people, things, and places will fade out of awareness and will lose its importance. This can reach a point when a piece of property or a physical body completely disappears from thought and the spiritual qualities are clearly present.

And thus it happens that enlightened people do not grieve. They do not have that great sense of loss when a loved one departs because the spiritual qualities are always present. They never die. "Blessed are they that mourn: for they shall be comforted" (Matthew 5:4), provided they come to understand that they haven't lost what is truly essential.

The way to heal grief is to spiritualize our concept of the departed one. The more clearly we are able to see the spiritual qualities of an individual, the less grief there will be because there will be no sense of loss. The real cannot be lost. If we are more mature in our love and ask ourselves, what do we love about our children or our friends, we will see that it is not their physical appearance but their qualities. Therefore, it is impossible to lose a loved one.

A mother of a college-age boy related the following experience: "Recently, we went to visit our son at his school. Lately, I was able not to miss him because I have learned to see him in spiritual terms rather than as a physical personality. But on our way down, as we approached the school, certain emotionalism invaded my consciousness and I couldn't wait to see him and to feel him near me. I wanted to be near his body. This was a great setback for me, and I realized I did him a disservice too, because all I was interested in was to make myself feel good by using him. It is incredible how that kind of thinking can take you out of spiritual consciousness and plunge you into the 'sea of mental garbage.' This experience was an eye-opener to me. Especially, I was keenly aware of my sadness at parting, which previously usually was not there."

The enlightened way of communicating love is without much physical contact, because the love which is communicated through the senses is, in fact, mutual exploitation for the purpose of sensory pleasure. Real love, being spiritual, needs no physical contact, and yet it communicates itself and has a powerful affirmative impact. The stimulation of the senses through bodily contact increases the desire for self-confirmatory experiences, and the more we love someone in this manner, the more susceptible he or she becomes to physical illness, because through physical love, petting, fondling, hugging, kissing, pampering, we are just whetting the appetite for self-confirmatory ideation. But spiritual love has a contrary effect. It lifts the loved one out of his body awareness into the consciousness of Divine Reality, where everything is perfect and man is not susceptible to illness and problems.

"Fail-Safe"

In everyone's life experience there are occasions of criticism, attacks, and rejection. The question is, How to cope with these or minimize their effects? Man has no right to influence anyone; it is, however, his duty to God to be influential. How are we to understand that? We become influential by embodying the right values and by making valid statements about what is intelligent, what is good, what is helpful, what is creative, what is beautiful, what is wholesome, and leaving it up to others to accept or reject. We can never be clever enough to prevent people from thinking the way they want to think, and even if we were, it would not be right to do it. Therefore, in order to be beneficial presences either in spiritual guidance, in psychotherapy, in marital life, in group life, or in life in general, we need to learn *the nonpersonal mode of being-in-the-world.*

Whatever ideas we present, we must know that those are not our own ideas. Good ideas come from God through inspiration. They are gifts of creative Mind. We present them for free consideration and allow people the freedom to respond to them positively or negatively. To some business people and politicians this, of course, would seem absurd because in the business world and in politics there is a belief that one has to sell ideas to people. But if we do sell our ideas to people, they will be troublesome; if we do not succeed, we will be troubled. In either case no good can come of it. The only solution is to be a nonpersonal beneficial presence, voicing whatever seems to be existentially valid in any particular situation. And then, if there is criticism and contention and opposition, it will in no way have an effect on us or on anyone else. The truth cannot be destroyed by criticism. It stands by itself. It is indestructible. And since we are not personal owners of it, we can in no way be frustrated or affected by its rejection. Interestingly enough, when the truth is presented in a personal way, it becomes unacceptable because we don't know where the truth begins and we end.

It is not easy to learn the nonpersonal mode of communicating ideas because we are so interested in our own personhood or in the personhood of other people. Often, when we try to be nonpersonal, we wind up being impersonal. The impersonal, however, is personal. When we are nonpersonal then the ideas are the focus of attention. When we are personal, we are pushing ourselves into the focus of attention. When we are impersonal we are sort of rejecting others and thereby making them the focus of attention. To reject or to accept is the same. If we reject someone, we are making him important as a person in a negative way. If we accept someone, we are making him important positively.

A beneficial presence in the world is a witness to the truth. It is not the witness that is important but the truth. The nonpersonal way is issue-centered, and people are given the right to misunderstand, even distort the issues, without this constituting a personal attack.

All these things sound rather simple. However, they are not really simple because the nonpersonal mode of being-in-the-world can be frightening. To most people it conjures up the fear of utter loneliness. Most of us have a fear of letting go of the old and facing something new. People can be attached to persons, places, things, and ideas, and these attachments can be unconscious and can be very strong. Anyone and anything that would tend to separate us from our attachments is liable to arouse a great deal of anxiety. In psychoanalysis this is called separation anxiety, but we call it existential anxiety. All of us have a tendency to lean on some person, some place, or some thing. We say we get used to certain relationships. When a necessity for a change arises, let us say, to part with some person — it could be a friend, or a spouse, or a child going off to college — we are often seized with tremendous anxiety. This anxiety can manifest itself in the form of some physical illness. We may believe that some outward circumstance is responsible for our condition and we do not realize that actually what we are confronted with is existential anxiety.

Sometimes, as we grow more mature and our values change, it is inevitable that we have to give up certain things which we have come to lean on for a sense of security. It can be a big issue or it can be something trivial. In teaching Metapsychiatry it sometimes happens that the viewpoints expressed point up the invalidity of some other viewpoints. If among the students there is someone who has developed an attachment to a certain psychotherapeutic school or a certain way of thinking, such a student may become disturbed, contentious, and defensive of his previous position.

Everyone is, to a certain degree, superstitious until he finds that power which can never be lost, refuted, or destroyed. And this power is God, omnipotent Mind, Love-Intelligence. This is the only way to attain a real sense of assurance. The Bible says: "Acquaint now thyself with him, and be at peace" (Job 22:21). If we do not have this acquaintance with omniactive Love-Intelligence as an existential Reality, we are forever reaching out for some invalid thing to cling to. The false systems of security are personal, materialistic, and intellectual. If we learn to lean on omnipresent Mind, we can never be separated from the source of our strength.

Here we can mention a startling fact, namely, whenever we find ourselves facing some physical symptom or any other kind of problem, we can be sure that we are in a state of fear. Some would say that the fear is generated by the threat to our health, or to our peace, but that is not correct. It is exactly the other way around. The fear is primary and the sickness or a distressing situation is just an indication of the fact that we are in a state of fear because something is threatening our security system. This can be a person, or the dawning of a new idea which is threatening to invalidate an old idea, etc. There is no sickness or problem that is not based on an underlying fear of the collapse of a false system of security.

Recently I spoke to a young lady whose great system of security was self-reliance. This young writer lived for the past two years in a primitive hut in the woods of Maine, all by herself writing a novel. She was proud to relate how she was able to take care of herself and all her needs fearlessly and efficiently, relying on no one at all, how she could surmount all obstacles in her life without anyone's help. However, lately she had come up against an enemy which she was unable to "handle." She had developed some kind of a spinal condition and no one seemed to be able to help her. This had completely disorganized her security system. She lives in great fear and with a sense of utter failure, not knowing which way to turn, whom to believe, and what to do.

Metapsychiatry is endeavoring to help her understand that self-reliance or ego strength, while it is universally extolled as a virtue, is actually just an illusory and unreliable security system. In order to be healed, one needs to find the existentially valid way of fearlessness, namely, conscious awareness of that "love [which] casteth out fear" (1 John 4:18). This alone is fail-safe.

A Sense of Humor

What does it mean when we lose our sense of humor? When we lose our sense of humor it is a sign that we have become involved with the cares of this world, that we have begun to take things seriously, that we are hypnotized and afraid. At this point we seem to be unable to transcend the material world and to take a higher view of things. We have also lost sight of God.

Some Zen Masters believe that Jesus was always joyous, even under the seemingly most trying circumstances. And indeed, they reveal to us that enlightened man is never serious; he is reverential, but his outlook is joyful, confident, assured, and peaceful.

To be serious is to be self-righteous. The foundation of healthy humor is joy. Before we can have a sense of humor, we must be joyous. If we are joyless, we are humorless. The question is now, What does it take to be joyous? This may become clear if we consider the fact that one of the most undesirable qualities anyone can manifest is that of a man who takes himself too seriously. Almost everyone finds this objectionable. What does it mean when we take ourselves too seriously? It is an indication that we believe that we live in our heads. There are people who have the illusion that they live in their heads. There are people who believe they live in their senses. Some believe they live in their emotions. These are the intellectuals, the sensualists, the emotional people, and the materialists. The stronger this belief is, the more serious and anxious such an individual will be and, as a consequence, he will be joyless.

Joy comes to us when we begin to see that we live and move and have our being in God, in infinite Mind. When these insights dawn upon us, we begin to see ourselves in a larger context, and with that, there is a growing sense of freedom and dominion.

It is important to distinguish between healthy humor and sick humor. Sick humor is not really humor. It is pseudo-humor and in actuality it is but a release of hostile feelings. It is a disguised way of expressing hostility and hurting people. It is a seduction to join in demeaning people or circumstances. Real humor is based on a sudden unmasking of the paradoxical nature of human experiences. This is tension releasing, enlightening, and uplifting. It liberates us from the danger of taking ourselves too seriously.

There is a Zen story which describes a monk who reached Satori, which is the experience of sudden enlightenment. This monk is described as having had a sudden spell of laughter lasting two days. It is safe to assume that from a divine perspective the human condition must appear quite ridiculous. At times we can catch a glimpse of this truth while reading historical novels, or seeing reruns of old movies which at one time were considered serious portrayals of real life.

Some humorless people tend to exert a hypnotic spell over others and intimidate them to the point where no one dares to be happy in their presence. Some religious leaders and evangelists have a tendency to mesmerize their audiences causing them to be joyless and fearful. They induce a sense of oppression, a gloom of doom. A characteristic feature of their mode of communication is that of pointing their fingers at people and waving their hands in an endeavor to personalize their message.

It is very important to understand how hypnotism works, so that one may become immune against this nefarious endeavor to deprive one of joy. Hypnotism works three ways: through seduction, provocation, and intimidation. We can tell when we are hypnotized by the fact that we find ourselves suddenly joyless, with no sense of humor. In this condition we are very susceptible to accidents, illness, and conflicts with our fellow men. Jesus warned us against mesmerism and admonished all to be sober and vigilant, to watch and pray.

Another powerful defense against hypnotism is compassion. Compassion understands that the would-be hypnotist is an ignorant individual — usually power-mad — and that his is a very troublesome condition. Compassion can see through the error and forgive because it is not threatened.

By understanding ourselves as manifestations of Divine Love-Intelligence, living in Divine Mind, we can transcend this human mockery and remain free. Then there can be joy, the laughter of release, and freedom in the knowledge that "none of these things moves me" (Acts 20:24).

A young lady remarked, "The more I struggle to be somebody, the more joyless I become and tend to develop backaches and headaches, etc. Things become especially bad when I start thinking about my background and the influence my parents had on me. Somehow I keep having the idea that because of my past, I am where I am and I cannot get out of it. These thoughts express themselves in painful spasms in my back. The question which plagues me is this — how can I disconnect myself from the past...?"

First we must realize that there is no such thing as cause and effect. The present is not caused by the past; it only seems that way. The moment we accept a "logical" cause-and-effect explanation, we are lost in a sense of victimization, which is self-confirmatory. We have descended into the quagmire of interaction thinking wherein there is no hope of healing. We are involved in thinking of ourselves as conditioned human personalities. On that level there are no solutions. The human condition is incurable. Real solutions are spiritual, not psychological. We must resist the temptation to diagnose our problems psychologically.

To find healing we must make a radical departure from the past, from psychology, and from the human condition, and recognize that we are spiritual emanations of infinite Love-Intelligence. We must let go of the past and of the illusion that we are human persons, molded by our parents. Man is a divine consciousness and the past never was, for God is not in the past, He is not in the future, and not in the present. God, life, and Reality are in the timeless now. We do not live in a time frame, for the past is pride, the future is ambition, and the present is vanity. Spiritual existence takes place in the timeless now and is therefore perfect.

The above-mentioned young lady was asked whether she cherished her past. She quickly answered, "I hate it." At this point she was confronted by the fact that whether she cherished her past or hated it, it was essentially the same thing because it means that she was involved with it.

This again demonstrates the paradoxical nature of the human dilemma, which can at times be very humorous when it comes into awareness as a surprise. On such occasions the light of the truth breaks through in consciousness, and we may receive a healing realization of the nondual nature of Reality. Here all human problems disappear, just as darkness disappears with the coming of light.

In Metapsychiatry we often talk of the good of God. Just what the good of God is, is not easily understood. For instance, we can understand what the good of an apple is because we can "sink our teeth" into it, but the good of God is more elusive. Yet it is very important to understand it and to develop the capacity to be aware of it.

What makes the understanding of the good of God difficult is materialism, personalism, sensualism, emotionalism, and intellectualism, for it is natural to think of the good things in life in terms of "tangibles." The Bible clearly states: "The natural man receiveth not the things of the Spirit of God: for they are foolishness unto him: neither can he know them, because they are spiritually discerned" (1 Corinthians 2:14). Therefore, if we have not yet developed this spiritual discernment which we all have but which is just hidden, we really do not know what we are talking about when we talk about the good of God. It is just words to us. But if we cultivate spiritual awareness, we can develop the faculty of spiritual discernment.

When we have awakened this faculty in ourselves, we leave behind the natural man. We are not human beings any more. We are spiritual beings. "Awake thou that sleepest, and arise from the dead, and Christ shall give thee light" (Ephesians 5:14). Materialism is deadness.

We seek to become aware of the fact that the good of God already is, always was, and always will be. But in order to know what it really is, we must have first-hand experiential awareness of it, and we speak of the awareness of spiritual blessedness and ask, What is it? Is it warm? Is it cool? What does it taste like? What does it look like? What is its shape? Where can it be found? Where is it located? How much does it weigh? It has none of these characteristics. Spiritual blessedness is a recognition of the fact that everything everywhere is already all right and all things are working together for good; that yes is good and no is also good.

When we have developed this awareness, we know that we do not have to agonize over what should be or what should not be; we do not have to control anything anymore. There is a higher intelligence present, active, operating, harmonizing all our affairs and blessing us.

Now the question arises, What does it take to have spiritual discernment at all times? We have to be willing to give up the natural man and welcome spiritual existence and identity, for we cannot serve two masters. For instance, we cannot be greedy for money and possessions and at the same time maintain spiritual consciousness. The more we are willing to leave behind the "five gates of hell" (sensualism, emotionalism, intellectualism, personalism, and materialism), the easier it is to wake up to the good of God, and the more real it will become to us.

The Bible says, "As in Adam all die, even so in Christ shall all be made alive" (1 Corinthians 15:22). We could paraphrase this passage by saying: As in Adam all are subject to sickness and suffering, to feeling good and to feeling bad, even so in Christ Jesus all are healed and live in spiritual bliss. The supreme good is *bliss-consciousness*, which is entirely separate from conventional human experiences. Bliss-consciousness is not a human experience. It is a spiritual condition.

Once we have discovered bliss-consciousness we are no longer interested in feeling good or feeling bad, being rich or being poor, being right or being wrong, having power or being powerless. We are interested in true happiness which "changeth not." This is not in the domain of feelings. It is not experiential. It is a state of consciousness which is the Kingdom of God. Therefore, we do not ask each other, How do you feel? And we do not speak about how we feel. We pay very little attention to these preoccupations of natural man.

At this point perhaps it would be helpful to remind ourselves what the word "spiritual" means. Spiritual is that which is neither material nor psychological, for psychology is the activity of the fleshly mind. So whatever is psychological is actually material. Spiritual is that which transcends the material, the psychological, the emotional, the sensual, and the temporal.

The right understanding of the good of God can turn our attention from the tribulations of this world to spiritual blessedness, and this may result in healing and comfort. We could say: In the world of "should" and "should not" we shall have tribulations but let us be of good cheer, for there is a way to overcome (transcend) this world.

Whatever we experience seems to us to be real. We say, This is real because I can experience it. But a hypnotist could make us experience anything he wanted to and it would not be reality. This proves that what we experience is a dream, whether it is food, or aches and pains, or time, or feeling good, or feeling bad. This is the dream from which Jesus Christ comes to awaken us. It is not really life. It is a dream about life. Therefore, the biblical statement says: "Awake thou that sleepest, and arise from the dead" (Ephesians 5:14).

The Curtain of Fear

A thirty-five-year-old man reported that he developed a bad cold on the occasion of his parents' visit with him over the Christmas holidays. During this time he became aware of the fact that his parents were neither interested in him, nor in his work, nor in anything else connected with his life, that they were only pursuing their private pleasures. He had a massive experience of abandonment.

The question may be rightfully asked, What does it mean to feel abandoned? A sense of abandonment awakens in us certain deep-seated fears of annihilation, stemming from childhood. The interesting thing about this is that it seems to be timeless. This unconscious fear does not diminish with time, and the experience can occur in adults just as easily as in children.

Often, when grown up, we may believe that we have outgrown our parents, that we have espoused entirely new ways of living, that we have come to live by different values, and that we are fully emancipated from our parents. This, however, is not as simple as it would seem. Occasional encounters with our parents may stir up deeply rooted anxieties and this may be accompanied by certain physical and emotional breakdowns and disturbances.

It is well known that at Christmas and other holidays, when families gather usually in anticipation of happiness and love, unpleasant side effects tend to develop. It is exactly the fear of abandonment which makes it so difficult to espouse values contrary to, or different from, those of our parents. We dare not abandon our parents' values lest they abandon us. Interestingly enough, this fear can be just as strong after the parents have died. There is deep-seated fear of abandonment, a fear of annihilation which we call existential anxiety.

Sometimes our parents live by weird value systems. For instance, if parents believe in physical beatings and abuse, a child may grow up with a conviction that he loves to be beaten and that he craves it. He may even pay someone to beat him. Being beaten is associated in his thoughts with survival. Therefore, he loves it. He may even get sexual pleasure out of it. If life depends on being beaten, then there is a love of being beaten.

These instances of irrational cravings may come in a variety of forms and are called compulsions. When survival is at issue, then there is a compulsion to perform whatever is required. Thus it seems difficult to change values, because it may mean separation from significant people in individual lives.

Actually, there is only one way to be healed of existential anxiety, namely, to really come to understand that God is our father and our mother, that we are offspring of omni-active Love-Intelligence, that we are individual expressions of divine consciousness. Once we understand that, then our parents become our sisters and brothers and we are not living in deep-rooted fear of abandonment, because our real father and mother can never be separated from us. We can never be abandoned by omnipresent Love-Intelligence. Without that realization we would be just deceiving ourselves about our independence. No amount of psychologizing will really bring about an emancipation of an individual from dependency on his parents. He may gain intellectual insight into his situation, but he will not be free. Without God this is not possible. With God all things are possible.

The questions may be asked, How can the realization of divine parenthood occur in the consciousness of an individual seeker? Is there anything that can facilitate this process? An important factor in the achievement of this goal is a willingness to be "scared." Our compulsions and our clinging to our human parents and their values are efforts at warding off our fear of abandonment.

A young lady lived with the conviction that she hates all men, particularly her husband. She was actually living the life of a compulsive man-hater and a sower of dissension. One day, while talking with her mother on the telephone, she became aware of, and actually heard her mother say that she would not come to visit her as long as her husband was in the house. After she hung up the phone, she became aware of a sense of intimidation. This alerted her to the problem and she began to pray by affirming: "God is my Mother; my mother is not God. My life is in God; I refuse to be intimidated. No one can make me hate my husband."

Thus, this example illustrates that first we must become aware of the fact that our compulsions are efforts at avoiding fear. We are afraid to be afraid. Just as we have to be willing to be embarrassed if we want to become humble, we also must be willing to endure the fear of annihilation in order to discover that beyond nothingness there is God. "The everlasting arms of Love" are awaiting us beyond the curtain of fear.

A free-lance photographer reported that his life was very disconcerting, especially on days when there were no assignments to fill. He wished he could have a regular job to go to in the morning and set hours of work every day. In other words, he longed for a structured life-style where time and space and activity were clearly circumscribed and under control.

There seems to be in man a universal longing for structure. There seems to be a fear of the formless and a corresponding desire to give form to every idea. Some individuals can feel comfortable only in the army or in jail or in some other severely structured setting. There are some who like to wear restrictive clothing; for instance, some women cannot function without wearing a corset, etc. In general, we can say the more structure the less life. A corpse is a completely structured man.

On the other hand, we could say that without structure

there would be chaos, anarchy, and confusion. Life would not be possible. Thus, we must admit that structure is necessary for intelligent and orderly existence. The question is, What kind of structure would be most compatible with healthy, fulfilling life? It seems that it would have to be a structure which would permit the maximum freedom of expression for the creative spirit.

This brings us to a consideration of the issue of order. From an existential standpoint we can distinguish two types of order: sick order and healthy order. In sick order there is tyranny and repression. It is based on human willfulness. It is a manifestation of "should" thinking. By this we mean thinking in terms of preconceived ideas of what should be or what should not be. This kind of sick order can be found in totalitarian systems of government, in which case we speak of pathological societies; or in family situations it can manifest itself in rebelliousness and obsessive-compulsive neurotic disturbances of individuals. Another form of sick order is the result of permissiveness which results in licentious disorderliness, or chaotic conditions of confusion, neglect, and criminality both in individuals and society, as for instance in some school systems under the influence of mistaken philosophies and educational policies.

Thus we see that structure, while absolutely necessary, remains a constant problem, and it seems almost impossible to have just the right amount of it at all times and under all circumstances. If there is too much of it, it leads to strangulation; and if there is too little of it, it leads to disorganization, anxiety, and chaos. We see that totalitarian regimes have their problems and the so-called "free" societies with democratic systems of government have their problems. Analogously, institutions, families, and individuals also suffer from either too much structure or too little.

Thus we have to consider the possibility of healthy order. As was mentioned before, sick order or structure is based on human willfulness or human will-lessness, overconcern or neglect, tyranny or permissiveness. Sick order is a disease of the human will. Sick order is man made. Pathological structures are indicative of the failure of the humanistic idea.

In contrast to this, healthy order is primarily characterized by *principles of aesthetics*. Here beauty, harmony, joy, intelligence, love, and the enhancement of the quality of life are the basic ingredients. For instance, a bouquet of flowers or a blossoming forsythia bush may be judged very unstructured, even haphazard; yet inherent in each is a higher type of order and structure signifying aesthetic value. Aesthetic structures are transcendent and independent of human volition and calculative thinking. When Mao Tse-tung proclaimed, "Let a hundred flowers bloom," he didn't realize what consequences this order would have on his ideological tyranny. Little wonder he had to rescind his statement shortly thereafter.

Healthy order is spiritual. Spiritual values and principles constitute the "infinite structure" which makes freedom and responsibility compatible with creativity and fulfillment. Healthy order is under the control of infinite creative Mind, cosmic Love-Intelligence.

The biblical warning against "graven images" can be understood as an attempt at counteracting the tendency of the human mind to give form to the formless and in the process lose sight of the true God, infinite Love-Intelligence.

The well-known tendency of various religions toward formalism and ritualism also belongs in the category of attempting to confine the infinite to finite structures. Whenever this happens, man stops asking, What is God? and starts asking, What should I do to please God? In this process he winds up worshiping himself as a worshiper.

The right understanding of "infinite structure" makes it possible to live and function in the world effectively in great freedom and usefulness. It is possible to become fearless, loving, and creative under most circumstances. When Jesus spoke of "being in the world but not of it," he may have been pointing to the possibility of transcendence of the restrictive structures of unenlightened existence. In a similar vein the Zen Masters speak of enlightenment as entering the "Gateless Gate."

When human consciousness awakens to Spiritual Reality, it comes into conscious at-one-ment with infinite Mind. This is also spoken of as Cosmic Consciousness. Here spiritual and aesthetic values govern man's functioning, and life is a manifestation of the divine order. All things are governed by creative Love-Intelligence. Here there is neither tyranny nor permissiveness.

"Infinite structure" makes freedom and responsibility compatible because responsibility is man's ability to respond to the beautiful, the good, and the true.

Jesus' heart-rending cry from the cross, "Why hast thou forsaken me?" (Matthew 27:46) has been a great problem to many sincere believers and students of the Truth. Many answers have been given. For instance, one reply was that Jesus was reciting the lines from the twenty-second Psalm, or that he was speaking for the world whose sins he took upon himself, etc. Somehow these answers do not seem satisfactory, and debates about the sentence have never stopped.

The question is usually divided into two parts: First, why did he say what he said? Second, how could he say it, since he himself was God, or the son of God, or the most enlightened man who ever lived and whose central theme was "I and my Father are one" (John 10:30)?

Whenever satisfactory answers are difficult to arrive at, it usually indicates that the wrong questions are being asked. An invalid question can never provide a satisfactory answer. Therefore, instead of asking, Why? and How? it might be preferable to ask, What is the meaning of the cry "Father, why hast thou abandoned me?"

Here it is helpful to remind ourselves that Jesus was an existential teacher. This means that he utilized every life situation to teach the world about the human condition and how to overcome it through the right understanding of God.

Since the cross is the symbol of human suffering, his outcry could be understood as a demonstration of what happens to all of us when confronted with severe pain. We all tend to cry out in agony that God has abandoned us. We have the impression of a separation between God and man. It is possible that Jesus endeavored to teach us that the meaning of suffering lies in an unawareness of man's inseparability from God. We do not suffer because God has abandoned us, but we suffer because we are ignorant of our at-one-ment with God, infinite Love-Intelligence.

At times when the importance of constant conscious awareness of God's presence becomes clear to a student of the Way, he may wish to avoid contact with people and other forms of distraction. The danger here is that of becoming a recluse. Monasticism has often been misinterpreted in terms of avoidance of the world and spiritual isolationism. However, Jesus clearly stated that we must be "in the world, yet not of it" (2 Corinthians 10:3). Metapsychiatry takes this to mean that an enlightened man is a participant in the affairs of the world as a "beneficial presence" rather than a beneficent person, which means that he is a constructive citizen without being a so-called "do gooder," or manipulator, or power broker. He is influential without influencing anyone. He neither seeks nor shuns social participation.

All things tend to work together for good around him for he is a focal point of harmony and healing. His consciousness is in constant relation to the source of all life, power, wisdom, and love. He is conscious of Omnipresence, which precludes the possibility of separation between God and man.

In order to participate in the world as a beneficial presence it is also needed to understand what constitutes healthy communication. For there are many forms of communication, for instance: debating, discussing, arguing, persuading, negotiating, selling, contending, propagandizing, boasting, baiting, bullying, bickering, etc. A beneficial presence in the world practices the art of *hermeneutic dialogue*, which is a joint participation in a process of shedding light on the truth at hand. As the Bible puts it: "Come, let us reason together" (Isaiah 1:18). The Buddhists speak of "tathata" or "true suchness," which could also be called issue-oriented communication, or Truth-centered living.

Sex Education

Our culture seems to be obsessed with sex. Recently there was a three-hour-long program on the educational television station devoted to the topic of sex. Elegant and sophisticated professional people talked with scientific authoritativeness about the desirability of sex. For three hours they advised the public on how to do sex. "How to do" was the basic consideration upon which the whole program was built.

How to? is an operational question. The existential question is, *What* is it? The sixth principle of Metapsychiatry is this: "If you know what, you know how." But if we are studying "how," we may never know "what." Therefore, whenever we approach any issue in life or in our profession, the first question to ask is, What is it? not, How do you do it? Suppose we then apply this existential inquiry to the mystery of sex and ask, What is sex? A panel member on the television program called it "pleasuring," which seems like a new word. Others called it recreation; someone else referred to it as "penile thrust."

The main idea that came through on that program was that the central issue in sex is orgasm. Assuming that the most important thing in sex is orgasm, they arrived at the conclusion that any kind of sex is desirable and good as long as it leads to an orgasm. So they were talking about sado-masochism, homosexuality, lesbianism, oral sex, sex "above the belt and below the belt," etc. On the surface it seems to be a liberation from Victorian and religious prudishness and hypocrisy. There is now the freedom of talking about and practicing sex without shame and guilt, and it has become the topic of conversation on all levels of society, even on television, where children of all ages are exposed to it.

Surely there is some good in freedom of expression because prudishness and hypocrisy were ways of repression and perpetuation of ignorance. But there are two types of ignorance. There is negative ignorance and there is positive ignorance. In the Victorian era and in the ages of religious hypocrisy there was negative ignorance; people just did not know anything. Ignorance is always troublesome. But there is a worse kind of ignorance and that is positive ignorance. It is when we think we know but we don't really know. As mentioned previously, the philosopher Heidegger speaks of positive ignorance this way: If a blind man knows that he is blind, he is safe because he knows that he cannot see and he proceeds carefully. But suppose that there was a blind man who believed that he could see. Wouldn't he be in grave danger of hurting himself?

Which ignorance is more dangerous, the negative or the positive ignorance? When we have an operational view of sex we are in a state of positive ignorance because we think we know and we proceed recklessly. It is very possible that many of the tragedies of marital life, which present-day statistics allude to, are based on attempts to lead a sex life in marriage based on positive ignorance. People think they know what sex is and they try to live accordingly, and it does not really work.

It is a very naïve assumption that sex is a physical act. If we give it a little thought, we notice that it is absolutely impossible to have sex without certain kinds of thoughts. It is absolutely impossible for a man to have an erection without some specific erotogenic thought. The Greek philosopher Heraclitus said: "Sine ratione nihil est," which means nothing can happen without thought. So the fundamental element in all sexual activity is thought. Since it is not possible to have sex without thoughts, therefore sex is a mental activity; it is not just a physical act. In the operational approach to sex this "minor" detail is completely overlooked.

If sex is not a physical act but a mental one, wouldn't it stand to reason that the primary issue to consider are those thought processes which underlie the sexual activity? We could say that the sexual act itself is but a shadow of thought. The essential element of sex is thought. Sex, therefore, is not physical but mental. If we want to understand good sex — and by good I mean healthy — then we have to study those mental processes which underlie healthy sexual expression. Any kind of sexual act which has unhealthy mental content, even though on the surface it is seemingly pleasurable, may be pathological and pathogenic, which means one could have seemingly good sex but actually become sicker in the process.

If we understand sex as a shadow of mental processes, then we will see that every sexual act, whether seemingly healthy or unhealthy, has a meaning. That is, it has a mental equivalent. Previously we defined meaning as a mental equivalent of a phenomenon. Sex is the phenomenon and the thoughts which underlie the sexual act comprise the meaning of that phenomenon, i.e., the mental equivalent.

Earlier we mentioned a case of a man who was developing many problems and who lived in a homosexual marriage. His favorite mode of sexual expression was sodomy. He claimed to love his partner. He claimed to have terrific orgasms. Sex to him was the focus and center of all creativity, and he built a certain romantic fantasy around it. As we were exploring his mode of being-in-the-world, we discovered that his fantasies revolved around having power to coerce, to subjugate, and to humiliate other people. And this fantasy was the mental basis for his sexual expression. But of course, sex is just one aspect of life. Fantasies cannot be limited to sexual expression. They tend to overflow into other areas of life experience. One cannot be a sadistic aggressor in bed only, and be an intelligent beneficial presence in the world and a healthy individual in one's social and professional life. Whatever the underlying fantasies that nurture the sexual desires are the same fantasies that will enter and color the mode of being-in-the-world, namely, the character structure and mental health. So the character and the mode of being-in-the-world of this particular man was that of a coercively interacting, willful-aggressive, hostile-demanding individual who had many other problems in life besides his particular mode of practicing sex.

We are as healthy as our thoughts are. Mental health depends on existentially valid thinking. What constitutes existentially valid thinking? How do we know what is a healthy-minded individual? Is there a way of being sure? Who is to tell us how we should think? The sex educators imply that whatever can provide man with the most pleasurable orgasm is healthy. However, a rapist gets his most powerful orgasm through raping. A masochist gets his orgasm through being defiled, humiliated, abused, even tortured. There is no limit to how far erotic fantasies can take man. The aim of erotic fantasies is the attainment of maximum orgiastic pleasure.

There is a general assumption that the greater the pleasure, the healthier the sex, and the healthier the sex, the healthier man is. Initially Freud believed that too. He postulated a criterion of mental health and called it genital primacy. He believed that if one can perform the sexual act genitally and get a big charge out of it, this is proof positive of health. Later he had to revise this naïve idea, and that is how ego psychology came into being.

But the above-mentioned television program, which may have been watched by millions of people throughout the United States, gave the impression that any kind of sex is good and desirable as long as it is pleasurable. However, pleasure and orgasm are in no way indicative of health. Metapsychiatry is not against pleasure but neither does it consider it to be a criterion of health. Suppose we put pleasure under the existential microscope and ask the question, What is it? We already discovered that sex is mental and now we ask, What is pleasure? We do not ask, How do you get pleasure, but, What is it? The answer is that pleasure is a thought, a self-confirmatory idea. Pleasure says: "I feel, therefore I am." Now suppose we ask the question, What is pain? It is the same thing. What does pain say? It says: "I feel, therefore I am."

It would seem that man's central preoccupation is the question, Do I exist, or don't I exist? Self-confirmatory ideation is the underlying dynamism which drives man to seek pleasure, pain, excitement, sorrow, remorse, hatred, feeling good, feeling bad, etc. Sex is just one of the many ways man seeks to confirm himself as actually existing as an individual physical person. Now we can understand how it is possible that to be a sadist or a masochist is the same, that to be a sex fiend or an ascetic is the same; sex and nonsex is the same.

At this point the question arises, Where do we go from here? The ancient sages, brilliant philosophers, various religious seers, and the Bible show us the way into the spiritual dimension of consciousness. What do we find there? We find truth, love, joy, harmony, supreme intelligence, creativity, peace, assurance, healing, perfect life, and freedom. Ye shall know the truth of existence and this truth shall make you free. Free from what? Free from pleasure? No. The Bible says: "For with thee is the fountain of life: in thy light shall we see light" (Psalm 36:9). "Thou wilt show me the path of life: in thy presence is fullness of joy; at thy right hand there are pleasures for evermore" (Psalm 16:11). The spiritual life is not devoid of pleasure, but this pleasure is qualitatively different because it is not self-confirmatory. It is confirmatory of the basic goodness of Reality. Reality is all good, perfect, wholesome, and without complications.

When we understand what Reality is, we are not losing anything that is good. We are only discovering what is really good and not what is good and evil. Ignorant man is crucified between good and evil, pleasure and pain, yes and no. Enlightened man knows the good which has no opposite. He knows the *nondual realm of Reality.*

Spiritual existence is not an operational idea; it is a fact of being. If we are to educate people about anything, it is important to start out with the right question. If we start out teaching and educating with the wrong question, we will not be educators. We will be miseducators. The television program was a massive example of miseducation offered to the nation under the pretext of authoritative scientific knowledge. And that is sad, because the people who got educated through that program will have to suffer the consequences of their positive ignorance.

Yielding

It has been often observed by individuals who are trying to lose weight that they run into a situation where they feel depressed if they don't eat, and they feel depressed if they eat. If they don't eat, they feel deprived of the pleasure of eating, and if they eat, they feel deprived of the prospect of becoming slim. Thus they are caught on the horns of a dilemma.

This predicament reveals an important aspect of spiritual progress. On the spiritual path we are required to give up many cherished notions with which we have grown up from childhood on and which we have come to consider vitally important for happiness, even survival.

I remember a little boy who used to stop at store windows displaying toys, and over and over again he would cry out: "I want this more than anything else in the world!" This little one is in all of us, and there are many "toys" which we believe to be absolutely essential for our happiness. On the path we must yield them up one by one. In the process we may experience depressions, episodes of feeling deprived and sorry for ourselves. If we don't understand the dynamics of this process, we may get scared about what is happening to us. Therefore, it is helpful to know that when we feel the worst, that is when we make progress. When we seem to be stagnating, we are not stagnating. We are gestating. We are in the process of parting with some cherished idea.

Sometimes this cherished idea is what we love, sometimes it is what we love to hate, and at other times it is what we love to intimidate ourselves with. These are three forms of self-confirmatory ideation which we have to yield up sooner or later, for *without yielding there is no healing*. No matter how much we know about the truth, no matter how well we understand the meaning of our problems, without yielding them up there can be no healing.

I remember a young woman, well advanced on the spiritual path and very receptive to spiritual truths, who had periods of depression and a sense of futility, hopelessness, and self-pity until it was discovered that she loved to hate her mother-in-law with such great passion that she was unwilling to give it up. She kept this consuming passion sort of encapsulated in her consciousness to avoid facing up to it until her periods of depression became intolerable.

When a healing does not come for a long time, it does not necessarily mean that the problem is serious; it may only mean that we are reluctant to yield certain cherished notions of what is important in life. To others these may seem silly and trivial, and yet we cling to them as if our very life depended on them. In one case it may be food, in another sex, or intellectualism, or secret ambitions, or anything else.

In the process of having to part with our cherished beliefs we have the impression that without them life would be completely empty and there would be nothing worth living for. When we reach the point of staring down into the abyss of absolute nothingness, then we can say: "But the good of life is spiritual. There is no other good but the good God gives." At first, of course, we may not believe it even if we say it, but if we persist we may begin to have a sense of being "uplifted." The truth of that statement begins to make sense and we realize that the good we seek is spiritual blessedness, and that actually nothing else is really good.

In proportion that our yielding to this truth is sincere and complete, in that proportion there will always be a healing, and more than healing. For as the Bible puts it: "My cup runneth over" (Psalm 23:5). There is a special meaning to this metaphor. Whenever a genuine healing occurs in our experience, we are not only relieved of a certain problem, but we become stronger and more assured about life in general. So it is always healing plus, because we have ascended a rung on the ladder of realization. Jesus did not heal people only in order to relieve their suffering, but to help them realize that life is God. He healed sickness in order to help people awaken to Divine Reality. Healing is just a byproduct of the process of awakening and of giving up certain cherished ideas hitherto clung to.

Occasionally we hear of some individuals who were able to discard their eyeglasses after many years of depending on them. It is interesting to contemplate the fact that many people find wearing eyeglasses — in a certain sense — ego gratifying; it enhances the impression and awareness of oneself as a physical person equipped with a symbol of scholarliness and intellectuality, somewhat like a pipe is for some psychologists. Many people find that they feel more secure while smoking a pipe, or a cigar, or wearing glasses.

It would seem then that a sense of eyesight has something to do with the sense of ego. In all of us there is a great desire to be seen and to be recognized as a tangible, significant presence. In turn, we have a desire to see those people who see us in this way. The internal dialogue goes somewhat like this: "I am a significant physical personality and everyone can see that I really am."

A common feature of the enlightened state is the absence of this desire. Enlightened man says: "It does not matter whether I am seen or not seen. What is important is to see what really is, because the visible world is but a world of appearances." He is interested not in illusions or phenomena but in Reality.

Under ordinary circumstances one of the greatest pleasures in life is seeing people, nature, art, beauty, etc. Life without seeing would be most frightening. The central point of human experience is the awareness of oneself as tangibly and visibly material. Jesus said at one point: "For judgment I am come into this world, that they which see not might see; and that they which see might be made blind" (John 9:39). In connection with this it is important to take note of the fact that physical infirmities tend to disappear when Spiritual Reality is discerned.

Jesus also is known to have said to some people: "Having eyes, see ye not? and having ears, hear ye not?" (Mark 8:18), and to others he said, "But blessed are your eyes, for they see: and your ears, for they hear" (Matthew 13:16).

Apparently, seeing is not just the function of the organ of the eyes. We can say "there is more than meets the eyes." Seeing is often used as a synonym for understanding, and understanding is clearly a spiritual faculty of consciousness. There is a mode of seeing which transcends anatomical structure and the physiology of optics. Whenever we have some difficulty in seeing with our eyes, we assume that the trouble is in the eyeballs and we seek to remedy it with corrective lenses, because we have a clear impression that the trouble is localized in the eyeballs, somewhat as when we have a running nose. It feels like the problem is in the nose, and we go to the pharmacy to buy some nasal spray or drops and apply them to the nose to fix it, so to speak. But we know that even though the symptom appears to be in the nose, the problem is not in the nose but in the thought of the individual.

Physical problems are mental. They always have a specific individualized meaning. We speak of mental equivalents of outward manifestations. If our vision is in some way impaired, this is a physical manifestation of a certain mind-set which can be understood and corrected. Thus healings are possible, for the problem is not in the eyes but in thought or in a specific belief system which governs us.

Everyone has grown up in certain specific belief systems which determine his mode of being-in-the-world, including his predilections to various physical illnesses and qualities. Eye problems are just as mental as any other physical phenomena.

The question may be asked, If our eye problems are mental, how is it possible that glasses can effectively improve our eyesight? To answer this question, the analogy with the running nose might again be helpful. We claim that the running nose problem is also mental; nevertheless, when nose drops or spray are applied to the mucous membrane, there is instant relief of limited duration. This is followed by rebound worsening of the condition. Similarly, the use of eyeglasses gives us instant relief with progressive deterioration of the condition. Corrective lenses do not heal the problem. They just mitigate it temporarily.

The body is a mental concept appearing in visible form. "The word was made flesh" (John 1:14), and anything connected with the body is just a variation of the mental concept. Therefore, eyesight is also mental; eyesight is "mindsight." It is the mind that sees. Concerning material man, the Bible makes the following statement: "Cease ye from man, whose breath is in his nostrils: for wherein is he to be accounted of?" (Isaiah 2:22). We can also think about it as saying, "Cease ye from man whose sight is in his eyeballs; for wherein is he to be accounted of," which seems to say that the material appearance of an individual is just appearance. It is nothing substantial. Therefore the material, fleshly mind which sees and hears and tastes and smells, calculates, imagines, schemes, and fantasizes, argues and debates, suffers and enjoys, is not to be taken as a reality, for it is illusion. It is not the real man.

The more we are able to see the mental nature of the universe and everything in it, the closer we are to Reality. Once we see the mental nature of the personal, fleshly mind, we have reached the point of transcendence. Then we become aware of the fact that the universe is governed by another mind, which is the mind of the universe or the universal Mind. And this universal Mind is infinite Love-Intelligence and it manifests itself in an infinite variety of ways which comprises all possible faculties, including perfect sight. A theory is useful only if it has practical applications and consequences. And here we see that the slightest glimpse of the truth of this theory frequently results in healing.

To pray effectively about sight, we can proceed somewhat along these lines: Only God can see. Man is an individualized divine consciousness. Therefore he partakes in all of the faculties of Divine Mind, which are individualized in everyone's being. God sees through man perfectly. God, the Divine Mind, and the faculty of sight are not subject to deterioration or any kind of imperfection. God is man's I am, and God is man's eyesight. Man sees with the same eyes with which God sees. God sees and man partakes in that seeing. Our faculties are not our faculties but are individualized expressions of the faculties of God.

The Natural, the Supernatural, and the Spiritual

In this day and age, when occultism is again in vogue in its various forms, it seems desirable to have a clear understanding of the difference between the natural, the supernatural, and the spiritual. Many people make the mistake of confusing the spiritual, and the metaphysical with the so-called "supernatural." When that happens, the Bible, the teachings of the prophets, and religion in general tend to be lumped together into a pejorative package under the title "the mystical, the irrational, the fantastic, the foolish."

However, this kind of confusion is tragic, because it tends to discourage people from seriously considering that dimension of consciousness which is the source of all that is beautiful, real, good, and existentially valid.

For purposes of clarity we can define the natural as that aspect of human awareness which is mediated by the senses. This area of inquiry belongs to the domain of the so-called "natural sciences." The supernatural is an area of human interest which is outside of sensory perception. This is the area of the so-called "paranormal" psychic phenomena, hypnotism, magic, witchcraft, satanism, demonology, necromancy, and such. The spiritual, however, is neither natural nor supernatural. It is a dimension of Reality which is neither sensory nor suprasensory; it is not normal or paranormal or abnormal. It is a faculty of awareness, uniquely human, consisting of man's inherent capability of appreciating aesthetic and spiritual values and principles. Love, honesty, harmony, beauty, compassion, justice, freedom, joy, gratitude are neither natural nor supernatural. They are spiritual qualities belonging to the domain of Divine Reality.

The study of the natural is the domain of scientific research and is motivated by man's desire to control his environment and secure his own physical survival. The study of the supernatural is motivated by man's desire to control his fellow man and secure his own superiority. The study of the spiritual is motivated by man's desire to come into harmony with the Fundamental Order of Existence and actualize in himself the optimum qualities which are potentially present and available to him.

The clear differentiation between the natural, the supernatural, and the spiritual is also important when we are studying the phenomena of healing. Medical science endeavors to heal on the basis of scientific research within the limits of the natural, material world. The scientific viewpoint is that man is part of nature, just like any other life form and, therefore, the only valid approach to his problems must be based on data gathered through sensory evidence.

Another approach to healing is based on the belief in the supernatural. These are sometimes called psychic healings, faith healings, miraculous healings, hypnotism, mesmerism, auto-suggestion, laying-on-of-hands, etc.

In the domain of the natural, healing power is sought in nature. In the domain of the supernatural, healing power is ascribed to individuals, or to locations and rituals, etc.

Spiritual healing is of an entirely different order. It is based on enlightened realization of transcendent Reality in individual consciousness. Essentially, spiritual healing requires at least a partial awakening of the patient to a recognition of some aspect of Spiritual Reality. It is important to emphasize that spiritual healing is not synonymous with faith healing or anything else.

It is safe to say that, except for spiritual healing, all other forms of healing are essentially based on phenomena of suggestion and hypnotism. Hypnotism is an experience based on man's belief in the power of a person, place, thing, or idea. Whenever hypnotism is at work, the healing is but an illusion, because the essence of hypnotism is illusion. Of course, many forms of illness, and other problems are essentially illusory. Therefore, when such a healing occurs, what happens is that an undesirable illusion is replaced by some acceptable illusion.

One of the most powerful instruments of hypnotism in our electronic age is television. The television exercises a powerful hypnotic influence on the viewer. It can encourage criminal behavior, it can propagate illness and it can sell remedies for illness. The right understanding of the difference between the natural, the supernatural, and the spiritual can provide us with a modicum of immunity against becoming victimized by the forces of suggestion, persuasion, seduction, intimidation, and provocation.

Enlightened man is able to observe these phenomena without being affected by them. He can preserve his integrity through the knowledge of the truth which indeed makes him free. But the Bible says: "The natural man receiveth not the things of the Spirit of God: for they are foolishness unto him: neither can he know them, because they are spiritually discerned" (1 Corinthians 2:14).

Innocence

We are often asked to define consciousness. In order to understand consciousness it is helpful to distinguish between consciousness and the content of consciousness. Consciousness is the faculty which makes us capable of becoming aware of the content of our consciousness. Consciousness is the faculty of being aware of being aware. Progress on the spiritual path essentially consists of an expanding faculty of awareness of the content of our consciousness and a growing ability to discriminate between valid and invalid ideas.

When the Bible speaks about laying up for ourselves treasures in heaven "where neither moth nor rust doth corrupt, and where thieves do not break through nor steal" (Matthew 6:20), it refers to a process of increasing appreciation of spiritual values and principles and a diminishing interest in materialism and psychological preoccupations.

Whenever we have a problem and we are helped to see its meaning, our faculty of awareness is being expanded. We are helped to become aware of the presence of certain invalid thoughts and thought patterns. This is a growth experience. From then on these invalid thought patterns can be replaced by valid ones. Whenever that takes place, a healing occurs. Not only does the problem disappear, but our consciousness has expanded and increased in its ability to discern its own content.

In Metapsychiatry we can avail ourselves of the method of "two intelligent questions." These two questions are: (1) What is the meaning of what seems to be? and (2) What is what really is? With the help of these two questions anyone can learn to heal himself by becoming aware of the content of his consciousness and improving it.

These two questions also reveal the tragic nature of the unawakened human consciousness which is subject to enslavement by an endless variety of hypnotic suggestions so that man falls prey to dreams. When human consciousness is invaded by a dream, man becomes unaware of God and suffers the consequences. We are continuously victimized by dreams of a multifarious nature. The Bible speaks of man's tendency to "fall asleep."

Most often we are inclined to blame ourselves for our problems as if we were the originators of them. Sometimes we say, "I am guilty of thinking the wrong thoughts and I am being punished for it." But actually this is not correct, for man cannot invent wrong thoughts to think. Adam and Eve did not invent the serpent. The serpent came and ensnared Adam and Eve. They fell victim to an evil thought.

The question may now be asked, Who made the serpent? If God were responsible for the appearance of the serpent, that would make God a very nasty creator, a miscreator. But God is Love-Intelligence. Therefore He could not have placed the serpent there to entrap Adam and Eve into sin by causing them to get befuddled. Similarly, it is helpful to realize that man is innocent. No matter how twisted he seems to be, essentially he is innocent.

It is a universal human experience to be invaded by dreams and invalid thoughts coming from the "sea of mental garbage." For instance, if someone manifests symptoms of power-madness, vanity, greed, contentiousness, etc., he did not produce these qualities in himself, and certainly it would not help to blame him. As long as man blames himself for his problems, or is blamed by others, he cannot be healed. For if problems had a creator, then they would be real, and Reality cannot be abolished or corrected. Reality is immutable.

To come back to Adam and Eve, let us reiterate that they

did not sin. They were victims of entrapment by an invalid thought. And this invalid thought, coming to them from the "sea of mental garbage," obscured their vision of Reality. Thus they are mythological prototypes of the human condition. Of course, many might say that this interpretation is an attempt at doing away with original sin and man's responsibility toward God. However, there is a difference between responsibility toward God and culpability. Man is not culpable but he is responsible, that is, he is able to respond to the good of God and consequently be redeemed.

Traditional religions have held to the idea that man is a sinner and that he is guilty, blameworthy, evil, and culpable. As a result of that, very little healing has actually taken place in the world. Experience has shown that reformation of character and redemptive healings are much more easily attained when man's fundamental innocence is recognized and instead of condemnation he is faced with compassion. "For God sent not his Son into the world to condemn the world; but that the world through him might be saved" (John 3:17).

Ignorance is not a sin but a tragic aspect of the human condition from which man can be redeemed. In Metapsychiatry we understand the word "sin" to be derived from the Latin *sine Deo* which means to live without the awareness of God. This does not make man culpable or guilty, but unenlightened.

The Bureaucrat and the Therapist

At times, if we work in an agency or in a hospital or in any other kind of institutional setting, it is easy to become confused and, under the pressure of internal politics, actually forget that we are therapists. Unwittingly we may become bureaucrats. It is therefore very helpful to have a clear concept in mind as to the difference between being a bureaucrat and being a therapist.

While bureaucracy is necessary, we have to know that being a bureaucrat and being a therapist are two mutually countervailing functions. A good bureaucrat works for society or for the institution where he is employed. A bad bureaucrat works primarily for his own advancement in the hierarchy of the institution in which he is employed. The good bureaucrat's aim is to benefit society; the bad bureaucrat's aim is to benefit himself. In either case, a bureaucrat is not interested in the welfare of his client. By definition the client here is a means to an end, a pawn in the hands of bureaucratic interests, even if well intentioned. Since the client is aware of the fact that he is being used, manipulated either in favor of society or the agency, or in favor of the bureaucrat's self-interest, he often develops an intense hatred of bureaucracy.

In contrast to all this, the therapist is primarily interested in benefitting the patient. While the bureaucrat is primarily thinking about what society wants, what the agency wants, or what he himself wants, the therapist thinks about what the patient wants. Having established to his own satisfaction what the patient wants, he seeks to discern what the patient really needs. There is an important difference between what a patient or client wants and what he needs.

Most often a patient's wants, especially in an agency setting, are primarily socio-economic. For instance, let us take the example of a divorced woman on welfare with a disturbed child of school age. She comes to an agency primarily seeking economic support and a solution to the child's school problems. The patient wants to survive. She wants to preserve her dignity in the community and to protect her child from diagnostic labels which would handicap him for the rest of his life. So the patient's concerns are primarily social and economic. This is what the patient wants.

But a therapist must go beyond all this and try to understand and, if possible, provide what the patient really needs.

It is helpful to contemplate the fact that, in general, God does not seem to be interested in what we want. Whenever we pray to God to give us what we want, He does not seem to answer. But God is ready and willing to give us always what we really need. And it is the therapist's job to discern the real need of the patient, to clarify it, and make it possible for the patient to receive what he really needs. Whenever the real needs are supplied, there is a healing, even in socio-economic terms.

It is important to repeat that bureaucracy is not really interested in what a client wants or needs; bureaucracy is mainly interested in perpetuating itself. There is no such thing as a generous bureaucracy; often there is only corrupt and noncaring bureaucracy. A therapist, however, transcends the limitations of bureaucratic systems and seeks to supply the patient's needs.

Needs are mostly spiritual. The need of the individual mentioned above would be, for instance, to come to understand that she is not a social parasite, that she can have genuine self-esteem, that she has inner potentialities which can be realized, that she can come to know that she is loved and worthy of being loved, that she is acceptable in the sight of her Creator, that it is possible for her to live a useful and dignified life. These realizations are her spiritual and existential needs. A therapist would focus on awakening her to a realization of her full worthiness and acceptability as a spiritual child of God. And out of that sense of self-worth there would come the solution to all her problems.

So the therapist aims at expanding the consciousness of the patient, because therein lie all solutions. Man is an individual divine consciousness. All this points to the fact that if someone is a therapist, no matter under what circumstances he may be functioning, his perceptions and his responses will be motivated by an entirely different system of values than that of a bureaucrat.

The bureaucrat and the client are inevitably in an adversary relationship, since their interests lie in opposite directions. However, a poorly trained or immature therapist may also find himself in conflict with the patient if he believes himself to be a "personal helper."

The Metapsychiatric therapist knows that there are *not two*. The therapeutic agent is the *Truth of Being*. In the realm of Love-Intelligence there is neither self nor other. Since there are *not two*, there is neither cooperation, collaboration, resistance, nor conflict.

Truth is not personal. Love is not personal. Intelligence, understanding, healing, are not personal. The Christ is not personal but universal. Thus a therapist can function as a beneficial presence regardless of the structure which society imposes on him.

Safety

The problem of safety is particularly timely these days when we hear and read about crimes, accidents, violence, and victimization in general. The seventh principle of Metapsychiatry states: "Nothing comes into experience uninvited." Many people find this somewhat hard to believe. Some are even offended by the idea. Nevertheless, let us look into it and try to consider the following seemingly outrageous statement: There are only two ways to become a victim — by wanting to, or by not wanting to. How is that possible?

The point is that, either way, the idea of the possibility of victimization is maintained in consciousness. Whatever we cherish or hate or fear tends to come into experience. Therefore, the question is, How can one be safe in a world seemingly rampant with crime? In what way can the knowledge of the above principle benefit us and provide us with protection? Some are beginning to understand that carrying a weapon, such as a gun or knife, not only does not afford protection, but actually tends to invite trouble. If we carry a weapon, it means that we have in mind the possibility of becoming endangered. Now if we have that thought in mind, that in itself tends to act as a magnet, attracting corresponding experiences.

Now the question may be asked, Should one just remain naïve and ignorant, and walk around without any idea of the possibility of danger? Is naïveté protection? Is ignorance bliss? No, naïveté and ignorance are not desirable either. Therefore, it would seem that there is no solution. This brings to mind a Zen saying: "Yes is no, and no is yes."

This paradox is particularly troublesome when parents try to admonish their children to be careful, to watch out crossing the street, or to drive carefully, or "do this, don't do that," because unwittingly they are implanting ideas of fear and danger into the children's thoughts. On the other hand, they cannot say, "Don't be afraid crossing the street, never mind the dangers," etc., because this would have the same effect. Neither would it be advisable for them to ignore the whole problem of danger.

This truly seems to be a conundrum. There is actually no solution to the problem of inviting experiences, as long as our viewpoint on life is purely human. A solution, however, begins to emerge when we consider what Jesus said to his disciples on one occasion: "Behold, I send you forth as sheep in the midst of wolves: be ye therefore wise as serpents, and harmless as doves" (Matthew 10:16). He did not say to his disciples, "Be careful not to be devoured by the wolves, or arm yourselves against the wolves." He recommended a certain quality of being. What determines the quality of our being? The quality of our being is determined by our state of consciousness. What determines the state of consciousness? Our state of consciousness is determined by the values we cherish. To be wise as serpents and harmless as doves means cherishing qualities which Jesus considered necessary for safety in a hostile world. What does the Old Testament have to offer in regard to safety? The ninety-first Psalm offers the safety of spiritual consciousness. It says: "He that dwelleth in the secret place of the most High shall abide under the shadow of the Almighty" (Psalm 91:1). "Because thou hast made the Lord, which is my refuge, even the most High, thy habitation; there shall no evil befall thee, neither shall any plague come nigh thy dwelling" (Psalm 91:9, 10).

It is not what others can do to us that is the problem, but what our own thoughts bring into experience. The enemy is not on the outside. It is in our own consciousness. We suffer the consequences of our own habits of thought rather than what other people do to us, or what conditions impose on us.

It is also very important to understand what Jesus meant when he said: "A man's foes shall be they of his own household" (Matthew 10:36). The most intimate aspects of our life are our own thoughts. Our own thoughts are the most dangerous factors which we must learn to beware of and to purify. Our own thoughts can make us or break us. Therefore, right thinking is of paramount importance for safety, for mental health, for physical health, for social integration, and for happiness.

How is an individual to know which thoughts are safe to entertain and which thoughts are dangerous to entertain? We can find out in the course of life that if we give hospitality to certain thoughts, these will bring disaster, or suffering, or discord, or illness into our lives. If we are ignorant, what usually happens is that we replace one set of invalid thoughts by another set of invalid thoughts, and we are forever looking around to find out what kind of thoughts other people entertain, in the hope that they may, perchance, have a solution. Then we find that there are certain trends in our culture which come in waves. Every now and then some kind of new fad appears. It becomes fashionable to think about this and that. All sorts of thought systems are sweeping the world. And if we have no solid anchor in understanding what is valid, we are repeatedly swept away by tides of trends. These can be political, philosophical, religious, pseudoreligious, etc. However, again and again we get disappointed.

There is only one way to cope with life, namely, to find that system of values which is not subject to fashionable trends, which is basically existentially valid, which will never change, and will always bear good fruit in terms of bringing us peace and health and assurance, even in the midst of a very insecure world.

It is impossible not to think of something, but it is possible to be so imbued with the knowledge and the awareness of spiritual values and the presence and the power of God that we can have a sense of safety and we actually can be safe.

Please note that we did not say that one has to know the Bible, or that one has to be religious, or be a theologian. We said we need the awareness of these values and the awareness of Divine Reality. Consciousness has to be imbued with these truths, and then one does not just know about them, but one actually realizes them. This is the only way we can be liberated from the conundrum of "yes is no, and no is yes."

Marriage and Parenting

In our modern times marriage is becoming a controversial issue. Many young couples ask themselves the question, Should we get married or shouldn't we get married? This, of course, is the wrong question. The right question to ask is, What is marriage? For if we know what marriage is, that is, if we have a clear understanding of what an existentially valid marriage is, then the right action will be easier to follow.

No one could hope to have a good marriage if he approaches it on the basis of "should" thinking. Here we may profitably seek to clarify the difference between making a decision to get married and committing oneself to a "mode of being-in-the-world" which includes being married. If one is making a decision, then whatever action follows is subsidiary to the ego; we call it self-confirmatory action. But if one is making a commitment, this is subsidiary to a greater idea. This we call God-confirmatory action.

The second Metapsychiatric principle states: "Take no thought for what should be or what should not be; seek ye first to know the good of God which already is." When a man and woman find a great deal of compatibility between themselves, they can ask the question, Is the good of God discernible in this situation? Can we find joint participation in the good of God? If the answer to these questions is yes, there usually follows a spontaneous commitment to this participation which is for all eternity. This constitutes an existentially valid marriage. The details follow as a natural unfoldment of the basic recognition that in this partnership the good of God is discernibly present. Thus one can get married without having to be pressured into it, or making agonizing decisions about it.

The idea of love between persons is an insufficient basis for marriage, but the idea of love as a contextual basis for living with someone is valid. The idea of love between two persons is a very narrow-minded way of seeing life, but love can be seen in a broader sense as constituting the spiritual environment in which a marriage can thrive and be securely founded.

It is also helpful to consider the concept of responsibility. On the human level responsibility has its opposite, namely, irresponsibility. But on the spiritual level responsibility has no opposite. In Divine Reality there are no opposites. All is nondual. On the human level responsibility is a burdensome idea of being obligated or ensnared, and it is closely associated in our thought with blame and guilt. However, the spiritual concept of responsibility is beautiful because it connotes the ability to respond to the good of God. We all have this ability. When two people find the good of God in their lives together, they can respond to this goodness with gratitude, joy, and commitment. They respond in a responsible way to the will of God.

Whatever we are interested in, we are responsive to and that is how commitment takes place. Someone asked, What if one of the partners is not interested in the good of God and they are already married? This is a situation where the spiritually minded partner must hear "the sound of one hand." The "sound of one hand" is a Zen Buddhist koan which stands for the ability to transcend the pressures and the temptations which enter into interaction thinking and behavior. It is based on a constant conscious awareness of the presence and the power of omniactive Mind, the governing principle of life.

This ability is also of great importance in enlightened parenting, because children have a tendency toward self-confirmatory, interactive, and provocative behavior. The enlightened parent will preserve his transcendent perspective and seek to be an inspiration to the children through prayer and right comportment, so that eventually the children will begin to appreciate the upright position in life and be inspired by the parents' way. If the parents are not sufficiently enlightened, they may have the tendency to mold the children, control them, and impose certain "shoulds" and "should nots" on them. The result of these erroneous ways is "the sound of two hands" which, as explained earlier, means collisions, conflict, rebellion, and strife.

Here we may very well remind ourselves of the eighth principle of Metapsychiatry: "Problems are lessons designed for our edification." Essentially, there are three kinds of parents: 1) learning parents, (2) teaching parents, and (3) daydreaming. The learning parent is an inspiration and a model for growth. The teaching parent is tyrannical and creates resistance in his children. A daydreaming parent is perhaps the most damaging one, for he rejects his children in favor of his own fantasies, and at times may set impossible conditions for love in a nonverbal way. For instance, there are parents who fantasize about having mentally retarded children, or insane, or sexually aberrant children and the children may be aware of these unspoken demands on them on a subliminal level and seek to comply. This, of course, leads to endless possibilities of suffering and misdirected modes of being-in-the-world.

Of course, no one can be blamed for these processes, whether conscious or unconscious, because they are just manifestations of ignorance. In general, we can add that children help their parents grow up. By the time the parents reach middle age, the children have finished their job and moved out.

There is a story attributed to Mark Twain, who supposedly said that when he was seventeen years old he was convinced that his parents were the most ignorant people in the world; but when he was twenty-seven, he was amazed to find how much his parents were able to learn in just ten years.

It seems vitally important that children have a chance to perceive that the parents' interests are focused on spiritual values. Whatever the parents are interested in will attract the children's interest. Thus there may follow a spontaneous unfoldment of the Christ-consciousness in them, provided the parents do not try to impose these values on them.

We do not indoctrinate; we seek to inspire. To influence is to trespass; it is tyranny. But to be influential is good. We seek to be inspiring and influential.

In the 1960's the feminist ideology deteriorated into a fashionable chic of women spending their time in groups complaining about their marriages and encouraging one another to take a dim view of men and the relationship of women to their husbands.

Under the title of "consciousness raising" many women fell into the error of becoming more and more unhappy and discontented in order to be fashionable. The constant rehearsal and advertising of problems is just as unhealthy as a medical diagnosis.

The fad of griping about one's marriage will in no way facilitate the attainment of harmony and conjugal bliss. Furthermore, politicizing of marriage and introducing civil rights concepts and legalistic fantasies result in the assumption that marriage is an adversary relationship where a power balance is the real issue. This, of course, is a complete perversion of the whole idea of harmonious living in an atmosphere of love and mutual approbation.

Marriage is not political, socio-economic, sexual, or legal; it is primarily an existential situation. What do we mean by this? Existential means that the real issue in marriage is survival under the most favorable and fulfilling conditions. The institution of marriage is ideally designed to improve the quality of life for both husband and wife and their offspring by creating a harmonious unit. Unfortunately, invalid ideologies are invading this institution and creating havoc in individuals' lives.

Marriage is not a place to fight for equal rights. It is not a battleground for ego-gratification, nor an arena for power-madness. Marriage is a situation where the beautiful, the good, the harmonious, and the intelligent life can be cultivated and realized. It is a joint participation in the good of God.

Recently someone said: "The only thing that is good in our marriage is sex. Everything else is rotten. We are both very unhappy, except for short moments in bed." This is an example of how invalid preconceived ideas about marriage can result in unhappiness. Without the right concept of marriage, people enter into this covenant with a wide variety of impossible expectations and fantasies. Therefore, it is very important to have a clear, existentially valid understanding of marriage and of life in general because only then is there the possibility of realizing and partaking in the good of God. The ideal marriage is without interaction thinking.

A great deal of suffering and illness in life comes from interaction thinking, so much so that whenever we get sick, it is a good idea to ask ourselves, "Who am I sick against?" It is helpful to realize that all interaction — even physical — is essentially mental. It is based on the belief of personal mindpowers acting against each other. Interaction is thinking about what another is thinking about what we are thinking.

When a marriage is based on joint participation in the good of God, the quality of happiness and well-being is entirely different from moments of pleasure based on ego-gratification. Ego-gratification is exciting and pleasurable (thus the word "heady"). This is counterfeit happiness; it is short-lived and has an obverse side of pain and disappointment. If a relationship is pleasurably exciting, then we are on an ego-trip. If in a situation there is an awareness of the good of God — which is spiritual blissfulness characterized by peace, assurance, gratitude, and love — then we are on the right track.

The right understanding of the good of God and the awareness of PAGL (peace, assurance gratitude, love) are very helpful indicators whereby we can judge whether our happiness is genuine or not. The poet Kahlil Gibran gives us two beautiful symbolic pictures of healthy marriage when he says: "The pillars of the temple stand apart," and "The strings of the harp vibrate separately to produce beautiful harmony." This illustrates the concept of being separate but not separated and of jointly participating in a harmonious marriage.

This also clarifies what a fallacy it is to think that marriage is an interpersonal relationship, or a sexual relationship, or a civil rights battleground, or a power struggle, or a legal contract. These cultural assumptions are existentially invalid and underlie a wide variety of problems and marital discord.

The Divine Context

Since Metapsychiatry is based on the metaphysical definition of man within the context of God, it is naturally important to have a very clear and existentially valid concept of God. There are many concepts of God, and they are mostly religious concepts. In the Old Testament God appears to be first a frightful judge, a warlord, and a legalistic authority. Later on He gradually becomes more benevolent and less punitive until, with the advent of Jesus, He becomes a loving Father. In fact, we can view the Bible as a record of man's evolving concept of God.

The more primitive the mentality of man is, the more frightful, intimidating, and even monstrous is his god, but Jesus speaks of God as a loving Father. Here we can already breathe a little easier, but still there is the problem of anthropomorphism. We can ask, What prompted Jesus to speak of God as a Father and thus give rise to male supremacist fantasies and reinforce the tendency toward anthropomorphism? We can theorize that the reason for this may have been the fact that Jesus was talking to very primitive people who were not yet sufficiently evolved to conceive of infinity or the possibility of an intelligence and power governing the universe and having no form.

It took many centuries for human consciousness to develop the capacity for abstract thinking and to conceive of a power and of an intelligence which is infinite, because infinity cannot be imagined. The moment we try to imagine something, it must assume a form. The formless cannot be imagined. Therefore it is very difficult even today for the average religious individual to conceive of God as an infinite presence, an infinite power, an infinite intelligence.

There was one man who went beyond Jesus in his definition of God. It was John who defined God as Love, not someone who loves, but simply Love. Thus, he is the first one to define God as a quality. Qualities do not have form. Here we already reach an evolutionary stage where individual human consciousness is able to speak of God without ascribing form to it.

It is interesting to remind ourselves that among the Ten Commandments in the Old Testament we find the prohibition against making "graven images" of God. Graven images refer to a mental process based on the power of imagination. In fact, it is a prohibition against the attempt to visualize God in some finite form. It is noteworthy that this commandment appears at a time when human consciousness was not yet ready to behold the formless. In order for something to be thought, it had to have a form. Abstract thinking was not a common ability. Undoubtedly there were unique individuals in ancient Egypt and in the Orient who were able to conceive of the formless and the infinite, but this was not true of the average human being.

In order to understand God in an existentially valid way — and this is crucial — it is necessary to reach such a level of mental development that one is comfortable with the idea of formlessness. We must come to know the unimaginable God, because that which can be imagined is purely imaginary, and we are not dealing with imaginary things. We seek to apprehend Reality.

To understand man in the context of God, it is important to understand God as unimaginable Reality; we have to be capable of knowing that which cannot be imagined. In Metapsychiatry we speak of God as Love-Intelligence. Love-Intelligence is a cosmic force constituting ultimate Reality. It cannot be given a form. This Love-Intelligence is the creative power from which everything real emanates. And man, as the image and likeness of God, is likewise unimaginable. The man that can be imagined is not man but a phenomenon, namely, an appearance. This man is formlessness masquerading as form. The famous Zen Master Suzuki used to startle his students with the mind-boggling statement: "Form is formlessness, and formlessness is form."

When we speak of masquerading, we imply that the form of the phenomenon is misleading and distracting and thus interfering with true perception. Jesus warned us, "Judge not according to the appearance, but judge righteous judgment" (John 7:24), which means if we judge man by his appearance, then we shall arrive at false conclusions about him and this will give rise to "many schools of psychotherapy." But if we judge righteous judgment, then there will be only one school of psychotherapy because then we will know the truth of what man really is, and the truth will make us free from error.

Thus, in order to have a solid, existentially valid foundation for a school of psychotherapy or spiritual guidance, we must know man as he really is, in the context of God. There is no such thing as man apart from God. It is impossible to arrive at any valid understanding of man when he is studied apart from his context.

Once I asked an artist, who had some problems, whether he could paint a picture without a background. He said, "Of course. It is very simple. I just take an empty canvas and paint the foreground and leave out the background...." He thought that if he did not paint the background, there is no background. But, of course, the empty canvas would be the background. It is impossible for anything to exist in the world in and of itself. It is impossible for man to exist without his creative background. And the creative background of man is infinite Love-Intelligence. And the background always determines the foreground. The foreground has no power over the background.

Man, in the context of God, is revealed to be a manifestation of Love-Intelligence. God can also be spoken of as Cosmic Consciousness. The quality of this infinite Love-Intelligence is consciousness and life itself. Cosmic Consciousness determines its infinite manifestations. Therefore, man is equipped with the capacity to be conscious. So infinite Cosmic Consciousness — which is the background — determines the foreground of an infinite variety of individualized consciousnesses. Man is a conscious expression of infinite Love-Intelligence. This is seeing man in the context of God.

The question may be asked, How can we see that which has no form and cannot be imagined? There is more to man than meets the eye. We all have the faculty to discern spiritual qualities in the world. We can see honesty. We can see integrity. We can see beauty. We can see love. We can see goodness. We can see joy. We can see peace. We can see harmony. We can see intelligence. None of these things has any form. None of these things can be imagined. None of these things is tangible, and yet they can be seen. What is the organ that sees these invisible things? Some people call it the soul, or spirit, or consciousness. Man is a spiritual being endowed with spiritual faculties of perception.

Recently I worked with a young woman who was blind from childhood on, and I told her: "You can really think of yourself as a sighted individual because Reality is available to you to perceive. In fact, you are able to see Reality because you are able to discern the spiritual attributes which comprise Reality, just as anyone else. Your spiritual faculties of perception are unimpaired." This was of great comfort to her. At once she felt herself closer to the rest of humanity and to God. She realized that all the essential elements of Reality are available to her to be "seen."

Our spiritual faculties of perception constitute the real essence of the good life. Whatever is good in life, whatever makes one happy, whatever is comforting, whatever is healing, whatever matters in life, is the awareness of these spiritual attributes of Reality. There is no human being who is not spiritual, but the vast majority of people are so involved with experiential living that they are distracted from the awareness of the spiritual dimension.

There is a radical difference between what is mediated through the senses — that which has form, is imaginable, and can be experienced — and that which is formless, unimaginable, and cannot be experienced but can be realized and spiritually perceived. It is the universal Love-Intelligence, man's true dwelling place. The apostle Paul said: "While we look not at the things which are seen, but at the things which are not seen: for the things which are seen are temporal; but the things which are not seen are eternal" (2 Corinthians 4:18), meaning real.

The universal tendency to desire and "experience" life is a great distraction which prevents us from using our spiritual faculties of perception. When a Metapsychiatrically oriented therapist sits down with a patient, he will not focus his attention on whether the patient is male or female, well dressed or poorly dressed, educated or uneducated, tall or short, heavy or slim, etc. His focus will be on the Reality of the individual and his concern will be to help him to awaken his innate faculties of spiritual perception and discover himself in the right context.

So the therapist views the patient in the context of absolute Reality, and that helps the patient to see himself in that context. When that realization is awakened in us, everything becomes transformed and healed.

In Metapsychiatry diseases are understood to be symptoms of misdirected modes of being-in-the-world. What we are helping people to be healed of are their modes of being-in-the-world, regardless of diagnostic labels. Misdirected modes of being-in-the-world can be recognized, regretted, and reoriented, and thus replaced by valid modes of being-in-the-world. These validate themselves through healings. Of course, no one can be healed against his will and it would be arrogant and intrusive to attempt to do so. The desire to be healed arises under two conditions — suffering and wisdom. Without them there is no motivation for healing, and the therapist has no right to attempt it.

In Metapsychiatry we see man in a larger context. In conventional psychological thinking man is seen as an autonomous unit, acting from his own mind and being affected by intrapsychic processes motivating him from the unconscious.

When we look at man as a psychophysiological organism, then we see that indeed there is such a thing as the unconscious. We do not see any place where a so-called "unconscious" could be located, but we are aware of the fact that there are many things we are not conscious of and there are things we are semi-conscious of, or more or less conscious of. There is a popular saying: "What you don't know can't hurt you." Thus, we say there is no unconscious, but there is unconsciousness. In Metapsychiatry, however, this is a triviality because the moment we see man in a wider context — in the context of God — then this issue disappears and what we have is God, infinite Cosmic Mind, completely determining man.

Many things which seem to be important in a narrower context completely disappear when the mental horizon is expanded to a wider context. In Newtonian physics, cause-and-effect relationships are a matter of fact, and in our everyday lives everyone knows that there is cause and effect. However, when we expand our mental horizon, we discover that there is really no such thing as a cause-and-effect relationship. In Metapsychiatry we seek to expand our mental horizon to the maximum possible dimension, that of Infinite Mind.

Let us consider, for instance, an object which we let drop to the ground. If we ask, Why did the object fall down? we are, in fact, asking what caused it to fall down. The answer is, the object dropped because it was let go of. This seems like common sense, cause-and-effect reasoning and an example of conventional, psychological reasoning. We always ask, Why do certain things happen? Why does someone have a headache? Why does someone fight with his employer? Why are we afraid of the dark? etc.

In Metapsychiatry we understand that there is no such thing as a cause-and-effect relationship. Therefore, we ask a different question. We ask, What is the meaning of what seems to be? If we ask, What is the meaning of an object dropping to the ground? we receive an answer, saying: This phenomenon reveals the existence of an invisible force called gravity. Or we may ask, What does it indicate that objects tend to fall to the ground? We immediately recognize that at this moment our mental horizon has become much broader than previously when we reasoned from the standpoint of cause and effect. The cause-and-effect dimension of reasoning is narrow-minded. It is applicable only within certain circumscribed, limited perspectives on life. Therefore, it is very important to know what questions to ask.

Metapsychiatry has isolated six questions, designated "futile" questions. These questions are universally asked in all schools of psychotherapy. As a result of these "six futile questions" our perspective on life and Reality remains limited. They keep us from expanding our mental horizon. The questions are as follows: What's wrong? How do you feel? Why? Who is to blame? What should I do? How should I do it? We have taken these questions for granted and it is time to question their validity. We are born ignorant and are educated to become increasingly so.

Just as cause-and-effect reasoning disappears in the context of Cosmic Consciousness, so the issue of conscious and unconscious thinking also fades away, and many other things tend to disappear when the mental horizon becomes wide enough.

We may now ask, If these "six futile questions" which are the foundation of conventional reasoning are eliminated, what is left? How are we going to function in life and in psychotherapy? Is it possible to live and function intelligently without these commonsense questions? Is it practical? Yes, it is. In Metapsychiatry we found two very useful "intelligent questions." These are: "What is the meaning of what seems to be?" and, "What is what really is?"

The "two intelligent questions" underlie and make possible the hermeneutic process of clarification, which is the basic method of Metapsychiatric therapy. To illustrate: A man comes seeking help for a marital problem. His marriage has deteriorated into a continuous state of discord. He hopes that the psychiatrist will find a way of straightening out his wife and making her do what he wants. This man, who happens to be a salesman and a hockey player, reveals a certain mode of being-in-the-world which could be best described as a "steamroller." It is pointed out to him that while he professes to be seeking guidance, he never gives the doctor a chance to get a word in edgewise, and that he continuously endeavors to instruct the doctor how he should "handle" his wife. After a while, it is explained to him that he is not really a hockey player and not even a salesman, because God never created such people, and that he happens to be a victim of miseducation concerning his own true nature, which is that of a man who could express peace, assurance, gratitude, love, and intelligence. At first, he finds this unbelievable. But slowly he begins to see that his marital discord reveals his misdirected mode of being-in-the-world and that this can be healed just as soon as he discovers the truth of his own being.

Many who read this may be tempted to reexplain what they are reading in terms of what they already know. Someone may say, But this is nothing new, it is not different from what others do. It is just a different vocabulary and attitude. Following is another example of the tendency to put "new wine into old bottles."

In Metapsychiatry mental health is defined as being a beneficial presence in the world. Whenever this definition is presented to an audience, shortly thereafter someone will invariably "correct" or reexplain it by speaking of a "beneficent person." When we inquire as to the meaning of this phenomenon, it is revealed to us that the concept of "beneficent person" is more in keeping with conventional thinking, which is operational and personalistic. Conventional psychological thinking views man as a self-existent personality, acting autonomously in the world, independent of God. But Metapsychiatry says, Let us expand our mental horizon and behold man in the context of God, infinite Love-Intelligence.

A beneficial presence is not an operator. Neither does he assume attitudes. We cannot make ourselves into beneficial presences. It is a quality of being arrived at through a liberated consciousness. What is our consciousness to be liberated from? We need to be liberated from the narrow confines of conventional thinking. We are all prisoners of conventional thinking. The bars of our prison window are built of the "six futile questions."

"The Nightmare Pill"

In Metapsychiatry the seventh principle states: "Nothing comes into experience uninvited." Occasionally, when this principle is presented to a group of people, someone will remark: "Do you mean to say that the victim invites disaster? Is the victim responsible for what is happening to him? Isn't this principle preposterous?"

In response to these questions it is important to explain, first of all, that a principle must apply under all circumstances, otherwise it is not a principle. For instance, if two and two is four, then two million and two million must be four million. Therefore, it is important to clarify the principle. When we say that nothing comes into experience uninvited, we are not saying that the victim is to blame for what happened to him. This would be a horrendous injustice, for it would seem to absolve the victimizers. We must understand that whether on an individual basis or on a national or international scale, whenever experiences are invited, it is not the person or persons who are doing it.

The real problem was and always is the existentially invalid thinking prevailing in consciousness. To repeat, it is always the existentially invalid thought, present in consciousness, which attracts corresponding experiences. It is always the thought which is the culprit. Mankind always has been and still is victimized by ignorance and by clinging to existentially invalid thoughts and mental images.

When we consider the various stories of miraculous escapes

of certain individuals and groups in history, we find that these people happened to be, to some extent, independent thinkers, not in conformity with the prevailing mental assumptions of their culture. Consequently, their experiences were at variance with those of the majority.

We can at this point clearly see that the victim and the victimizer have this in common: they are both driven by ignorance. It is also important to understand how the victimizer invariably becomes a victim in the end. Thus error destroys itself. Invalid ideas are not viable. Unfortunately, this problem is rampant in the world.

We see that the problem lies in man's insufficient understanding of what constitutes existentially valid thinking, in spite of the fact that the Old Testament contains the ninety-first Psalm, which is a clear presentation of what the remedy to this problem is. Unfortunately, the ninety-first Psalm and other important passages in the Bible are not considered in the context of their existential meaning. Few realize that the Psalmist intuitively discovered what is existentially valid for man, giving us a blueprint for survival and protection from illness, accidents, disasters, and even terrorism.

In the 1980's there was a great deal of publicity about atomic warfare in connection with a television movie. Millions of people had an opportunity to read about it, to see it, and to experience all the gruesome horrors by watching it on the television screen. The general assumption was that this exposé increased the sense of abhorrence in people and, hopefully, would insure that such things would never happen.

In considering this logic we may ask, Suppose scientific progress were to arrive at a point where someone developed a little pill which could produce a uniform nightmare of horrendous violence in all the people of the world. Would this pill cure mankind of wars, once and for all? Looking at it from this standpoint, we must regretfully face the fact that filling our consciousness with thoughts of violence, brutality, injustice, and evil will not heal these problems, just as studying psychopathology will not bring about mental health. Only the study of mental health can result in mental health. Only the study of what is existentially valid can bring about a transformation of human character in individuals and nations alike.

It is therefore clear that watching such television programs and saturating consciousness with images of pathology on a planetary scale — or any other scale for that matter — is not beneficial to anyone. There is a difference between the study of history and the exposure of the mind to the influences of television imagery. The study of history is nothing but information dealt with by the intellect; but the television screen has the power to change information into experience and that has existential implications for the viewer. Consequently, instead of having a beneficial effect for world peace, it tends to have a harmful effect, particularly on the mental and psychosomatic balance of individuals.

When we understand that all mankind is suffering — or, as the Bible puts it, "groaning" ("For we know that the whole creation groaneth and travaileth in pain together until now," Romans 8:22) — in disastrous experiences due to ignorance, then we have great compassion. We do not take it lightly; we are not callous or indifferent. Just because we refuse to swallow the "nightmare pill," it does not mean that we have no compassion for mankind.

In the history of civilization there have been only a handful of spiritual giants able to rise above the sea of ignorance surrounding them and provide mankind with some guidance. These are the Hebrew prophets, Jesus Christ and his disciples, and the Oriental spiritual luminaries. We must gratefully acknowledge the fact that in this period, in spite of all the horrors of recent history, the light of spiritual enlightenment shines brighter than ever and is seen by increasing numbers of people. And this is the hope of the world.

Fearlessness

In a class of projective techniques a teacher used a method of projecting certain pictures onto a screen and asked individual students to reveal their thoughts about what they saw. To her surprise, a number of students refused to respond to this request and a few others "drew a blank." The teacher explained that these students were exhibiting a "fear of self."

In conventional psychological thinking there is a tendency to ask two futile questions: one is, Why am I afraid? the other, What am I afraid of? Whenever these two questions are asked, many explanations can be found. If we explain something, this gives us the illusion of understanding. However, this is not so. In order to reach understanding of certain phenomena we must know the right questions to ask. In this case we would ask, What is the meaning of drawing a blank? In this case it would be revealed to us that it is a form of resistance and fear of being tricked into self-disclosure and being made into an object of investigation without conscious consent. We don't like to be objects of investigation.

The psychotherapeutic situation is set up according to the medical model, where the therapist functions as an investigator, seeking to find out what is wrong with the patient. He intrudes into the patient's personal life in order to find faults; he explores the most intimate details of the patient's past and of his present life. Unless one is just an outright exhibitionist, this is a very unpleasant experience. If we visualize the original Freudian set-up with the patient lying flat on his back and the doctor sitting behind him, out of his visual field and making notes and asking probing questions, it conjures up a picture of some sort of medieval inquisitory scene where the assumption was that man is an object, filled with some evil ideas which need to be brought out in order for him to be purified.

This kind of approach inevitably creates the well-known phenomenon of resistance. This also explains the generalized misgivings people tend to have about psychiatry, psychology, and psychotherapy, for these are perceived as forms of intrusion into the privacy of individuals and families under the guise of scientific helpfulness.

Projective tests are particularly suspect, because they are perceived as tricky ways of eliciting confidential information from unsuspecting patients, students, and applicants for jobs and promotions. The basic assumption is that therapists have a right to "help" people whether they like it or not, whether they want it or not. Of course, many patients believe that they want to be objects of scientific exploration, but if that were true, there would be no phenomena of resistance.

In traditional forms of psychotherapy resistance phenomena appear to be ubiquitous. They come in the form of many disguises, such as drawing blanks, missing appointments, hostility, contentiousness, even feigned cooperativeness. And then, of course, psychotherapy assumes that what is needed are more skilful techniques of resistance analysis to detect and break down these resistances.

Resistance occurs whenever a therapist is treating a patient or a disease. But there is a better way. We do not have to treat the disease and we do not have to treat the person. We can help the patient to see his mode of being-in-the-world, for the problems he encounters in life are manifestations of misdirected modes of being-in-the-world. When a patient is able to see the connection between his suffering and his erroneous mode of being-in-the-world, then he becomes interested in reorienting himself in accord with what is more existentially valid.

For instance, earlier a salesman was mentioned whose mode of being-in-the-world was reminiscent of a steamroller. It was not necessary to therapeutize the patient, nor to discuss his problem, which was a marital one; instead, his mode of being-in-the-world was clarified to him. It was explained to him that misdirected modes of being-in-the-world are manifestations of certain assumptions about life, arrived at through miseducation. The salesman was educated to be very articulate and to "snow" people with words and clever arguments. He was very good at it. Furthermore, he absorbed the value system of the game of ice hockey, which is known to be one of the more aggressive forms of sport. These factors played an important role in his mode of being-in-the-world, which, being existentially invalid, resulted in marital discord. As all this became clear to him, he naturally became interested in finding a better way and thus there was no resistance whatsoever. There was just recognition, regret, and reorientation.

The better way is found in the model of perfect being manifested by Jesus Christ. The qualities and values which he taught the world are available to anyone to contemplate and to accept. The result is healing for all concerned. Not only was the patient in the above case healed, but his family was relieved of the pressures which he used to bring home from work.

When we treat modes of being-in-the-world, we preserve the patient's integrity. He does not feel threatened. He is not in the position of being an object of tricky investigations and intrusions into his privacy. He is just learning to perceive reality in a more valid fashion. Therefore, problems of resistance do not arise. Neither are there any transference and countertransference phenomena to cope with.

So now we have to consider again the issue of fear and fearlessness. As we mentioned, it is important to ask the right question in order to get a valid answer. In order to become fearless, we must come to understand what fear is. Millions of people suffer from fear unnecessarily. Fear is self-concern. It is the habit of being concerned about oneself. In Metapsychiatry we call it "self-confirmatory ideation." From childhood on we are conditioned to ask ourselves two questions: How do I feel? and, How am I doing? These questions are always present in the background of our thinking.

Interestingly enough, if we are in the habit of fearfully contemplating our condition in life, this thought is present in consciousness, and whatever is present in consciousness acts as a magnet attracting corresponding experiences to reinforce that mental preoccupation. The more we are in the habit of fearfulness, the more we shall attract experiences of intimidation. All sorts of little experiences will come our way to increase our fearful self-concern until we may develop a full-blown anxiety neurosis. We are trained from childhood on to be fearfully preoccupied with ourselves. One young lady came to her session and said: "When I arrived here today, I got very scared because I noticed that I forgot to be anxious."

If we unmask fear as a chronic form of self-confirmatory ideation — and as such it constitutes a misdirected mode of being-in-the-world — then we can slough it off. Jesus often said to people: "Fear not: believe only" (Luke 8:50). Is that possible? Is it possible to shake off fearfulness and be rid of it once and for all?

Fear is a prolific source of illness of every kind: emotional, mental, physical, social, economic, etc. Behind all our problems lies the unfortunate inclination toward self-confirmatory fearfulness. If we could be fearless and loving we could truly be healthy all the time. How is this possible? What did Jesus mean by saying, "Believe only?" We have to realize that fear is nothing other than misdirected interest. When we are fearful we are interested in ourselves. Even if we are concerned with the welfare of others, we are still interested in ourselves, and when we are interested in ourselves we are fearful. When Jesus says, "Believe only," he actually says: "Shift your interest to something higher, more valid; turn your attention to something that is existentially more valid; reorient yourself mentally toward God, infinite Mind, Love-Intelligence, the source of your existence, the foundation of all life."

So when we realize that what we suffer from is a misdirected interest in self instead of in God, the Transcendent, then we see that it is possible for man to be healed of self-confirmatory mental preoccupations and thus become fearless, loving, intelligent, and joyful. He can attain his full and conscious spiritual identity. He can become conscious of himself as a spiritual being, a divine manifestation of Love-Intelligence, and thus attain the ability to be a beneficial presence in the world, which is mental health. Hence we see that fearfulness, while inevitable, is actually not necessary.

In conclusion, it seems desirable to point out the difference between fearlessness and courage. The difference can be understood if we compare the philosophy of Stoicism with Christlike meekness. The courageous Stoic relies on willful resistance to fear, thus struggling against it. The Christlike meekness is based on a higher understanding of life as divinely governed wisdom and love. Therefore it is effortless and free. The enlightened man is naturally fearless and loving.

The Love of Being Loving

Traditional psychotherapies see love as requiring an object. In psychoanalysis one speaks of a love object, which is very strange because if we turn our loved one into an object, we have denied his basic humanity and ignored his spirituality.

Someone could say that we don't really turn people into objects, that this is just a semantic license. However, this is not just a semantic refinement; actually, the prevalent mode in love relationships is that of objectification. This is one of the main themes of Martin Buber's work. His most important point is that man has a tendency to deal with his fellow man as if he were an object. Instead of "I-thou" relationship, which is Martin Buber's idea of love, unenlightened man tends to function on the presumption of "I-it." We tend to turn our fellow man into an "it." And what happens when we deal with one another as objects? We become manipulative.

To be manipulated is not a pleasant experience; it is dehumanizing, humiliating, even infuriating. The hostilities and resentments and strife which we can observe in everyday life have much to do with an erroneous approach to our fellow man. It is the manipulative object-relations approach. In psychoanalysis, especially the interpersonal theory of psychoanalysis of Sullivan and others, this terrible term was made respectable. It has become respectable to talk about an "object-relations theory" of psychoanalysis. It simply means that we treat our fellow men as if they were objects. If they are objects,

189

like for instance a chair, they can be pushed around, turned upside down, even smashed.

Now someone may say, But a man can defend himself; he can resist our manipulation. To this we can answer that if we were to encounter such resistance, we would want to improve our skills of manipulation to such a point as to make it impossible for our love object to resist. Rape could be considered an extreme case of object love. Combined with murder, it would carry the theory of object-relations to its ultimate point of absurdity by rendering an animate "object" into an inanimate object. If our assumptions about life were based on such theories, the result would be indeed disastrous.

Without realizing it, people are led to believe that a loved one is an object who is here for our personal gratification. If we love someone, we have the right to use that individual to make ourselves feel good. Love thy neighbor as if he were an object. This is what it comes to.

Many of the phenomena of resistance, so widely discussed in psychoanalytic therapy, have much to do with the fact that the patient is being treated as an object of exploration and manipulation. Psychoanalysis has not introduced the idea of object-relations but psychoanalysis has legitimized it and made it respectable as quasi science. This tendency was always present in human relationships. This explains the need for the commandment: "Thou shalt love thy neighbor as thyself" (Leviticus 19:18). What does this command mean? It means that we must know and see our neighbors as spiritual beings or manifestations of God, just as we are. Then there will be a different situation at hand. There will be no objectification of the loved one. There will be no manipulative abuses. There will be just the love of being loving.

True love is not object-related. We do not love anybody or anything. God is not somebody who loves somebody. God is love and man is the expression of God's love. Therefore, man loves to be loving. What happens if a therapist loves to be loving? What "technique" is he going to use on his patients? How is he going to "handle" them? Of course, these are utterly objectionable words. A Metapsychiatric therapist does not use techniques, he does not handle people, he does not influence people. He is, however, influential.

Metapsychiatric therapy is not interpersonal. The focus of Metapsychiatric therapy is not the patient, not the therapist, and not the relationship. It is the *truth of being*. The task of the therapist is to continually shed light on the truth of what really is. How does healing take place in such a nonpersonal therapeutic situation? Let us put it this way: A traditional psychotherapist could be compared to someone who discovers that the statement "Two and two is five" is erroneous and who then proceeds to work on making two and two not to be five. He may work hard at it for years, exploring all the whys and wherefores, and the historic background, and the blameworthiness of this condition. In Metapsychiatry we are not trying to make two and two not to be five. We say that two and two is four, and this truth abolishes the five and the whole problem.

It is not the therapist who abolishes the error but the truth. Therefore, one of the principles in Metapsychiatry is: "The understanding of what really is abolishes all that seems to be."

The Healing Environment

We are often asked about the treatment of children in Metapsychiatry. In Metapsychiatry we consider children to be extensions of parental consciousness and, later on, of significant adults in their particular lives. Therefore, the best approach to the treatment of children is through the consciousness of the parents. If children have problems, the best thing to do is to work with the parents, particularly the one who has the greatest impact on the child.

The parental consciousness constitutes the context in which the child experiences life. The child does not have the ability to transcend the context of parental consciousness and attain a different mode of being-in-the-world. Therefore, from this vantage point conventional child psychotherapy does not seem to make much sense. Sometimes, when a significant rapport is established between a therapist and a child, it can happen that the therapist becomes a parent substitute and actually takes over the process of child rearing. This, however, is not psychotherapy.

The great tragedy nowadays is that parents tend to be so impressed by psychotherapy that instead of being parents they become amateur psychotherapists to their own children. Child raising disappears and is replaced by a clinical form of parenting. The fundamental difference between a psychotherapist and a parent is this: Loving parents seek the good in the child; the psychotherapist is oriented toward finding out what is wrong with the child. Parents who espouse the clinical approach thus become habitual fault-finders and inflict upon a child the idea that he or she is sick. If parents become impressed by professionalism, then love, which is a positive viewpoint, is shoved into the background and a negative, clinical attitude takes over.

Children need to be seen through loving eyes and not through clinical eyes, because love sees the beautiful, the good, the harmonious, the intelligent, the divine qualities. The clinical eye is harmful even if it is practiced by a legitimate psychotherapist. This also applies to the therapy of adults.

As mentioned before, Metapsychiatry has isolated "six futile questions" which are to be consistently eschewed if we are to be helpful, and the first of these questions is, "What is wrong?" The Metapsychiatric therapist seeks to understand an individual's mode of being-in-the-world, not whether it is wrong or right, but as an indication of his way of perceiving reality. We do not condemn it but ask, Is this individual's mode of being-in-the-world valid? If we find that it is existentially invalid, it does not mean that it is wrong or that the individual is to be blamed for it. Nobody is to be blamed. We are born in ignorance. We grow up in ignorance, and through miseducation we become increasingly ignorant. As a consequence, we develop certain world-views (*Weltanschauungen*), that is, certain ways of looking at life and perceiving reality. If these perceptions are not valid from the standpoint of existential principles, then we are going to suffer. Therefore, the entire question, What's wrong with someone? is not necessary and not asking it makes it possible for us to be nonjudgmental.

The usual diagnostic approach to people places us in a position where we are scientifically entitled to pass judgment on others. Whether we are scientifically entitled or not, it is damaging to the patient to be judged. It is well known that the Bible admonishes us not to judge. "Judge not, that ye be not judged. For with what judgment ye judge, ye shall be judged" (Matthew 7:1, 2). "For wherein thou judgest another, thou condemnest thyself" (Romans 2:1). It is possible to be a psychotherapist and remain nonjudgmental. Thus we preserve a positive regard for patients. Positive regard is compassion and love.

If the therapist has the freedom to be nonjudgmental, compassionate, and loving, then the patient or client finds himself in a therapeutically helpful climate. The climate in which the therapeutic process is taking place is determined by the quality of the therapist's consciousness, not unlike a child who lives and grows and actualizes his potentialities in the context of parental consciousness. The therapeutic tool and the therapeutic environment is the therapist's consciousness. The power which heals the patient is the truth which the therapist knows. When we say that the therapist knows the truth, it must be understood that we don't say that the therapist knows *about* the truth. Knowing about the truth would make the therapist religious. This has little beneficial effect. But knowing the truth will make the therapist free and make it possible for him to set the patient free. Therefore, the education of a therapist is neither intellectual, nor operational, nor academic, but existential. What do we mean by that? By existential we mean that the knowledge which we acquire through an educational process must have a transforming effect on our lives and character. It is not enough to be well educated and to know techniques. We must actually be healed and transformed by what we have learned, for there are two kinds of education. There is education which is information and there is education which is transformation. Academic education is essentially based on information. Real education must bring about transformation of character and mode of being-in-the-world, so that the quality of consciousness of the therapist might become a therapeutic environment in which patients can be healed.

What is environment? What determines it? Suppose an interior decorator comes into an empty room and decides to create an environment by decorating that room. We may ask, What determines the particular environment which he will create? The answer is that his value system and aesthetic concepts will externalize themselves in a certain specific form and determine the environment. This indicates that environments are mental, whether in a room, a house, an institution, a community, or a culture. All things are externalizations of mental processes revealing the underlying value systems governing the thinking of the significant individuals who participate in the creation of the environment. We live and move and have our being in a universe of Mind, and everything depends on the value system which fills that mental climate. Our perceptions are determined by our values.

Recently I read a quotation attributed to Albert Einstein, who in 1926 in a conversation with Heisenberg said: "Our theories determine what we shall observe in our experiments." Thus even research in atomic physics cannot be said to be objective, but is mentally determined. The consciousness of the observer determines what will be seen. The experiments take place in a mental environment. Internalized values and thoughts determine perception. External reality is not objective.

In psychotherapy it is the mental climate which governs the therapist's environment that determines the effectiveness of the healing process. There is no such thing as an objective scientific procedure. This would explain the mysterious fact that in spite of the number of various schools of psychotherapy, effective therapists can be found in all of them, notwithstanding "party affiliations."

It is known that Freud never cured a patient in his entire career; apparently he didn't have a therapeutic consciousness. He was essentially an investigator. And it is said that the psychoanalytic method which he devised is not a healing method, but a method of investigation. Certainly, an investigator is not a therapist.

The greatest therapist was Jesus Christ. He never analyzed people. He never investigated anything. He never asked futile questions. The special faculty which he had was an infinite outpouring of nonpersonal love. The quality of his consciousness created a climate of love around him and anyone who came into contact with that love was instantaneously healed. The Bible describes the story of a woman who was bleeding for twelve years and no one could help her. She sneaked up behind Jesus and touched the hem of his garment, which means she reached out for contact with that mental climate and was instantaneously healed.

The ideal therapist seeks to cultivate within himself the maximum possible loving, compassionate, intelligent consciousness, so that anyone who comes into contact with that environment, which takes place in his presence, will become affected in a favorable way.

It is not necessary to investigate our patients to find out what is wrong with them and why, and who is to blame for it, and what we should do about it, and how one should do it. Whatever is invalid in a patient's thinking reveals itself spontaneously in the right mental climate. If we know that two and two is four, we can instantaneously spot that two and two is not five. But if we don't know that two and two is four, we wouldn't know that two and two isn't five. In a therapeutic climate whatever is existentially invalid reveals itself spontaneously as error.

A Metapsychiatric therapist asks himself two questions: "What is the meaning of what seems to be?" and "What is what really is?" The meaning of what seems to be cannot be figured out through calculative thinking. We have to wait till it reveals itself to us. If we have learned to live in the right consciousness, the meaning of every problem will reveal itself spontaneously. The work is without effort.

The tenth principle of Metapsychiatry states: "The understanding of what really is abolishes all that seems to be."

The question is sometimes asked, What role do drugs play in psychiatric treatment? There are many people who are not interested in a healing, but only in temporary relief. For instance, suppose someone likes to be domineering and push other people around. He may enjoy hurting other people, but he himself does not seem to suffer until such time that he comes up against someone whom he cannot tyrannize. At that point he may begin to suffer. He may go to a doctor and the doctor may find that he has high blood pressure or some other physical symptom. On that basis this individual might try to take some tranquilizing drugs and for a little while get along that way. But eventually the drugs become less and less effective and his problems may increase until, finally, he runs into an existential crisis of some sort. At that point he may be forced to recognize the error of his ways, regret his ignorance, and perchance reorient himself and thus be healed.

Thus the healing process consists of three steps: recognition, regret, and reorientation. Reorientation means coming into harmony with the Fundamental Order of Existence: peace, assurance, gratitude, love, freedom, wisdom, joy, beauty, goodness, and being a beneficial presence in the world. This is the Christly standard of being healthy.

Lately there have been widespread discussions in the nation about the issue of capital punishment. All sorts of arguments have been raised pro and con. In general, we can distinguish positions based on pure vindictiveness, on crime deterrence, and on economic issues (it is claimed that a prisoner in jail costs $30,000 a year to the taxpayer). Certain religious arguments are also brought up. And then there are others who are convinced that capital punishment has no effect on discouraging crime. The arguments seem to go on endlessly.

It appears that, by reasoning from the standpoint of human emotions and human logic, it is not really possible to arrive at an intelligent answer to this problem. Consequently, it is not possible to be for or against any of these positions in a clear-cut way. A Zen Master would say: "When it comes to the issue of crime and punishment, yes is no, and no is yes."

In contemplating this issue we may ask, What does it take to become the victim of a crime? There are only two ways to become a victim: by wanting to or by not wanting to. Therefore, if we could find an alternative to these two conditions, this might provide us with some valid answers. In answer to this dilemma we can say that the solution lies in being interested in something other than wanting or not wanting to be victimized. Thus when we are faced with the decision of whether to vote for capital punishment or against it, we cast our vote for crimeless living. In the universe of Mind crime is not known. There is brotherly love, harmony, peace, assurance, gratitude, freedom.

Someone may object and ask, Yes, yes, but what about in the meanwhile? In the meanwhile we suffer the trials and tribulations of living in an ignorant world. Thus the issue boils down to this: not how to punish criminals, but how to live in safety in spite of the crime-ridden environment. In order to be safe, we rely on our meditation which we have called the four "Ws": Who am I? What am I? Where am I? What is my purpose in life? The answers to these questions are as follows: I am an image and likeness of God, a manifestation of Love-Intelligence. I am a divine consciousness. I live and move and have my being in omniactive Divine Mind. My purpose is to be a beneficial presence in the world.

It is a well known and widely observed fact that animals react to the quality of consciousness in people. For instance, if someone is afraid of a dog, the dog may — more often than not — behave in a hostile, threatening way toward him. This indicates how important the state of consciousness is when it comes to safety.

So when we meditate sincerely and with understanding on the four "Ws," then we dwell in the "secret place of the most High ... under the protection of the Almighty" (Psalm 91:1). And this is the secret of safety and a remedy to the crime problem. Nothing will ever stop crime except if individuals in large numbers learn to dwell in the secret place of the most High.

An unprotected consciousness is exposed to mental contagion propagated by the news media or hearsay, which captures the imagination and perpetuates and magnifies the adverse experiences of the culture. Today we have epidemics of terrorism, of arson, blue collar crime, white collar crime, government corruption, etc., perpetuated by a marvelous system of communication. The blessings of scientific progress are always accompanied by the cursed problems of its side effects. Purity of good, however, can only be found through spiritualized consciousness, which is the essence of what we have called the healing environment. In such an environment neither illness nor crime can endure.

The Riddle of the Sphinx

Whenever new ideas are presented in a seminar or at a lecture, it invariably happens that someone will attempt to reformulate them in terms of what has been previously learned. This is often spoken of as "putting new wine into old bottles." We could say that concepts are containers for ideas. For instance, let us consider the concepts of attitudes, integration, and holistic wholeness. These concepts have no existential usefulness. Nevertheless, they keep cropping up in discussions.

In existential Metapsychiatry we cannot speak of attitudes because the concept is an operational one. An attitude is something that we can assume. It can be done. Whatever we can do, we call operational. It is a transaction. We can assume an aggressive attitude, or a passive attitude, or a friendly attitude, or an unfriendly attitude, etc. We can do it. There is a certain autonomy about it which is very appealing to us because we would like to be able to do whatever seems helpful to do. In juxtaposition to operational concepts there are existential realities.

The second concept mentioned was integration. This is a marginal word which suggests that we can bring together something old and something new, as well as some other factors and ideas, and put them together and make something valid out of it. So it is a marginally operational idea, but whatever is operational is not existential.

Nowadays we hear about a concept called holistic health and wholeness. We have to view this concept with a grain of salt, i.e., carefully, because it depends on what we consider wholeness to be. In general usage wholeness is conceived of as an expanded view of man in the context of his environment. Metapsychiatry does not consider this to be valid because man is not a plant, nor an animal, nor a rock. Man is not natural. While it is true that being in conflict with nature would make man sick, nevertheless, coming into harmony with nature would not make him whole.

Man is radically different from all other life forms on earth. Therefore, we can speak of wholeness only in terms of consciousness. The central fact of human existence is the quality of consciousness, and to understand human wholeness we must see it as consciousness which is in harmony with the Divine. Jesus has put it succinctly: "I and my Father are one" (John 10:30). "I am in the Father, and the Father in me" (John 14:11). To understand this we may ask, What was so special about Jesus? Certainly it was not his physical organism. Neither could we think of him as a "nature boy." He represented the spiritually enlightened man whose wholeness was based on the quality of his consciousness. We certainly appreciate ecology and nature in the admirable unity and delicate interrelatedness of its elements, but our appreciation of nature is essentially aesthetic rather than biological. This fact also points up the radical difference between man and other life forms. Only man seems to have the faculty of aesthetic appreciation and only man is capable of artistic expression. These are spiritual faculties in man. Even primitive man, who is usually very close to nature, gives evidence of expressing himself artistically and reveals a capacity for aesthetic appreciation.

To understand human wholeness we must consider the fact that this wholeness is entirely different from all other ideas of wholeness. The wholeness of man is attained when he is in conscious harmony with the Fundamental Order of Existence, which is Spirit, God, infinite Love-Intelligence. Interestingly enough, when we approach that state of realization, we find our health improving in every possible way — emotionally, mentally, physically, socially, economically, maritally, etc., which is proof positive of the fact that we are moving in the right direction. Metapsychiatry seeks to help people to attain or to approximate that kind of wholeness which we call conscious at-one-ment or union with God, infinite Love-Intelligence. Love and intelligence are basic qualities of God which man can realize, actualize, and express. To the extent that we succeed in bringing our lives into alignment with this transcendent Reality, we approach the Christly standard of wholeness.

This, of course, is not an attitude which we can assume. If we tried to do this in terms of assuming an attitude, the best we could achieve would be religious hypocrisy. But we are concerned with existential realization, namely, we are seeking to become what we have truly understood. Knowing is being. What we really know, that is what we really are. What we just know about, we pretend to be. Pretending is one of the great mistakes which lead to attitudes. The operational approach to knowledge leads us into believing that we already are what we only know about. This is called behaviorism. There is a school of psychotherapy called behaviorism where people are being trained to assume certain attitudes and to behave in certain ways which are considered socially desirable. The more successful we are in terms of behavior, the less authentic we become, because we are then just a set of conditioned reflexes, like the Pavlovian dogs. The school of behavior therapy seeks to help man by turning him into a functional animal.

In general we can distinguish three kinds of people, depending on the level of their spiritual development. There are animal people. There are human people. And then there are spiritual beings. Of course, everyone is a spiritual being, but we are not all on the same level of development in terms of consciousness. For many centuries the Sphinx was considered a great riddle. The Sphinx appears to be a very mysterious and fascinating creation of ancient man, endowed with some deep knowledge of the secrets of life. Many people report that they are awe-struck facing the Sphinx and cannot understand what it is that elicits this reaction.

A well-known writer and philosopher by the name of Ouspensky describes in detail his own fascination with the Sphinx. He spent prolonged periods of time standing in front of it and trying to fathom the meaning of the Sphinx by seeking to understand his own reaction to it. He seemed to have come very close to understanding it, but he didn't make it quite clear enough in his descriptions. If, however, we consider the Sphinx in terms of the three levels of human consciousness which we have described above, we may find an adequate explanation of the riddle of the Sphinx. As is known, the Sphinx has an animal body and a human head, but what is most mysterious about it is the peculiar gaze in its eyes. The animal body could be thought of as symbolizing or representing animal man. What is animal man? Animal man is "nature boy," namely, sensual, emotional, material, animalistic, instinct-ridden man, seeking instinctual gratification and expression. Animal man is primarily concerned with instinctual gratification. On the second level is human man. The Sphinx progresses from an animal body to a human head. What is a human man? Human man is psychological man, a man who "uses his head." By that we mean commonsense thinking, cleverness, craftiness, calculative thinking, manipulativeness, deviousness, political ideation. In other words, human man is a man who uses his head and lacks creativity. The highest attainment of the human man is politics and psychology.

The Sphinx seems to represent the development of man from animality through psychology to transcendence. The eyes of the Sphinx do not focus on anything in the material world. They stare into infinity. Spiritual beings have their focus on infinite Love-Intelligence, the source of all wisdom, creativity, aesthetic perceptivity, divine consciousness. We could say that behaviorism deals with animal man, and psychology deals with human man. Metapsychiatry seeks to elevate the entire being of man to the level of divine consciousness, to awaken within him the dormant faculty of spiritual awareness which reminds us of the Bible passage: "Awake thou that sleepest, and arise from the dead, and Christ shall give thee light" (Ephesians 5:14).

The meaning and purpose of life and Metapsychiatric therapy is to help us attain the highest level of consciousness through right understanding of Divine Reality. This understanding results in a transformation of man: he becomes a spontaneous expression of Divine Love-Intelligence.

Approbation

An attractive young lady reported the following: "I find that my happiness most of the time depends on whether or not I am being fed compliments. When no one is complimenting me, then I feel awful. I know that all these things are totally futile and childish, but this is how it is anyway. I can talk myself into really being depressed just because I am not getting any compliments. I would like to be free of this roller coaster. I have recently read a book entitled *Zen in the Art of Archery*, written by a Westerner by the name of Herrigel. In it he is told by a Zen Master that he must rise above the buffetings of pleasure and pain. I wonder how I could do that?"

There is a more precise way of looking at the problem. We have to rise above the habit of self-confirmatory ideation. If we rise above the buffetings of pleasure and pain, we don't know where we are. We could find ourselves in a position of stoicism, or catatonic self-mortification, or apathy. These are not felicitous solutions. But if we rise above self-confirmatory ideation, then we find ourselves in a dimension of consciousness which is aware of and acknowledges God's allness. We call this the God-confirmatory mode of being-in-the-world. In this situation we are aware of pleasure and pain, but they have lost much of their importance. Our interest has shifted toward an appreciation of spiritual bliss: peace, harmony, assurance, gratitude, love, transcendent joy.

This, then, is the healing of vanity. Vanity is a desire to be admired, which is an eminently self-confirmatory idea. Pleasure and pain are just two sides of the same coin, which we have called self-confirmation. Self-confirmation is self-destruction, and self-destruction is self-confirmation. These two constitute two sides of the same coin.

Sometimes we can observe an animal licking himself and biting himself intermittently, thus trying to heal himself and destroy himself at the same time. Such are the dualisms of unenlightened life.

Some people are constantly fishing for compliments, in a way asking to be licked, but often they wind up getting bitten because they provoke and irritate others. So licking and biting belong together, and in this duality yes is no and no is yes. Vanity is a thin-skinned balloon filled with hot air.

Recently, a young man was cornered by his mother who insisted on knowing whether or not he liked her new blouse. Being thus put on the spot, he remembered that it would not help to say yes, and it would not help to say no. After thinking a while, he hit upon the following answer: "I understand that you would like me to compliment you." This response brought about the collapse of the balloon of vanity and enabled our friend to break the "double bind" of his mother's demand.

It is interesting to note that the concept of self-confirmatory ideation, which is so helpful to us in coping with these problems, cannot be found anywhere in the literature, neither in the East nor in the West. While the term is linguistically not very attractive, it is nevertheless worthwhile because it clarifies and pinpoints an important source of human suffering. The explanation of this omission may be found in the fact that most philosophical systems endeavor to explain the human condition and its transcendence without a forthright and explicit acknowledgment of the existence of God.

It is advisable to point out here the difference between the God of traditional religions and the God of enlightenment. In traditional religions man is seen as separated from God and as seeking to establish a relationship with God through prayer, ritual, and conduct. In enlightenment there is no relationship between man and God. Enlightenment is based on a realization of at-one-ment of man with God. God manifests himself in the world through man. As the rays of the sun are one with the sun and the waves of the sea are one with the sea, so God and man constitute an inseparable unity. This, of course, is easier to conceptualize than to realize. The moment this oneness is realized, vanity becomes impossible. The gratification of vanity could be compared to a thirsty man drinking salt water; the more he drinks, the thirstier he becomes until he may die. Modern psychology has come up with a new method of controlling children in schools and prisoners in jails. It is called operant conditioning or behavior modification, and it is based on the principle of focusing attention on good behavior and continually rewarding it with praise and gifts, and not punishing bad behavior. The results seem to be promising, except if we understand the underlying issues, we see that while the behavior may temporarily improve, the children are actually being trained to expect continuous and ever increasing ego gratification. This, of course, must inevitably lead to problems. It may succeed in producing large numbers of ego-maniacal individuals.

The fact is that praise is not good and punishment is not good. Pampering is not good and persecution is not good. Complimenting is not good and criticizing is not good because they are the same. They are all ego-confirmatory modes of thinking. The more we feed the ego, the sicker we get. This indeed is a great problem in education, in parenting, and in life in general.

Now the question is, Is there a valid way of approbation, which means acknowledging the good? Of course there is. But who can do it? Only the "right man" can do it. The "wrong man" can try to do it but it will be phony, manipulative, and it will backfire, for "if the wrong man does the right thing, then the right thing works the wrong way" (Chuang-tzu). Now, teachers, psychiatrists, executives, and parents need to become the "right man." How do we become the "right man"? What does it mean to be the "right man"? The right man is capable of acknowledging the good of God wherever something good occurs, not the good of persons, but the good of God. The right man acknowledges it and rejoices in the fact that God's good is in evidence.

In *Zen in the Art of Archery* there is a scene described in which the student finally succeeds in hitting the bull's eye in perfect form, and the Zen Master, noticing a self-satisfied smile on the face of the trainee, says to him: "Let us bow to perfection," and together they bow. This, then, is the model of existentially valid approbation. Perfection is not personal; it is the manifestation of the divine impulse acting through man. We honor the good of God wherever and whenever it becomes manifest.

The Question of Affectivity

Most of our knowledge is based on judging by appearances. If we look at ourselves just with the naked eye, we see that we are highly emotional people, and feelings constitute a very impressive aspect of our humanness. We are keenly aware of our feelings and, as a consequence, we have assumed that we are controlled by our feelings, and that emotional reactions determine our judgment and our mental health.

It is not surprising then that this phenomenon has assumed in psychology the significance of an a priori fact. As it is with many things in life, that which seems to be is not necessarily what really is. And again it goes back to the question, What is man? Is man what he seems to be, or is he something else? Many schools of psychology have been developed on the basis of what man seems to be. But we are coming to realize that judging by appearances can be highly misleading.

Conventional psychological thinking states that feelings are primary and thoughts are secondary. It assumes that feelings and sensations give rise to certain thoughts. We, so to speak, interpret reality by the impact things have upon our feelings and sensations, which means that sensory perceptions appear to be the primary mediators of our contact with reality. Even Paracelsus, the famous medieval physician, believed this to be so. He said: "Nihil est in intellectu quod primum non fuerit in sensu," which means nothing can be in the mind which has not been first in the senses. So what Paracelsus took for granted, conventional psychology has accepted.

However, Metapsychiatry sees it otherwise. It states that thought is primary, and feelings and emotions are byproducts of thought processes. This, of course, is a revolutionary realization which turns everything upside down — or better yet — right side up. This realization brings hope and possibilities of healing within reach. If feelings and emotions were primary, then our situation would be hopeless. How many times have we heard people say: "I can't help how I feel!" For instance, someone may say, "I feel like strangling that person. I can't help it, that's the way I feel." If it were true that feelings and emotions are primary, then man would be at the mercy of his impulses. But if we come to understand that thought is primary and that our feelings and emotions — and even sensory perceptions — are determined by our thought processes, there is a possibility of healing because thoughts can be improved. With the improvement of thought processes, emotional responses and even sensory perceptions and cognition improve.

Let us now examine how it is that feelings and emotions are byproducts of thought processes. In considering this issue, it is helpful to remind ourselves of a famous quotation attributed to Einstein: "Our theories determine what we shall observe in our experiments." Thus, even sensory perceptions and cognitive processes depend on our thinking. In psychotic conditions we have come to understand that hallucinatory experiences are not primary feelings and sensations, but perceptualized thought processes. This realization made it possible to heal such conditions by improving the thinking processes of patients, either through chemical intervention or through skillful psychotherapy.

When our thought processes are existentially valid, then our feelings, emotions, perceptions, and cognition improve and we are healed. "For as he [man] thinketh in his heart, so is he" (Proverbs 23:7). Just as bowel movements are byproducts of digestive processes, feelings and emotions are byproducts of thought processes. This leads us to the important discovery that man is not a perceptual organism relating himself to reality with his senses and with his feelings, but that man is consciousness. Man is an individualized divine consciousness. And the quality of his consciousness determines his mode of being-in-the-world. The quality of our consciousness will determine what we see and how we interpret what we see, and what reactions we have to what is going on around us.

In the Old Testament God seems to be subject to emotional reactions. He is capable of wrathfulness, vindictiveness, jealousy. He seems to have many psychological problems. But as we have evolved over several thousand years, we have come to understand God in a more advanced way. God is totally devoid of emotionalism and sensualism. God is just pure consciousness. The attributes of this pure consciousness are love, intelligence, creativity, life, beauty, harmony, joy, perfection. This understanding of God in its pure form helps us to understand ourselves. While in the Old Testament God is man-like, our present-day understanding of God helps us to see man as God-like.

Divine attributes must not be mistaken for emotions. They are spiritual qualities existing in consciousness and manifested through realized man. By contrast, emotions and feelings are psychophysiological processes occurring in the neurovegetative system of the organism. These processes do not exist in God. Man, as an individualized aspect of divine consciousness, is capable of being aware of spiritual attributes and even expressing them. Joy, love, creative intelligence have nothing in common with affectivity. They are qualities of consciousness and they are spiritual rather than organismic. To understand this is very helpful. For instance, if we misunderstand love and believe it to be an emotion, we can be subject to rapid changes of experience. Our love can quickly turn to hate and our joy into sorrow. If someone makes us feel good, we love him. If someone makes us feel bad, we hate him. Thus we are unstable. But real love is steadfast. It has no opposite. It is a quality of being which is focused on the good of God unconditionally. It is a mode of being-in-the-world.

If we assume that the primary issue in mental health is

affectivity, we may become psychologically disturbed. This unfortunately happens in those instances when the psychotherapeutic method used consists of focusing the patient's attention on his feelings and emotions. The more we try to help someone to feel good, the sicker he gets. "Where a man's treasure [interest] is, there shall his heart [problems] be also" (Luke 12:34).

In Metapsychiatry we are not dealing with emotions, because these are secondary. The focus is on the quality of consciousness, because that is primary. How do we improve the quality of consciousness? If we would improve our consciousness we must learn to see life in an existentially valid context. Oddly enough, the most existentially valid context that has ever been revealed to us comes from the teachings of Taoism, of Zen Buddhism, and of Jesus Christ. These happen to overlap to a great extent. The right perspective on Reality requires us to come to recognize the existence of God and our absolute contingency and inseparability from the divine context. Anyone who tries to understand man apart from God is sadly mistaken.

If we want to see reality in an existentially valid way, it is inevitable that we come to understand life in the context of God. That does not mean that we have to go to church, or that we have to espouse a particular religion, or that we have to perform certain rituals. What is required is learning to see ourselves and others in the context of God, Divine Reality. And this must be an existentially valid concept of God, that is, a fundamental power, a force which underlies all life processes, creativity, intelligence, and love, in the universe. Without this force nothing can exist. Neither can we very well survive.

Recently there was a debate on television between a well-known representative of American atheism and a panel of religious leaders of various denominations. The members of the clergy were trying very hard to discredit the opinions of the atheist. However, she was very articulate in her counterattacks and succeeded in rendering her opponents quite ineffectual in their arguments. What these religious scholars failed to notice was that the atheist, in fact, was quite religious, except that she worshiped scientific materialism as her god.

Everyone worships something. It is impossible for man to be an atheist. There is no such thing, but we have a variety of choices of what to worship. If we have a multitude of gods we can choose to live by, how can we know which god to choose? Since there is no such thing as a godless individual, the question boils down to this: Which god is the real God? And how can we know Him? We have three ways of worshiping our private god: whatever we cherish, whatever we hate, and whatever we fear. But surely, we all need to know whether we are worshiping the right God. All religious intolerance and strife indicates that mankind does not know for sure which is the valid God. Knowing which god to worship is of supreme importance to man. The God which validates Itself existentially must be the true God.

What is existential validation? Existential validation is a way of coming to know what really is. That which truly is, validates itself by healing, by its power to bring harmony and fulfillment of man's potentialities.

We could ask, What is the meaning of Jesus' healing work? What was he trying to do? He was demonstrating the existential validity of his God. In proportion that our understanding of God is existentially valid, in that proportion do we become healthier, more harmonious, more loving, more intelligent, more fearless, more perfect in every possible way.

So the process of Metapsychiatric therapy, focusing attention on the quality of consciousness, simultaneously helps people to understand God and themselves as a unity of man and God in an existentially valid way. Whatever enhances life is existentially valid, and the central issues of life are not emotions, feelings, and sensations, status, competition, jealousy, sex, gender identity, but consciousness.

The Physical Is Mental

One of the frequent complaints we hear is the experiencing of tension. If we ask, What is tension? the explanation offers itself that tension is the experiential aspect of intentionality. There is no tension without intention. Thus we can see that tension is not physical but mental. It is a thought.

There are various forms of tension; we speak of tension headaches, muscular tension, hypotension, and hypertension. The most frequent forms of medical treatment of these problems consist of attempting to alleviate these tensions at the point of their manifestation. For instance, tension headaches and high blood pressure are most frequently treated by specific types of medication designed to relieve the condition at the point of its appearance. Thus the phenomenon of tension with its multitude of manifestations such as backaches, kidney troubles, cardiovascular disease, respiratory problems — as in asthma and emphysema, etc. — is a very important illustrative point which can help us understand that the physical is mental.

Unfortunately, physical symptoms tend to create such alarm and fascination in us that we get hypnotized into believing that we are dealing essentially with organismic disturbances rather than epiphenomena of certain mental processes. This explains the fact that when an illness is approached on a purely medical or surgical basis, the problem is at best alleviated but never really healed. Cures alleviate conditions, which is not synonymous with healing. But if we understand that physical problems are mental, then there is the possibility of getting to the core of the issue. For instance, if someone suffers from migraine headaches, we would not therapeutize the head of a patient with drugs, but we would deal with the meaning of the problem.

There is, however, universal resistance to facing up to meanings. For instance, a man developed a severe dental condition with complications which involved going from a dentist to a root canal specialist and finally to a dental surgeon, with a resultant alarming swelling of his face. This individual is not a student of Metapsychiatry, but his wife is. At the height of his suffering he kept pleading with his wife to look into his mouth. She resisted this request because she knew the problem was not in the mouth. But he insisted, so she yielded to his request twice, but she saw nothing. This, however, did not reassure the patient. We could ask, What could be the meaning of this patient's insistence on this action? The meaning was that the patient wanted to have his wife confirm his own belief that the problem is a dental one and is located in his mouth. But his wife knew that this problem was not what it seemed to be and was not where it seemed to be; it was some festering thought in her husband's consciousness which happened to flare up and assume alarming proportions. His insistence was — in a sense — a desire to defend himself against facing up to the meaning of the condition.

If a problem is physical then the patient can think of himself as an innocent victim of some adverse circumstance which has befallen him. But if the problem is mental, then there is a tendency to blame oneself for one's thoughts and feel guilty for having brought upon oneself such suffering. What most people do not understand is that even though we are responsible for our problems, we cannot be blamed for them. For example, in the above case it was discovered that this patient entertained hidden antisemitic prejudicial thoughts about his son-in-law, who happened to be a Jewish dentist. His prejudicial thoughts festered in his consciousness for a long time until at one point the whole package of impurity flared up at the root of his teeth. But certainly it would be a mistake to blame this man for his problem, or for his prejudicial thoughts, because prejudice is only a common form of ignorance to which most of us are easily subject.

Nevertheless, to be healed, this ignorant pocket of impurity must be cleansed out from consciousness and the truth of spiritual identity in God must be recognized and accepted as a fact. This would result in complete healing.

The process of purifying our consciousness is called the prayer of beholding. This must be distinguished from wishful thinking. Wishful thinking is preoccupation with what should be; the prayer of beholding is an endeavor to realize what really is. Wishful thinking is self-deception, beholding is prayer. The consciousness which beholds Reality becomes aware of its own purity as an aspect of the Christ-consciousness. This realization manifests itself in healing. Whenever one individual attains the purity of the Christ-consciousness, everyone around him is blessed, including, of course, himself. Such an individual becomes a beneficial presence in the world. His being is a focal point of harmony and healing. In beholding there are neither others nor self, there is only the awareness of God's perfect Reality as the infinite background upon which manifest themselves all life forms in absolute perfection and beauty. "In the realm of Love-Intelligence there is neither self nor other, there is only that which really is."

The Healing Factor

Metapsychiatry views all phenomena as modes of being-in-the-world. If we are healthy, we have a certain mode of being-in-the-world. If we are neurotic, we have a certain mode of being-in-the-world. And if we are psychotic, schizophrenic, or whatever, all these conditions are expressions of a certain mode of being-in-the-world. This way we do not have to label people with preconceived diagnostic categories, which may or may not fit them. Instead of labeling people with diagnostic categories and obscuring the real issue, we seek to discern the specific and particular mode of being-in-the-world in every case.

When we discern an individual's mode of being-in-the-world, then we really understand him, and only when we understand him can we truly be helpful to him. By pinning a label on someone we are making it harder to help him. And certainly he will feel judged, condemned, and pigeonholed, and he will lose a sense of his specific unique individuality. So we reserve our official diagnostic labels for purposes of intraprofessional communication and for insurance and legal purposes. Let us understand that when we say that someone is a schizophrenic or a neurotic, we are only "rendering unto Caesar what is Caesar's" ("Render unto Caesar the things which are Caesar's..." Matthew 22:21). Just because we are able to fill out forms to the satisfaction of bureaucratic demands, that does not mean that we can already help someone. More often than not, the contrary is true. To be really helpful

217

we must understand the specific mode of being-in-the-world of every individual who seeks our help.

What do we mean by "mode of being-in-the-world"? In contrast to official diagnostic categories, which are based on symptomatology, the Metapsychiatric view is based on the *meaning* underlying the clinical picture. In other words, the mode of being-in-the-world is determined by an individual's belief systems, which may be conscious or unconscious. Belief systems determine the quality of thoughts and the extent of cognition. The Bible says: "For as he [man] thinketh in his heart, so is he" (Proverbs 23:7). And indeed, our thought processes determine our mode of being-in-the-world.

When we understand an individual's mode of being-in-the-world, we know whether his fundamental outlook on reality is existentially valid or invalid. Then we know that the therapeutic process will consist of finding a way of helping him shift his perspective on reality into the sphere which is existentially more valid. A basic presupposition, of course, is that the therapist is imbued with a value system and a world-view which is existentially valid. Otherwise the "blind would be leading the blind, and together they would fall into the ditch."

There is one interesting aspect of Metapsychiatry which is all-important. If one is properly trained in it there is no transference or countertransference reaction, which makes for a very clean work situation. It is well known that transference and countertransference reactions tend to create complications in psychotherapy. What makes it messy is the irrationality of these reactions. In Metapsychiatry, if we understand what we are doing, there is no occasion for transference and countertransference to develop.

Many experienced therapists of other schools would say that this is impossible, but the most wonderful feature of this work is the nonpersonal nature of it and the total absence of any manipulative intention on the part of the therapist. Since the therapist's focus is not on the patient but his value system and his belief system and his mode of perceiving reality, there is no possibility for any kind of interpersonal complications to occur. For instance, if the Metapsychiatric therapist says: "Two and two is four," he does not say: "I tell you that two and two is four, and I want you to believe it," or "I want you to know that two and two is four." He only says, "Two and two is four. I didn't make it that way, and you cannot change it. It is."

In Metapsychiatric therapy it is not the person of the therapist and not the person of the patient that is the issue, but Reality. Jesus said: "Where two or three are gathered together in my name, there am I in the midst of them" (Matthew 18:20). Many think this to be a religious statement, but actually it is a statement of a principle of Metapsychiatric therapy. It is the nonpersonal principle, which means that truth and Reality do not belong to anybody. Reality just is.

What does it mean to gather in Jesus' name? It means that two or three or more people gather with the aim of understanding existentially valid Reality. If the Christ is in the midst of us, he takes over everything. There is no self and there is no other. There is only the truth of being. Thus the attention of the patient and the therapist is focused on that which really is. In Buddhism this is called "tathata" — true suchness.

The tenth principle of Metapsychiatry, which is worth repeating, goes as follows: "The understanding of what really is abolishes all that seems to be." Thus it is not the therapist who abolishes the patient's problems and it is not the therapist's viewpoint which changes the patient's belief system. There is no interpersonal encounter here. There is only an encounter with the truth of what really is. It is the discernment of the truth of what really is that abolishes all that seems to be.

The healing factor in Metapsychiatric therapy is the Christ-truth. The Christ-truth transcends all religions. It is existentially valid Reality. When someone is healed in Metapsychiatry, he does not necessarily become a religious man, or a Christian, or a Jew, or a Buddhist. He becomes capable of seeing what is valid in life and what is not valid in life. He is free to choose any form of religious organization or practice.

This explains the mysterious fact that, while we are deeply immersed in the Bible as a source of understanding of Reality, yet we are not advocating any particular system of religious worship. Metapsychiatry is truly transdenominational.

Malicious Hypnotism

Children live in the climate of parental consciousness. If children suffer, it is always the parents that need to be healed. When parental consciousness is brought into harmony with the Fundamental Order of Existence — which is spiritual love — children are healed. The story of Abraham and Isaac speaks of such a situation. God, in a sense, said to Abraham: "If you continue being possessive and proud of your son, he will have to die. If you want him to survive, you must correct your thinking and know that he is not your son but God's son, and that he is not a material possession but a spiritual being, a divine consciousness, belonging to God. If you are willing to love him in this manner, then he will not have to die."

This mental influence extends not only to children but also to material possessions. If we cherish our car, for instance, and are proud of it, then something will surely happen to it. There seems to be such a mental influence extending itself even into the inanimate sphere of life, and we have to learn to be intelligent owners of our homes, furniture, automobiles, etc. We must see these things in the context of God. People who do not understand this principle tend to encounter a great many difficulties with their possessions. Not long ago there was an advertisement on television which went as follows: A man was sitting on his bed, staring out of the window. His wife asked him, "Sam, what are you doing? Why aren't you sleeping?" He replied, "I am watching our new car so that no one scrapes the fenders." "But you never used to do it before when we had the old car," said the wife. The husband replied, "Don't be silly. Nobody scrapes the fenders of an old car!" This advertisement reveals a widespread belief that whatever we cherish tends to attract some untoward events or experiences.

The question may now be asked, What happens when we hate someone or something in a malicious way? If there are mental influences emanating into the world to our loved ones and cherished items, there must then be a corresponding mental influence emanating into the world of a malicious, destructive nature from us also. Of course, we all know that it is not a healthy condition to entertain malicious and hateful thoughts. But strangely enough, other people can be adversely affected if we entertain evil thoughts about them. This is called malicious hypnotism, and hypnotism seems to work either through direct contact or through indirection. For instance, if it is directed toward someone's possession and if that individual is not sufficiently spiritually minded, then that possession can be destroyed. We are all very susceptible to hypnotism as long as we are materially minded. But if we are spiritually minded, then hypnotism has no effect on us. It is important to recall here a remark Albert Einstein once made: "Arrows of hate ('fiery darts') have been shot at me many times, but they never touched me because they came from a world with which I have nothing in common." What did he mean? Where was he dwelling that these arrows of hate couldn't reach him? He was dwelling above and beyond interaction thinking, in the land of spiritual consciousness. An ancient Chinese proverb says: "A poisoned arrow can find no place to lodge itself in an enlightened man."

Love and spiritual mindedness, far from being just religious clichés, have great existential value. Not only are they blessings for us and others around us, but they make us invulnerable to malicious hypnotism. In the material world people frequently hurt each other, even kill each other, not only physically but also mentally. In the Caribbean region the process of mental assassination has evolved into a religious cult known as voodoo. Voodoo is murder perpetrated through mental means on people who are susceptible to these influences, and it is apparently effective either in direct contact or even at a distance through telepathic communication. Sometimes we are not fully aware of the fears and beliefs we entertain, and these unconscious factors make us susceptible to hypnotism.

Most of us have seen hypnotists work in a theater in front of an audience. They often start hypnotizing a whole crowd, and a certain number of people will immediately respond to their suggestions. These people are more susceptible than others; the others may also be susceptible but to a lesser degree. This indicates that it is not the power of the hypnotist which is at play here, but individual susceptibility of those who believe — consciously or unconsciously — in the so-called "mind-power" of the hypnotist.

Following are some of the factors which render us particularly susceptible to hypnotism: pride, vanity, ambition, lust, greed, envy, jealousy, materialism, admiration, contempt, malice, sowing of dissension. The only protection from all these is increasing spiritual mindedness. Jesus said: "In the world ye shall have tribulation: but be of good cheer; I have overcome the world" (John 16:33), which means that we have to rise above the petty narrow-mindedness of interaction thinking which characterizes the world of the unenlightened materialist.

There are several statements in the Bible which point to protection against malicious hypnotism. One is: "Your life is hid with Christ in God" (Colossians 3:3). Anyone who can understand this line will realize that one who is hid with Christ in God is out of the reach of all malicious intentions and is protected. In the Old Testament we have the ninety-first Psalm, which says: "He that dwelleth in the secret place of the most High shall abide under the shadow of the Almighty.... He shall cover thee with his feathers, and under his wings shalt thou trust: his truth shalt be thy shield and buckler.... Because thou hast made the Lord, which is my refuge, even the most High, thy habitation; There shall no evil befall thee, neither

shall any plague come nigh thy dwelling.... Thou shalt not be
afraid for the terror by night; nor for the arrow that flieth by
day; nor for the pestilence that walketh in darkness; nor for the
destruction that wasteth at noonday" (Psalm 91:1, 4, 9, 10, 5, 6).

———

Semantics

In the Bible we read: "Wisdom is the principal thing; therefore get wisdom: and with all thy getting get understanding" (Proverbs 4:7). It is important not to fall into the error of assuming that the Bible recommends an acquisitive approach to wisdom and understanding. Acquisitiveness interferes with understanding. Understanding cannot be acquired since it is spiritual. Only material things can be acquired. Spiritual treasures unfold in receptive consciousness. Understanding comes by grace to those who are receptive. Receptivity and acquisitiveness cancel each other out. They are mutually exclusive. If we are materialistic in our view of the good of life, then we are inclined to be acquisitive. We tend to transfer the acquisitive idea into the spiritual realm. We can acquire books containing a great deal of knowledge in the form of information, but we cannot acquire understanding.

There is another semantic curiosity related to this issue, and that is the word "apprehend." This word attempts to straddle the issue between acquiring and understanding. It sort of refers to acquiring understanding. It is good to know that neither understanding nor true realization can be acquired.

The materialistic approach to the spiritual life can be a serious stumbling block to progress, and it often goes unnoticed for years. Therefore, semantic analysis such as we have undertaken up to this point is not just a frivolous play on words, but actually can unmask certain modes of being-in-the-world rooted in materialistic presuppositions which hamper individ-

225

ual progress on the spiritual path. The right understanding of receptivity is of central importance. The Bible says: "But as many as received him, to them gave he power to become the sons of God, even to them that believe on his name" (John 1:12). It does not say, "to them that acquired his knowledge," but "to them that received him." The emphasis here is on receiving.

In considering the issue of receptivity, it becomes clear to us that acquisitiveness is greedy and aggressive and willful, whereas receptivity is humble, grateful, and alert in the expectancy of good. The greedy, acquisitive, aggressive, anxious materialistic approach defeats itself. It is not unlike catching a pigeon. In order to catch a pigeon, one must be quiet and patient with one's offering, whereas an aggressive reaching out to catch one invariably turns out to be futile. Understanding requires reverent loving receptivity and responsiveness to that which reveals itself from moment to moment.

Interestingly enough, the materialistic approach tends to be self-defeating even in the material world. For instance, if we are very acquisitive about money, it may elude us; but if we are receptive to money, it will come to us. This also applies to jobs and other opportunities. It may be a common experience that if we go shopping determined to buy certain specific items we may go from store to store not being able to get them. But if we are receptive to certain ideas about items of usefulness to us, we may just stumble over them while strolling by a store. I know a young lady who spent many an hour searching in department stores for a piece of furniture and could not find what she wanted. After she had given up on it, she noticed from her window that across the street from where she lived there was a small furniture store featuring the very item she was hunting for, and at a discount, at that.

The acquisitive approach is an aspect of an existentially invalid mode of being-in-the-world. The receptive, grateful, spiritual mode is valid.

It is a great blessing to be able to discern the spiritual essence of all reality. When we can see the spiritual basis of life, then our vocabulary will undergo a corresponding change, and, as the Bible says, we shall speak with "new tongues" (Mark 16:17). We could speak of vocabularies of materialism, operationalism, and in juxtaposition, the language of the spiritually minded. The aim of semantic analysis is to bring about an altered mode of perceiving life and participating in it. Our language affects our ways of seeing, and our seeing affects our language. "As thou seest, so thou speakest; and as thou speakest, so thou seest."

Another pitfall of materialistic thinking is the constant expectancy, even demand, to "get something out of" every endeavor. This is the so-called "profit motive." One student remarked: "I have been studying hard and laboring on the spiritual path for a number of years and getting nothing out of it. I still have the same job, I still live in the same crummy apartment, and I still haven't found the right girl." The profit motive does not apply to spiritual progress. It is not a "getting something out of it" process. Spiritual enlightenment is its own reward. It expands the boundaries of awareness, transforms characters, alleviates suffering, and inspires with wisdom and love.

The Body

It is not possible to emphasize enough the importance of mental discipline. If we realize that nothing comes into experience uninvited, we clearly see how vitally important it is to discipline our thoughts and thereby gain dominion over what will be admitted into consciousness and what will not be permitted to take root in consciousness. Everything depends on the quality of consciousness. God gave us the power to be stewards of our consciousness.

Sometimes it seems like a very hard struggle to give up pleasurable fantasies which provide, for instance, erotic sensations in various parts of the body. Interestingly enough, in most harmful thinking the issue is mostly physical sensation. No matter what kind of imaginings we are partial to, in the final analysis, what we are aiming at is some kind of special physical sensation. In other words, fantasies have one common denominator, namely, the confirmation of the physical self. If we do not understand the importance of spiritualized consciousness, we are forever hurting ourselves with our thoughts. The more pleasurable the thoughts, the more harmful they may be. Where a man's pleasure is there will his pain be also.

As mentioned above, mental discipline is not easily attained. It requires years of devotion and practice, plus a real, deep understanding of what it means to be a human being and what it means to be a spiritual being. Human beings are preoccupied with their physical sensations. Everything in the human condition revolves around feelings and sensation in the body; therefore, human beings are forever thinking about how to invite pleasurable experiences. They are thinking, for instance, about what they will eat, drink, what they will wear, how they will improve their bodies, etc., and how to have more and more interesting, exciting, and pleasurable experiences. This is what human existence revolves around — sensations, feelings, emotions, etc.

Discipline must not be confused with control. Control is based on "should" thinking which is willfulness. Discipline is based on wisdom, love, and understanding of what is good. "Discipline" is derived from the word "disciple." Discipleship means following the teachings of a master. When we love the wisdom of the master, we become naturally disciplined.

The most remarkable physical sensation, of course, is sexual arousal and climax. Therefore, sex plays an important role in the quest for human pleasure. All sorts of complicated methods and practices are invented to achieve orgiastic sensation. The few seconds of intense physical sensation are often considered the ultimate good of human existence — the *summum bonum vitae*. When we gain a little perspective on the human condition, we see the futility and emptiness of this entire quest. In addition to the short-lived nature of the pleasurable experience, there are longer lasting consequences of an unpleasant nature connected with this mode of being-in-the-world.

Interestingly enough, our physical illnesses are part and parcel of our preoccupations with physical sensations. Therefore, sooner or later, we have to lose interest in these pursuits and we must come to discover what it means to be a spiritual being. God did not create human beings. God knows nothing about human beings. God knows only spiritual beings because God is Spirit, and anyone who wants to communicate with God must be spiritual.

Natural man cannot commune with God. As long as we believe ourselves to be human beings, we can only theorize about God. Jesus said: "God is [a] Spirit: and they that worship him must worship him in spirit and in truth" (John 4:24). The truth is that we are spiritual beings. Spiritual beings are not interested in physical sensations. They have long left that behind. What are spiritual beings interested in? Spiritual beings also are interested in happiness, but the happiness of a spiritual being is not sensual or emotional. It is spiritual. Therefore, his thoughts are on an entirely different plane. The aim of his thoughts is PAGL (peace, assurance, gratitude, and love), not orgasm or other pleasurable experiences. A spiritual being has a different notion about the good and what is important and what is desirable. His thoughts move in a different direction. The good he seeks is in consciousness, not in the body.

PAGL contrasts with physical sensation in that it is not short-lived, there is no let-down, and it is not pathogenic (illness producing). On the contrary, it is healing, harmonizing, health-promoting, inspiring, liberating. It is not an experience but a realization. To understand this difference is a great blessing, and the more clearly we understand this difference between being human and being spiritual, the easier it will be to discipline our thoughts for the attainment of this realization.

The mental discipline we are referring to is called "mind fasting," which means refraining from entertaining thoughts which lead to the confirmation of one's self as a physical body. Having suffered for a while, we may be willing to engage in the practice of mind fasting and thus emerge gradually from the darkness of materialism into the light of spiritual consciousness. "In the world ye shall have tribulation: but be of good cheer; I have overcome the world" (John 16:33). It is possible to overcome the world. To overcome the world means to transcend the body, because everything in the human dream revolves around the body.

It is becoming clearer that the more ignorant we are of Spiritual Reality, the more painful our living and our dying is; whereas when we realize that we are spiritual beings and truly understand it and have transcended the body, there is a loss of fear of death, and dying is not an agony but a more or less peaceful process of transition. Grief also is less of a problem. Therefore this has great importance.

The whole human race seems to be evolving toward the attainment of universal Christ-consciousness. Some are driven (through suffering) and some are drawn. Blessed are they who are drawn. A famous Zen koan (riddle) says: "There is a goose in a bottle. How does the goose get out of the bottle? ... "

Anger

Anger is an epiphenomenon of frustration. The meaning of anger can be found mainly in one single phrase — "I want." Another source of anger is the habit of "should" thinking — thinking in terms of what "should" be and what "should not" be. Habits of thought and words are our tormentors.

An interesting example of an angry man was Saul of Tarsus, who was a known persecutor of the early Christians. On the road to Damascus he had a remarkable experience. He saw a blinding flash of light all around him and heard a voice saying, "Saul, Saul why persecutest thou me?...It is hard for thee to kick against the pricks" (Acts 9:4, 5). We understand this to mean that willful aggressiveness and anger are self-defeating ways of living, resulting in painful experiences. The victimizer becomes the victim of his own aggressiveness. Typically, Saul responded with an operational question, "Lord, what wilt thou have me to do?" And the answer was: "It shall be told thee what thou must do" (Acts 9:6). But the task required of him was not an operational one but an existential one, namely, study, prayer, reorientation, and transformation of character until the "scales fell off his blinded eyes" (Acts 9:18), and he learned to see Spiritual Reality. Then he understood that the way to do is to be. Finally, he reached the point where he could say: "I live; yet not I, but Christ [liveth] in me" (Galatians 2:20).

It is helpful to point out here that aggressiveness and passivity are two sides of the same coin because both are ways of ignoring the power and the presence of God. If there were no God, there would be no third alternative. In such a context man is either victim or victimizer, persecutor or persecuted. Someone said, "If there were no God, we would have to invent him." Without the third alternative, life would be a miserable condition. No wonder Sartre called his play "No Exit." In that play there are three people in a hotel room from which there is no exit, and they are doomed eternally to endure each other's aggressiveness and passivity. Sartre called that condition hell and said: "Hell is people." But to those who have God-consciousness there is an exit, for God, infinite Mind, is the controlling power in all our affairs. To understand this makes "shouldlessness" possible, while without it shouldlessness seems unattainable.

Conventional psychology assumes that the best way to deal with anger is to express it. This amounts to saying "You will feel better if you make someone else feel bad." Unfortunately, the more anger is expressed, the more there is of it. However, keeping it bottled up is also not the answer; we can't let it out and can't keep it in. Some people believe that being angry is good because it makes it possible to have courage (Eric Hoffer, the longshoreman-philosopher). In a Godless frame of reference this seems to be true, but in the context of God, omniactive Love-Intelligence, the alternative to animal courage is loving fearlessness. Salvation is found in the Christly perspective on Reality, which says, "Perfect love casteth out fear" (1 John 4:18). Spiritual beings are fearless because they are loving. They are neither passive nor aggressive. They are responsive. Courage, rooted in anger, is unintelligent, whereas fearlessness, rooted in love, is based on a sound mind and clarity of vision.

It is very important to be aware of our self-identity as emanations of the universal Mind, and to be aware that the firmness and forthrightness and the ability which we express is God manifesting Himself through us.

At this point the question may be asked, Is it possible for man to be free of the tendency toward anger? The answer is: Yes, in proportion to his understanding and conscious awareness of God's omnipotent, controlling, governing presence. In order to attain this realization it is helpful to conceive of God as omniactive Mind. This dynamic concept facilitates our cognitive awareness of a power and presence, a mental force, always present and active in our affairs. This leads to the realization of two principles: the third principle of Metapsychiatry, which states, "There is no interaction anywhere; there is only Omniaction everywhere," and the fifth principle of Metapsychiatry, "God helps those who let Him."

Anger and passivity are forms of interaction. In juxtaposition to this, Omniaction becomes a reality to us. When a theory becomes existentially valid for us, we have attained its realization.

Alcoholism

If we are to consider the problem of alcoholism, we must first view it in the context of addictions in general because alcoholism is just a special form of addiction. Let us then consider the meaning of this addiction. Alcoholism is an attachment to a chemical substance and its effects upon the mood and the thought processes of an individual.

All men have a tendency and an urgent desire to find some way of managing their moods and their thoughts in order to find contentment, happiness, and freedom from undesirable mental preoccupations. It is a remarkable thing that what man suffers from most are his own thoughts. It is not so much conditions or people that torment us but rather our own thoughts about them. The Greek philosopher Epictetus already knew this. He said: "Man does not suffer from conditions, but rather from the views he takes of them." For instance, if there is a rainy day, some people get depressed. Now rain will not cause us to be depressed, but the thoughts which we may entertain about the bad weather can torment us.

So man is burdened with the universal problem of managing his own thought processes in such a way as to escape suffering. Certain thoughts make us happy, while other thoughts can make us miserable. Of course unenlightened man does not realize that and he has a tendency to think in terms of cause and effect. When he falls into the trap of cause-and-effect thinking, he is inclined to blame some external factors for his internal torments. To the extent that his primitive thinking has him under control he blames external conditions for his unhappiness and, naturally, he is inclined to seek external remedies for his problems.

The meaning of all addictions could be defined as endeavors at controlling our life experiences with the help of external remedies. These remedies can be persons, places, things, and ideologies. Places, persons, and things are symbols, and their effect is ideational. Chemical substances affect the functioning of the organism by altering perceptivity and experience. So alcohol is a chemical substance which man uses to control his experience of life.

Unfortunately, all external means of improving our life experiences are doubled-edged swords: they are always good and bad. No external remedy improves our condition without, at the same time, making it worse. When Eve saw the beautiful apple on the tree of knowledge, she reached out for it to enhance her life experience, and by using this external means, she discovered good and evil. This is the original prototype of man's quest for happiness — seeking the Kingdom of God on the outside rather than within consciousness.

In considering the story of Adam and Eve, it is helpful not to omit the role of the serpent. It was the serpent which was suggesting to Eve to reach out for external means. What does this talking serpent stand for? It stands for a mode of thinking based on sensory impressions, that is, judging by appearances. The universal tendency to judge by appearances is the source of all ignorance. Judging by appearances, man jumps to false conclusions and becomes a victim of his own errors.

Let us consider someone who has reached the point where he is unable to snap out of his depression. He may reach for a drink of alcohol and find, indeed, that his thinking has changed, his mood is lifted, and suddenly he feels better. As the Bible says: "Then your eyes shall be opened, and ye shall be as gods, knowing good and evil" (Genesis 3:5). This is the beginning of alcoholism. The moment we reach out for alcohol as an external remedy for our internal distress, we have found a wrong solution. The same goes for smoking, pill-popping, drug taking, etc. The basic issue in all addictions is the desire to control the quality of inner experience with the help of external remedies.

Interestingly enough, traditional medical thinking about addictive substances is as follows: If one substance is harmful, let us find another substance, less harmful, which might perhaps replace the previous one. A most blatant example of this is the present day endeavor of substituting the drug methadone for heroin. The results of this treatment, of course, are highly unsatisfactory — as could have been expected.

There is only one remedy to all addictive problems of man, and it is to return to that condition where life is lived in the original purity of consciousness. Man has a God-given power which is called "dominion." What does that mean? It means that we don't need to resort to external means in order to manage our internal conditions. It is possible with this God-given power to manage our thought processes in such a way as to live in the constant conscious awareness of peace, assurance, gratitude, love, freedom, wisdom, joy, beauty, goodness, and truth. We have the power to be spiritually minded; we have the power to turn our interest in the direction of transcendent values. We are capable of inspired wisdom and creative intelligence. We can learn the art of management of our internal affairs.

What are the methods of attaining control over our internal affairs? They are prayer and meditation which includes "mind fasting," which means refraining from entertaining certain harmful thoughts and fantasies. Thus we see that prayer and meditation are not just forms of religious observance, but a method of survival. It is a mental hygiene technique par excellence. It is hard to imagine how anyone could survive without prayer and meditation. It is the most important thing to learn in life if we want to be healthy and effective. Without it we are at the mercy of all sorts of erroneous remedies which the world (the talking serpent) is constantly offering us.

There is a story about a teenage girl who was overheard talking on the telephone and saying: "I don't know what to do;

should I take a benzedrine and go out on my date, or should I take a phenobarb and go to sleep?" This may be called "scientific progress" and "better living through chemistry...."

The healing of any addiction requires getting to the point where one is willing to forsake all external remedies and turn with absolute sincerity toward internal remedies, which are spiritual. This process is facilitated through supportive guidance either by recovered fellow sufferers and/or experienced therapists who understand the dynamics of spiritual healing.

Jesus has described in one single statement both the phenomenology and the healing process of the addictive individual. He said the following: "For this people's heart is waxed gross, and their ears are dull of hearing, and their eyes they have closed; lest at any time they should see with their eyes, and hear with their ears, and should understand with their hearts, and should be converted, and I should heal them" (Matthew 13:15). He beautifully describes the condition of the addict who doesn't want to hear, who doesn't want to see, who has become callous in his absolute self-centeredness, who does not care about anyone, and only thinks about his own comfort.

What has to happen in a therapeutic process is that the addict has to begin to hear, to see, and to become responsive to positive values. He has to begin to understand. He has to undergo a conversion from externally oriented remedies to internal remedies and then he can be healed. Thus the rehabilitation process is essentially a conversion process.

Sometimes we hear that psychologists recommend that certain attitudes be assumed by the family of an alcoholic. It is important to understand that attitudes are really operational concepts and manipulative devices to be employed on behalf of a patient. This can never be helpful because no one likes to be an object of manipulative intervention. More often than not, this provokes a patient and aggravates his condition. A family, of course, could be helpful just as an Alcoholics Anonymous group, when sincerely working together, can be very helpful, not on the basis of assumed attitudes, but on the basis of understanding what the underlying issues are.

The remedy is *existential*, not operational. We do not believe in the effectiveness of "right attitudes." They are just pretensions of helpfulness. It is not what we do that is helpful, but what we know.

Levels of Cognitive Integration

Human consciousness seems to exert its influence throughout the planet earth and even beyond. Ignorant human consciousness seems to exert a devastating influence everywhere, and we see it even in the animal kingdom. Beastliness in the animal kingdom may very well be an expression of low-level human thinking. When man reaches enlightenment, then the Christ-consciousness will become manifest throughout the world — as the utopian picture which the prophet Isaiah paints for us reveals that animality will vanish even among the so-called "wild" beasts: "The wolf also shall dwell with the lamb, and the leopard shall lie down with the kid; and the calf and the young lion and the fatling together; and a little child shall lead them" (Isaiah 11:6).

Thus we see that the world we live in reflects the qualities of consciousness which prevail among us. Therefore, there is only one task ahead of us, namely, the purification and elevation and spiritualization of our consciousness to the highest possible level. We can distinguish six levels of cognitive integration. These are: (1) the sensual, (2) the emotional, (3) the intellectual, (4) the materialistic, (5) the personalistic, and (6) the transcendent. By cognitive integration we mean, "As thou seest, so thou beest." On a sensual level we are primarily concerned with the pursuit of pleasure and the avoidance of pain. These are the pleasure-seeking ways of life. This is the lowest form of existence. Then there are those of us who see life in terms of feelings and emotions. On a little higher level is intellectualism, where life is seen in terms of the intellect. This includes craftiness and fraudulency of mind. Then there is materialism, where the value of life is seen in material possessions. Next are the psychologically minded, who see life in terms of personal relationships and interaction thinking.

The highest level of cognitive integration is the level of transcendence. On this level the central issue of life is awareness and spiritual discernment of transcendent values, such as: peace, assurance, gratitude, love, freedom, wisdom, joy, harmony, beauty, etc. The human race is evolving toward this level of cognitive integration. The closer we come to it, the more harmonious and wholesome life becomes, not only for mankind but for animals and plants and the whole earth as well.

It is interesting to consider the fact that traditional psychological thinking considers mental health to be based on the ability to function primarily on the first five levels of cognitive integration. Mental diseases are seen as consisting of fixations on any one particular level. As someone remarked, "You are only in trouble if you specialize, but you are O.K. if you can enjoy being polymorphously perverse."

Life on the first five levels can be experienced as good and bad. Sooner or later the bad tends to become aggravated and there is a desire to shift from one level to another. More often than not, life consists of traveling up and down this ladder of cognitive integration. But then there are those who are willing to forgo the experiential life and seek to attain the level of transcendence where the central issue is not experience but awareness. These individuals seek to understand that man is an *individualized aspect of divine consciousness,* just as a raindrop is an individualized aspect of the seas. Here, being is synonymous with knowing. Awareness is the central function of enlightened man. Such consciousness becomes a luminosity and a beneficial presence in the world.

Zen literature abounds with interesting stories describing such individuals and their modes of being-in-the-world. For example, there is a story about a fishmonger who was poor, ragged, and smelled of fish. This man was a student of Zen and became enlightened. People were talking about him in the fish market, and one day one of his friends came to him and said, "I heard that you became enlightened through your studies of Zen, but I see no difference in you. You are just as poor as ever and you are still selling fish, so wherein lies your enlightenment?" The fishmonger answered: "To tell you the truth, I don't know myself, except that I have noticed one thing. Wherever I walk even the dead trees come alive."

Another Zen story tells of a laundryman who was known in his neighborhood as the man with the heavy bundle on his back. This man studied Zen with a Master for some years. One day he came to his teacher and said, "I had my enlightenment." The Zen Master said to him, "All right, so tell me what is the meaning of Zen?" Whereupon the student threw his bundle to the floor. "That's good," said the Master. "Now tell me what is the meaning of enlightenment?" In answer to this, the student picked up his bundle and walked out....

A third story is about a very saintly Zen Master, living in a cave above the village. In the village there was a young girl who became pregnant. In her distress she made up a story that the Zen Master was the father of her child. When the child was born, the villagers became incensed and took the child and dumped him in the Master's lap, accusing him of being guilty of this shameful act. When the Master heard these accusations, he looked around and said, "Is that so?" and accepted the baby without protest. Years passed and the young woman had a change of heart; she confessed in the village that she had lied about the Zen Master, whereupon the villagers became incensed again, and a crowd of angry men and women came to the Zen Master, accusing him of keeping the child unlawfully for himself, whereupon the Zen Master, having listened to their accusations, said, "Is that so?" and returned the child.

All these examples describe that mode of being-in-the-world which we have called the transcendent level of cognitive integration. On this level man is a beneficial presence in the world. His yoke is easy. His burden is light. He is fearless and loving.

Friction

Today we are asked to consider the meaning of being attacked. If we are prone to experiencing attacks against our person, then our love, our joy, and our sense of security are precarious. Human existence in general seems to be very precarious. At any moment something may happen that can destroy not only our mood, but life itself. Recently, a man was passing by a bank in New York City and a bomb exploded and killed him. And a woman was walking near the Pan Am building when a helicopter crashed onto the roof and a fragment of the propeller fell to the street, killing her.

In psychology there is a well-known concept called accident proneness. We may ask, What makes an individual accident prone? This question is answered in Metapsychiatry by the seventh principle: "Nothing comes into experience uninvited." There are only two ways to get into accidents, by wanting to or by not wanting to. How can that be? In the book of Job we read: "For the thing which I greatly feared is come upon me, and that which I was afraid of is come unto me" (Job 3:25). How can we make any sense of this? Some people would quickly conclude that we are indulging here in magical thinking by ascribing power to our thoughts, the power to make things happen just by thinking them. This, of course, is not what we are talking about.

In order to understand this principle we might profitably consider the problem of friction. In daily life we experience a great deal of friction. People constantly come physically and psychologically close together, and they experience either pleasurable or painful forms of friction. To caress someone or to hit someone is essentially the same thing; it is friction of various intensity.

Friction is also spoken of as interaction, which can be gentle or abrasive, even violent. Friction, then, is a fundamental element in human experience. It would seem that what we dread above all is frictionlessness. Frictionlessness is experienced as being ignored, or as nonbeing. What we dread most in life is the experience of nonbeing, or being nothing. Therefore, we all have a craving for friction. One lady of my acquaintance is in the habit of saying: "A kick is as good as a boost."

We pay lip service to a desire for peace and harmony but actually we seek friction. Even flight requires friction of the plane against the atmosphere, and a bird needs the air currents in order to fly.

There is a story about Chuang-tzu, the famous Taoist sage. One day his students reported to him that in the neighboring province there lived a man who was so enlightened that he could ride on the wind. Chuang-tzu was unimpressed and said: "He still needs the wind!"

The philosopher Heidegger wrote about the "dread of nothingness." The dread of nothingness impels us to seek friction, and the more fearful we are of nothingness, the more urgently we seek friction. Children who are afraid of being ignored tend to make pests of themselves, become hyperactive, provocative, even violent, and of course, accident prone.

Psychology proposes to teach people how to live in a relationship with minimal friction. This is called "getting along with people," or "learning to relate," but this is just a technique. If we learn how to be smooth operators in society, this is not synonymous with liberation from existential anxiety, which is another way of speaking about the dread of nothingness. Social functioning tends to break down and complications do arise because there remains in man the fear of becoming insignificant, rejected, and ignored.

So, from time to time, when we become anxious about being nothing, we may reach out in clumsy ways for some kind of approbation from our fellow men and get rebuffed and hurt. And that's how life may proceed as a process of coping with an undercurrent fear of nothingness or insignificance. Man cannot be healed of his problems unless he learns to think in existentially valid ways.

So let us now consider the issue of attack and ask again, What is the meaning of being attacked? Attack is nothing else but an incident of heightened friction of short duration.

Elsewhere a case was described of a young man who, while driving on the road, was attacked by a pheasant which smashed into his windshield. A few miles further down the road, while stopping at a red light, another car bumped into his car. Later on that night, his parked car developed a flat tire in front of his house. When we explored his thought processes and his entire mode of being-in-the-world, we understood that this man was very anxious for admiration and sought to get it from people. He realized that to get admiration or to get attacked is essentially the same, because if one is the recipient of intense admiration, this can actually amount to an attack. A good example are the rock stars who are literally assaulted and their clothes ripped apart by admirers. So then to get a compliment or an insult are really just variations on a theme. And the basic theme is friction.

Let us now recall the above-mentioned principle, which says: "Nothing comes into experience uninvited." The Bible says: "For he that soweth to his flesh shall of the flesh reap corruption" (Galatians 6:8). We may ask, What is the basic seed of life? It is thought. Whatever thoughts we entertain in consciousness and communicate to the world will manifest themselves in corresponding experiences. They will not *cause* these experiences to happen, but they will manifest themselves as such experiences according to the principle of transmutation of energy. A thought as a seed of life is a unit of energy.

The Bible also gives us the healing remedy to the dilemma of friction and all its complications. It says: "But he that soweth to the Spirit shall of the Spirit reap life everlasting" (Galatians 6:8). This points up that the solution to safety, harmony, freedom from accidents and violence as well as illness, is "sowing to the Spirit," which means that our thoughts must be imbued with spiritual values and we must see ourselves in the context of Divine Reality where nonbeing is unknown. Therefore, the dread of nothingness is healed and we are no longer afraid of being ignored. As a consequence, we are no longer driven to crave friction.

The fear of nonbeing can be healed by understanding the following statement: "God is cognizant of us while we are mindful of Him." If anyone wants to be healed of the dread of nothingness, he must learn to be mindful of his oneness with and inseparability from the love of God.

God never ignores us, but we can ignore God by allowing ourselves to be distracted by the "five gates of hell" which, as mentioned earlier, are: (1) sensualism, (2) emotionalism, (3) intellectualism, (4) personalism, and (5) materialism. When we allow ourselves to be distracted by any of these means, we become susceptible to existential anxiety and an urgent craving for friction. Friction is a form of self-confirmatory striving. But Omniaction is the power and presence of Divine Love-Intelligence expressing itself through individual beings. This is a different dimension of reality and is free of the dread of nothingness. Therefore, it is harmonious, intelligent, wholesome, and perfect.

Perfection is not only possible but actually the only Reality there is. What is needed for man is to awaken to its realization and then he will be able to partake in it. Otherwise, all we will have is an endless variety of friction with its disastrous consequences.

The Other Cheek

From time to time we hear certain sincere individuals say, "I would like to be a good Christian, but there is one thing I cannot do — I cannot turn the other cheek." This saying of Jesus: "Unto him that smiteth thee on the one cheek offer also the other" (Luke 6:29), has been interpreted as a requirement to be either masochistic or arrogant or stoically unfeeling and hard, a collector of injustices. In order to understand this most unusual utterance and recommendation, it is helpful to ask ourselves what the meaning of "cheek" is. Cheek is the quality of thought which we present to the world.

Unfortunately, there are individuals who — without realizing it — are very much attached to the experiences of being persecuted, so much so that they misinterpret even friendly gestures as designed to persecute them. They are so attached to this idea of being victims that it is hard for them to turn *another cheek*. Human nature tends to be rather perverse, and we know that pain is just as self-confirmatory as pleasure; however, most people would be embarrassed to admit this. There is a form of mental disease in which the individual interprets everything as cruelty and persecution. This disorder is called paranoia. There is a desire here to be the butt of persecution, and a strange refusal to distinguish between kindness and cruelty. There are various degrees of this kind of thinking, but the real issue in this condition is self-confirmatory ideation. Thus we can say that here everything becomes grist for the mill. It makes no sense to call such an individual a masochist because he will enjoy the feeling of being accused of masochism. There is a universal inclination in man toward self-confirmatory ideation. And this could be considered the "original sin."

Occasionally someone gets incensed against Metapsychiatry because it reveals this secret of self-confirmatory ideation. The remedy to self-confirmatory ideation is transcendence of the ego and commitment to God-confirmatory living. *This is the other cheek.* In practice this means being issue-oriented in our responses. When we are personally slighted, tempted, provoked, or intimidated, we turn an "other cheek" and deal with the issues at hand. In order for this to come about there must be a willingness to be embarrassed about secret self-confirmatory desires. The heat of embarrassment is the consuming fire of "hell" in which the ego is annihilated.

The pilgrimage on the spiritual path is in the direction of realizing that we are not what we seem to be. We are not autonomous persons in interaction with other persons. We are individual spiritual beings, emanations of divine consciousness capable of nonpersonal intelligent responsiveness to situations and issues.

It is possible to awaken — and indeed we must — from the dream of interaction living and realize our spiritual individualities as manifestations and instruments of omniactive Love-Intelligence which is the Metapsychiatric name for God. We do not live in dreams of interaction, but we coexist harmoniously as living Souls in the universe of Mind.

Persons react personally. There is a Latin saying: *Argumentatio ad hominem et argumentatio ad rem,* which means that we are either debating personalities or issues. Interpersonal relationships tend to be troublesome. They constitute the dream of life as interaction. Spiritual beings, on the other hand, respond to issues nonpersonally.

Anxiety

Because anxiety is a universally discomforting, unpleasant experience it is generally assumed that it shouldn't be. Unfortunately, if we accept that proposition, our problem will get worse, and in proportion to our antagonism to that experience, it may loom as a formidable adversary to the point of paralyzing constructive activity, or social participation. Thus, while the problem seems to be anxiety, it is actually not the problem. It is our antagonism to it which creates the difficulty.

If we examine the meaning of anxiety phenomenologically, we see that it is actually just a heightened state of alertness, connected with an anxious desire to succeed in some project. Therefore, it is actually healthy to be anxious. We can say, It is all right to be anxious as long as we are not timid. Timidity is a fear of appearing anxious, and it gives rise to a desire to stifle and cover up the anxiety. Anxiety can be accepted as something positive and timidity can be refused as something cowardly, unproductive, and self-indulgent. It is always good to know the enemy, because then we can see what the real issues are.

Timid people often blame anxiety for their suffering, but if they realize that the foe is timidity hiding behind anxiety, then they can simply refuse to be timid and the whole problem disappears. Therefore, we can say that it is all right to be anxious as long as we are willing not to be timid. Anxiety is eagerness to do well. Timidity is a desire not to feel bad. "God hath not given us the spirit of fear [timidity]; but of power, and of love, and of a sound mind" (2 Timothy 1:7). Thus we do not have to be against anxiety. We can make friends with anxiety. We must learn to welcome it as a heightened state of alertness which makes creative responsiveness more available.

As it is with anxiety so it is with the problem of pain or dis-comfort of any kind. If we take an antagonistic position against pain and try to stop pain, thinking that it shouldn't be, it will get worse, because we have accepted the reality of an illusion. The harder we try to get rid of it, the more we confirm its reality. But if we say, "I am aware of pain, but I am not against it. I want to understand its meaning," then we shall befriend the pain and it will reveal to us something about our mode of being-in-the-world which is important for us to know at that particular time. And when we have understood the message and corrected our thinking in a certain specific way, the pain will cease because it has accomplished its mission.

It is good to remember that problems thrive on attention. Therefore, we must learn the art of transcending them and seeking to understand the meaning behind them. The impor-tant thing is not to get ensnared into preoccupation with the symptom, but to turn away from it and focus attention on Real-ity. The more we learn the art of focusing attention on Reality, the greater dominion we gain over distractions of physical ex-istence. Every symptom is an invitation to be preoccupied with oneself.

In the final analysis all problems require us to come to understand the truth of being and our self-identity as individ-ual expressions of God.

A young woman said: "I have a strange problem. I seem to enjoy having colds. When I have a cold I enjoy staying in bed, drinking tea and pampering myself. This in spite of the fact that I am well aware of the three 'Ps' which I have learned here, namely, that praise, pampering, and persecution go together and are inseparable experientially."

This is a good example of the perversity of the human con-dition, where feeling good and feeling bad are actually the same, with the common denominator being self-confirmatory ideation. If we do not understand this, then we naturally assume that the remedy to feeling bad is finding a way to feel good. The devil is portrayed as having two horns. We could say that this symbolism points toward the trap of dualistic thinking in unenlightened man. Divine Reality, however, is nondual. Therefore the solution to human problems lies in taking refuge in Divine Reality and transcending the tendency to be preoccupied with how we feel.

Upon meeting someone we are in the habit of asking each other, "How do you feel?" This is actually a harmful custom because it suggests that it is important to feel good and to avoid feeling bad. It suggests that our feelings are arbiters of our state of health. As a consequence, the vast majority of people are constantly preoccupied with finding ways of feeling good.

This brings to mind a story about a Zen Master who, when asked how it feels to be enlightened, replied: "When I am hungry, I eat, and when I am tired, I rest." Whereupon the inquirer asked, "Isn't this what everyone else is doing?" The Master said, "Not at all. Everyone else eats when he feels hungry, and rests when he feels tired." "So what's wrong with that?" asked the inquirer. And the Master said, "Don't you see, you can feel hungry right after you have eaten, and you can feel tired after a night's sleep."

Unenlightened people, without realizing it, base their lives on how they feel. They are guided by their feelings. Enlightened man is guided by Reality. The word "tathata" means that which really is, or "true suchness." As long as you take your feelings as a measure of reality, you are a "goose in a bottle" — which means that you see yourself as living in the body.

As long as we are anchored in our feelings, we cannot possibly conceive of any other index by which to live. If the Zen Master does not concern himself with how he feels, how can he know when he is hungry, or how can he know when he is tired? Surprisingly enough, it is possible to know the difference between being hungry and just feeling hungry and similarly, between being tired and just feeling tired. The secret lies in a heightened awareness of our thoughts. It is possible to know whether or not we are using food and rest for self-confirmatory purposes or for valid reasons of nourishment and recuperation. Enlightened man does not think about how he feels and does not talk about how he feels.

Returning now to our story about the Zen Master and his interlocutor, we hear the interlocutor say, "But Master, I still don't understand the difference." Whereupon the Zen Master says, "When enlightened man eats, he eats; and when he rests, he rests. But unenlightened people think of ten thousand things when they eat, and dream of ten thousand things when they rest."

The consideration of this issue can be quite illuminating in the context of marriage and family life. When members of a family are governed by their feelings, then there is constant jockeying and striving to get pleasure from each other. Everybody wants something from everybody else in the hope of feeling good (or bad). There is a natural tendency to use not only food and rest, but people also, for the purpose of feeling good. And it is generally assumed that this is natural and right and that's how things should be, for what is life without feeling good? There seem to be only two choices: either one feels good or one feels bad. In such a marriage there is constant pressure and mutual manipulation, as a result of which endless complications may arise.

For some time now this emphasis has dominated the thinking of lay people, starting from the "hippie" movement of so-called "doing your own thing," through the fad of encounter groups all the way to respectable psychotherapy. For instance, one of the pet phrases one heard from psychotherapists was "get in touch with your feelings." And in encounter groups the basic assumption was that whatever one feels is the truth; therefore an honest man would always speak about how he feels and "tell it like it is." The result was that large numbers of people were trained to express unabashed and ruthless egotism. One of the oddities of television at that time was a weekly program where a young woman — very sexy — would sing a few songs and wind up her show with the following pearl of wisdom: "And remember folks, our saying: If you feel like doing it, do it!..."

The Origin of Man

What practical value is there in considering the question of the origin of the human individual? Buddha said: "We are what we think, having become what we have thought" (Dhamapada). However, it would be more correct to say that we seem to be what we are thinking, having become what other people have been thinking about us. But this only refers to our appearance and to our experiences. It is not really what we are and it has little to do with our true selfhood. Our true selfhood was never born and it never dies. It just is. It is a manifestation of God in the world.

The philosopher Heidegger said that man is a place where God reveals Himself in the form of existence (*Lichtung des Daseins*). And that is what man really is, while the other just seems to be. If we speak about the origin of man, it is important to ask ourselves: "What is man?" Who are we talking about — man who is a thought, or man who is a place where God can manifest Himself as Presence?

What are the practical implications and consequences of understanding this? Is it just fanciful speculation for philosophers and theologians to argue about, or does it have practical relevancy to our lives? If we think that we are what other people have thought about us — which seems to be so — then we can become disturbed, trying to blame certain individuals from our past for having thought the wrong way about us, and we may engage in a futile endeavor of attempting to change the past, which is an impossibility. A great deal of suffering can flow from such ways of thinking about ourselves. It is therefore of great value to understand that the Buddha was not precise in his historical statement. We are not what we think and we are not what others have thought about us. That is what we just seem to be. We really are emanations of Divine Love-Intelligence, or we are places where God reveals Himself as a presence of intelligence and love. If we see ourselves this way, then all problems tend to disappear and Jesus' injunction, "Be ye therefore perfect, even as your Father which is in heaven is perfect" (Matthew 5:48), does not strike us as an impossible demand.

We have to realize that God's thoughts constitute our true being and not our parents' thoughts, nor our teachers' thoughts, nor our brothers' thoughts, nor our sisters' thoughts. It is therefore very helpful to learn to distinguish between human factors and divinely inspired ideas. When we are fearful, when we are envious, when we are jealous, when we are superstitious, prejudiced, malicious, etc., we know that this is not what we really are, that these thoughts are no part of our true being, and we can disassociate ourselves from them and affirm passionately the truth of our being.

Divine consciousness gives us immunity against seduction, provocation, and intimidation. As long as we maintain an awareness of our true selfhood, we transcend the tendency to have human reactions to various stimuli, which are part of the everyday experience of unenlightened man.

Sometimes symptoms of illness can have an enticing effect on us and we are tempted to indulge ourselves in them. Sometimes they frighten us and sometimes they get us angry and upset. In either case we must quickly take refuge in divine consciousness and this way we may learn to deal effectively, quickly, and competently with human problems.

The tragedy of the human experience is the universal tendency to judge by appearances, which results in a misperception of reality in which we have the impression that we are separated from God. If one were so enlightened as

to know the truth of being perfectly, there would be no
more need for prayer and meditation. Prayer and meditation are but endeavors to reestablish our sense of at-one-ment
with God.

The Line and the Circle

Recently, in an adult education class, the story of the prodigal son came up for discussion. Interest became focused on the good son who was faithful to the father but who, upon the return of his rebellious brother, became jealous and complained about the reception accorded to him. The class asked whether the meaning of the story is a lesson in humility.

That is the usual moral and religious interpretation of the parable. However, the spiritual meaning of it is this: To be good or to be bad is the same. Sometimes children are very good, while at other times they misbehave. What is the difference? Essentially nothing. For when a child is "good" he seeks to be praised, and when a child is bad he seeks to be punished. The common denominator is a desire for attention, which we call self-confirmation. We can confirm ourselves by being bad or by being good.

Let us consider the meaning of the father's statement in the parable. He didn't say, You must be humble, or, You shouldn't be jealous, or, You should be nice to your brother. He did not make any reference to moral or ethical behavior or religious sentiment. His answer was aimed at clarifying the truth of what really is. He said: "Son, thou art ever with me, and all that I have is thine" (Luke 15:31), which means that the good of God is infinite, spiritual, and always available to everyone. No matter how many people are getting how much, it is limitless. Envy, jealousy, greed, pettiness, rivalry, make no sense whatsoever. If we are faced with infinite good, there is noth-

257

ing to quibble about, and enlightened man knows the good of God is limitless. There will never be a time when God will run out of love, intelligence, joy, beauty, health, harmony, peace, assurance, wisdom, or happiness.

The two brothers in the parable were reasoning from the standpoint of material limitation. Once life is understood in its spiritual dimension, humility, arrogance, goodness, and badness become insignificant. Trying to improve a human person is like trying to straighten out a snake. How long will a snake remain straight?

In this context it is interesting to contemplate the various systems and institutions which man has evolved in the hope of improving the human race. Efforts at improving the human person are not very effective and often disappointing. This indicates that our assumptions about man must be inadequate. Man clearly is not what he seems to be. According to the Bible, man is image and his substance is spirit. How are we to understand this?

One way to attempt the clarification of this mystery would be to imagine a circle, or a loop. This circle, when viewed at an angle to a source of light casts a shadow. When the circle is at a right angle to the source of light, the shadow will be a line. A line has a beginning and an end; a circle has neither beginning nor end. A line can be straight or crooked and still remain a line. In a way, we could speak of a sick line or a healthy line. A straight line is a healthy line, while a crooked line could be considered a sick or distorted line, but it is still a line. A circle, however, must remain perfect at all times. Otherwise it cannot be considered a circle. A perfect circle can cast a shadow in the form of a straight line or a distorted line, depending on the surface upon which the shadow falls. In other words, environmental factors can affect the appearance of the line.

The circle, however, has no beginning and no end, and is perfect all the time. It represents our true selfhood in the context of Divine Reality. The light represents divine consciousness. In the context of divine consciousness we are all perfect and immortal. The line represents the human personality. The circle is not accessible to sensory perception. All we see with our eyes is the shadow and its problems. When we have a crooked line, we may try to improve the environmental situation — this could represent medical science and psychology, or social engineering, etc. — but we are still engaged in trying to improve a shadow, a phenomenon.

What is the substance of a shadow? It is nothing. It is an optical illusion. Therefore, it is insubstantial. The visible is insubstantial and the invisible is substantial. "We look not at the things which are seen, but at the things which are not seen: for the things which are seen are temporal (illusive); but the things which are not seen are eternal" (timeless, infinite, perfect, real immutable) (2 Corinthians 4:18). What is needed is the realization of what really is in contrast to that which seems to be. It is not a simple reversal of facts, but a cognitive awakening to an awareness of God's omnipresence and man's perfection in the context of divine consciousness.

As long as attention is focused on other shadows, all we see is shadows. In order to discern the divine consciousness — the light and the circle — attention must be turned away from interaction to the awareness of omniactive Mind.

There is an interesting parallelism between the shadow and money. A dollar bill is but a piece of paper indicating the existence of a corresponding value, either in the form of gold or other monetary standard which is kept by the government. So a dollar bill is not really a value, but a symbol of value. Our currency transactions and economic life proceed on the level of symbolic logic. The human personality is a symbolic structure indicating the existence of the real being which is spiritual man in divine Consciousness, the governing Principle of the universe. Our activities on the level of human personality are, therefore, symbolic gestures expressing in a symbolic way certain values and witnessing the existence of these values in the realm of the real.

Work is an activity aimed at expressing usefulness, intelligence, and beneficence. Income is a symbolic appearance of the flow of God's good to man and man's receptivity to it. Therefore, income is not directly related to work; work is related to usefulness, and income to receptivity. The more useful we wish to be, the more opportunities will arise for work. This is a spiritual solution to idleness and unemployment. The more receptive we are to the good of God which is spiritual, the more income will be manifested in our experience. This is the spiritual remedy to a sense of lack.

Enlightenment

Ordinarily, life is thought of as proceeding on four levels: First is the level of self-awareness, self-consciousness, pre-occupation with oneself — how one feels, what one is thinking, what one wants, what one needs, what one would like. The second level is concerned with relationships of the self with others. The third level is a concern of man's relationship to the environment, and the fourth level is the relationship with God.

The world of the self is the domain of psychoanalytic inquiry. The world of relationships or interactions with others is the domain of social psychology. The world of the environment belongs to ecology. The world of man's relationship to God is the domain of religion.

Enlightenment is none of these things, and none of these things can lead to enlightenment. Enlightenment involves radical iconoclasticism. Iconoclasticism means the destruction of cherished symbols.

There is no self and other, and no relationship of self to other. There is no relationship between man and God. There is no God apart from His creation. There is only God manifesting Himself in the universe in multitudinous life forms. God and His universe are one. Man and God cannot have a relationship; man is a direct expression of God. There is no relationship between the sun and the sunbeam; the sunbeam is an emanation of the sun. The sun and the sunbeam are one. So God and man are one. Jesus said: "I am in the Father, and the Father in me" (John 14:11). "I and my Father are one" (John

10:30). If we are one with the divine Godhead, how can we have a relationship?

In enlightenment all symbolic structures and relationship ideas are discovered as nonexistent. They are only appearances. The third principle of Metapsychiatry says, "There is no interaction anywhere; there is only Omniaction everywhere," and if we really understand it, we are enlightened. When we can understand, behold, and realize reality as Omniaction, then we have completely transcended the world of symbolic structures. And indeed, Jesus said: "I am with you always, even unto the end of the world" (Matthew 28:20). Furthermore he said: "Heaven and earth shall pass away, but my words shall not pass away" (Matthew 24:35, Mark 13:31, Luke 21:33). This is usually interpreted as referring to some historical event in the future, but Jesus was talking about the process of enlightenment in individual consciousness.

At the point of enlightenment we realize that the material world is a conglomeration of symbolic structures, pointing beyond themselves. Problems in human experiences arise from unwittingly confusing symbolic structures with Reality.

In the process of approaching enlightenment we come to a realization that indeed, as the famous Zen Master Hui-neng said, "From the beginning nothing is." This is one of the most radical Zen statements ever uttered. Enlightened man sees that *everything is nothing, and nothing is everything.* The Zen Buddhists avoid referring to God. The Hebrew religion also has a prohibition against naming God. It is a sin to name God, and it is an even greater sin to portray God pictorially. St. Paul said we must not try to use imagination to imagine what God looks like. In the Moslem religion, likewise, there is a severe prohibition against making images of God. This prohibition resulted in the limited presence of representational art in the Moslem culture; there is mostly abstract art, usually in the form of geometric ornamental designs.

The use of the word "God" in our culture is both helpful and unhelpful. It can become a stumbling block if it is an intellectual concept, for it tends to conjure up anthropomorphism in thought. It creates a tendency to imagine God in human form. When Hui-neng proclaims: "From the beginning nothing is," he really says: "In the beginning God, and besides Him nothing." ("All things were made by him; and without him was not anything made that was made," John 1:3).

In Buddhist meditation the aim is to attain a realization of "emptiness," which is synonymous with "nothingness," where one has seen through the world of symbolic structures. At this point, man's Buddha-nature emerges. The Buddha-nature is synonymous with the Christ-consciousness. Instead of love, the Buddhists prefer to speak of compassion, which is synonymous with spiritual love (agape). This compassion is combined with wisdom and understanding, and thus man becomes spontaneously a beneficial presence in the world. This is the point where Christianity, Buddhism, Sufism, and all other spiritual disciplines converge in the same truth.

The question is sometimes asked whether it is possible to perform daily tasks and still preserve a constant conscious awareness of God. To understand this issue, it may be helpful to distinguish between thinking about God and being aware of God. If we are thinking about God, we are religious. A religious individual will from time to time think about God. An enlightened individual will be in a state of constant conscious awareness of God as the source of all intelligent ideas flowing to him and enabling him to function effectively.

When we speak of God it is also important to point out that we are not talking about a corpse hanging from a cross, nor of a personage somewhere in outer space, nor of a plastic Jesus on the dashboard of a car, nor of a rabbit's foot. God is the source of all intelligence, power, wisdom, understanding, love. Enlightened man does not have to think about God. He is an open channel of awareness, and he is constantly listening for intelligent ideas to obtain in his consciousness. These intelligent ideas make it possible for him to function. In fact, Jesus said: "My Father worketh hitherto, and I work" (John 5:17).

Religious man has a relationship with God; enlightened individuals are at-one with God. Relationship implies two. At-one-ment is one. God is All-in-all; therefore, whatever good work we accomplish, the credit goes to God. We can never boast about it. Whatever mistakes we make, they are due to ignorance. We take neither credit nor blame. This leaves us in the realm of nothingness.

The question may be asked, Is it desirable to attain a consciousness of our nothingness? a complete freedom from self-confirmatory strivings? Certainly. Ordinarily, we all want to be somebodies. A great deal of energy is being expended to establish oneself as somebody. When we seek enlightenment we desire to become nothing. We go against the stream of prevalent thinking. We suddenly realize that the greatest, most glorious freedom is being nothing. When we are nothing, *God is all;* and when we become nothing, we become divine, and that is the Christ-consciousness.

When we are nothing, we don't have to make anything happen. There is no need to influence, to pressure, to fight, to worry; *there is no interaction, only Omniaction.* All things work together for good to them that love to be nothing. "He that loveth his life shall lose it; and he that hateth his life in this world shall keep it unto life eternal" (John 12:25).

As long as we want to be somebody or something, we live in interaction and we are crucified. When we want to be praised, pampered, and persecuted, what is it that we want? We are seeking self-confirmation through interaction. It is quite amazing what a hunger there is in most of us for interaction experiences. It seems to be built-in into the human condition because there is a tendency in man to interpret reality within a horizontal perspective. Some people get panicky when alone, even for a short time. It is a dread of solitude. On the other hand, there are those who seem to avoid contact with others. These are spoken of as "loners," "antisocials," "schizoids."

When we avoid interaction, we are engaged in interaction. Avoidance is a negative form of interaction. Yes is no, and no is yes. Enlightened man neither seeks interaction nor shuns it. To him it is just a dream of life as a person.

Solitary Man

A businessman reported the following experience: He spent a weekend sulking over the fact that his family had not made enough of a fuss over his birthday. On his way to work the following Monday morning, he stopped his car at a curb and stepped out to buy a newspaper. While his back was turned, someone jumped into the car and drove off with it.

It was pointed out to this man that nothing comes into experience uninvited and that, therefore, the incident had a special meaning, relevant to the quality of his thoughts. Whereupon the businessman said: "You mean I caused this to happen? Am I to blame for this? Was it my fault that my car was stolen and that my family deprived me of my birthday party?..."

The difference between cause and meaning is not easily understood. To get beyond cause-and-effect thinking requires a certain degree of developed consciousness. At certain levels of mentation we begin to see that there are no cause-and-effect relationships, only meanings. There is no interaction, only Omniaction. The more we see, the more we can see that there is less and less to see until, finally, we come to see that there is nothing to see. And then we can really see.

In other words, in order to see Omniaction, we must begin to suspect that there is no such thing as interaction. In order to discern meanings, we must begin to suspect that there is no cause and effect. In order to participate intelligently in a dialogue, it is necessary to see that it is impossible to ask a question while making a statement.

There are many ways we ignorantly try to do the impossible, or claim responsibility and accept blame for something that we could not have done, especially if we believe in cause-and-effect thinking.

One of the more common forms of mental disease is power-madness. That, too, is based on the illusion that man has the power to make things happen, to influence people and events, and to be a prime mover. The Bible says: "A double-minded man is unstable in all his ways" (James 1:8). Double-mindedness seems to be almost a social requirement if one is anxious about being "in" with the crowd and not being isolated. In this connection it is helpful to consider the difference between being lonely and being solitary.

Contrary to general belief, the remedy for loneliness is not companionship but solitariness. The Bible speaks of it by saying: "Come out from among them, and be ye separate" (2 Corinthians 6:17). The more one relies on companionship, the more one tends to suffer from loneliness. It is like drinking salt water when we are thirsty; the more we drink, the thirstier we become.

Daniel (the Book of Daniel) is a model of the solitary man who is never lonely. Solitary man is a man who never seeks companionship, has no need of friends, and is always available to everyone in need. Daniel was a great blessing to all around him. He never had a friend and never sought one, yet he was never lonely. He was a model of spiritual excellence.

Solitariness is not synonymous with solitude. Solitude can be experienced either as pleasant or unpleasant, depending on the state of one's consciousness. But solitariness is a realized mode of being-in-the-world. Solitary man is always with God and with the world, at one with the universe. He does not use people to make himself feel good. He lives in the consciousness of the presence of omniactive Mind. Solitary man can be male or female, married or unmarried. Solitary man enjoys solitude, but he also enjoys company, and though he does not seek friends, he is very friendly. Truly, this is freedom and dominion.

Whenever Daniel is mentioned, people tend to associate him with the story of his survival in the lions' den. Some think that he was a skillful hypnotist or animal tamer. But the real meaning and importance of Daniel is not in that, but in his mode of being-in-the-world. The lions' den is best understood in a symbolic way. Since he had no need for companionship, he was untouchable, immune to the animal or beastly tendencies of people around him. He was immune to gossip, intrigue, and malice, which abounded at the royal court where he lived. Nothing could touch him. He was invulnerable. He called it "innocency." He said to the king: "My God hath sent his angel and hath shut the lions' mouths, that they have not hurt me: forasmuch as before him innocency was found in me" (Daniel 6:22). This is the power of solitariness to make one immune to the mental poisons which fill the atmosphere in organizations and in political and cultural institutions, etc.

Daniel demonstrated that it is possible to be in a vicious mental climate and remain completely untouched by it. As a matter of fact, the whole empire collapsed around him and he remained unscathed. He is like a man standing in the midst of an earthquake, with everything tumbling around him, and not a speck of dust falling on him. He was not a do-gooder. He was just good.

Daniel demonstrated that a solitary man cannot be victimized since he does not crave interaction and confirmation by his fellow man. The above-mentioned businessman, however, sought to be the focus of human solicitude, and thus there was an unconscious vested interest in victimization. This mental set acted as a magnet attracting corresponding experiences into his life. His mode of being-in-the-world was that of a man anxiously seeking self-confirmation through solicitude.

Decision or Commitment?

In traditional Protestant revivalist religions we hear a great deal about "deciding for Christ." The Bible, however, speaks of commitment. At first glance, it would seem that making decisions and committing oneself are synonymous terms. However, there is an important difference. Decisions are usually willful, arbitrary, and voluntary. In contrast to this, commitment could be spoken of as semivoluntary. Decisions seem to be more autonomous actions than commitment. Decision is an ego function. The ego cannot decide to be egoless. Commitment to a higher power is an act of letting be what is.

Commitment becomes greatly facilitated by understanding the fourth principle of Metapsychiatry, which says: "Yes is good, but no is also good." This is not a statement of fatalism or renunciation; it refers to the nondual nature of Divine Reality, the will of God. Having understood that the will of God can only be beneficial under all circumstances, commitment becomes a simple matter of trusting what has been realized about the nondual nature of omniactive Mind, God, the harmonizing principle of the universe.

A very good example of such a committed mode of being-in-the-world is the biblical story of Joseph, who was exposed to a series of negative experiences — being sold into slavery, being falsely accused and thrown into jail — and yet every negative experience unfolded higher evidences of God's blessings. What was characteristic of Joseph was his constant conscious awareness of God's sustaining presence.

Today, when we endeavor to maintain a constant conscious awareness of omniactive Mind as the governing power and principle of our lives, we may be challenged by apparently very intelligent and erudite people, and thought of as being superstitious wishful thinkers. We may be judged as believing in magical incantations and religious shibboleths. The challenging questions and opinions of our skeptical friends must be taken seriously, and we must ask ourselves, What evidence is there of the validity of our position? How can we be sure that we are on solid ground? Is there a way of understanding and proving the validity of our claims? Is there a way of communicating, or even just attempting to explain? Are we just believers or wishful thinkers, or do we really understand something which to many others may seem absurd and illogical?

Jesus was in a similar position when he was challenged by the Pharisees and the scribes who were the contentious skeptics of his time. At one point he was accused of bearing record of himself, and he was told, "Your record is not true because you are bearing record of yourself." Whereupon Jesus answered: "Though I bear record of myself, yet my record is true; for I know whence I came, and whither I go" (John 8:14).

Now we may ask ourselves, Do we know where we came from and do we know where we are going? Certainly. Those of us on the spiritual path know full well that we came from the land of suffering, which we have identified as based on self-confirmatory ideation; and we move toward the land of peace, assurance, gratitude, and love, which we have found to be the "God-confirmatory" enlightened consciousness. It is the promised land of conscious awareness of omniactive Mind, the harmonizing principle of the universe.

So the answer to the skeptics consists of explaining the process of transformation of human consciousness and its beneficial consequences. It is no mystery. It is not superstitious belief. It is verifiable truth, available to any sincere seeker. With increasing understanding there is growing commitment. With growing commitment there is increasing understanding. This is a process of unfoldment rather than willed deciding.

Guilt

The general belief is that the capacity to feel guilty is very important and is a sign of mental health. It is also believed that psychopathic personalities and criminals are incapable of feeling guilty and, therefore, they are incurable.

It is important to differentiate between guilt on the one hand and regret or remorse on the other hand. There is no such thing as healthy guilt, or neurotic guilt, or insufficient guilt because all guilt is boasting. It is a self-confirmatory mode of ideation. It is also presumptuous, devious, and self-promoting. It is presumptuous because it is based on the presumption that man is capable of being knowingly evil. It is devious because it claims not to be ignorant; and it is boastful because it is self-referential, i.e., self-confirmatory.

It is possible to observe a universal eagerness to feel guilty. People are easily convinced that they are guilty. The Viennese psychoanalyst Steckel observed a frequent symptom among his patients which he called "the compulsion to confess." Confessions are nothing else but formalized boasting.

The more guilty a criminal feels, the less will he be receptive to rehabilitation. It is difficult to reform someone who feels guilty, for the rehabilitation process itself becomes an occasion for self-confirmatory boastfulness. If a man says, "I know that I am bad," there is no hope for him. Only if he is able to say, "I know that I don't know," is there hope for him. This brings to mind the words of Jesus: "Father, forgive them; for they know not what they do" (Luke 23:34).

The real issue is ignorance, but people in general would rather admit to guilt than to ignorance. To admit to ignorance requires humility.

The issue of guilt is a hoax which the "devil" plays on mankind; and there will never be any effective rehabilitation of criminals as long as they are allowed and even encouraged to feel guilty.

Psychopathic personalities commit crimes and the world expects them to feel guilty. But they refuse. Psychologists and criminologists have assumed that these criminals are unable to feel guilty. They think that there is some kind of defect in their personality make-up which makes it impossible for them to feel guilty. Of course, if we understand the workings of self-confirmatory ideation, we can see that to not feel guilty and to feel guilty is really the same. In either case the ego is being asserted and gratified.

A psychopathic personality has such contempt for social conventions that he refuses to abide by the expectations of society to feel guilty, thereby asserting his ego. The hypocrite says: "I feel guilty because I am bad." The psychopath says: "I am bad and I refuse to feel guilty." Essentially, both of them would loathe to admit to ignorance.

The question may now be rightfully asked, What are the requirements of a healthy response to a misdeed? The healthy response to a misdeed is comprised of the following three steps: (1) recognition, (2) regret, (3) reorientation. We recognize our mistake, regret our ignorance, and reorient ourselves by forsaking our errors. All these take place in the privacy of our consciousness.

The more clearly we understand that two and two is four, the less likely we are to make the mistake of thinking that two and two is five, or six, etc. The more clearly we have been given to know what the truth of life is, or what Reality is, the more clearly it will stand out to our eyes whatever does not conform to that standard. In Isaiah we read: "When the enemy shall come in like a flood, the Spirit of the Lord shall lift up a standard against him" (Isaiah 59:19). We must be edu-

cated in the Christly standard of values and the understanding
of Divine Reality. And the clearer this is established in consciousness, the more perceptive we shall be of whatever does
not meet this standard.

Moses gave the Israelites the Ten Commandments to have
a standard of right and wrong. Jesus gave us the Sermon on
the Mount. Jesus also gave us the Lord's Prayer (Matthew 6:9–
13) as a standard mode of contemplation of Divine Reality and
man's place in it. Unfortunately, the Lord's Prayer tends to
conjure up an anthropomorphic image of God and man's relationship to God, notably concerning the issue of forgiveness,
when man seeks forgiveness for his misdeeds.

The Lord's Prayer is a form of meditation about Divine Reality and how man can come into greater harmony with the
laws governing Reality. On the basis of what has been said
before about guilt, regret, and reorientation, we now propose
the following interpretation of the Lord's Prayer, based on
Metapsychiatric insights.

Meditation on the Lord's Prayer

Our Father which art in heaven, Hallowed be thy name.

> I cherish the knowledge of God as omniactive Love-
> Intelligence.

Thy kingdom come. Thy will be done in earth, as it is in heaven.

> Heavenly harmony is available here and now to the
> "shouldless."

Give us this day our daily bread.

> The good of God is realized daily as inspired wisdom,
> peace, assurance, gratitude, and love (PAGL).

And forgive us our debts, as we forgive our debtors.

> I abandon the error of interaction thinking.

And lead us not into temptation, but deliver us from evil;

> God consciousness is immune to seduction, provocation, and intimidation.

For thine is the kingdom, and the power, and the glory, for ever.

> God-centered living is the only alternative to self-confirmatory ideation.

Multitudes recite the Lord's Prayer every day without ever giving a thought as to what it could mean. The routine recitation of the Lord's Prayer could be considered a form of conceptual expression where the meaning is lost. It is words without meaning. In juxtaposition to this, there is a form of communication which consists of meaning without words, and that is music. Music is nonconceptual communication of meaning. What does music communicate? Sound? No. Sound forms the basis of music. Music communicates musical ideas which are nonconceptual and yet universally understandable. There is sensual music, there is emotional music, there is intellectual music, and there is spiritual music.

God can be conceptual to some people, but existential to others. To theologians God is conceptual. To religious people God is symbolic. To enlightened people God is existential awareness. Enlightened man seeks to know God in a direct awareness as a presence and a power affecting every phase of existence all the time.

Jesus expressed it in a most simple but infinitely inspiring way when he said: "I and my Father are one" (John 10:30) ... "I am in the Father, and the Father in me" (John 14:11). The right understanding of these statements can provide a healthy solution to practically every problem. When that happens, we have partaken in an existential, epistemological, spiritual realization of God as Reality, a power, and a presence which governs the whole universe. It is not just a theory any more. It is not just a ritual. It is not just an intellectual scholastic idea.

It is Reality. We are seeking the realization of Reality; that's what life is all about. Problems arise only to show us that we have not yet reached a sufficient degree of realization of this Reality.

Evil

Experiencing evil is inevitable, even though it is not necessary. The Bible says: "Thou art of purer eyes than to behold evil, and canst not look on iniquity" (Habakkuk 1:13). The transcendent Ego is completely devoid of evil and knows nothing about it. God knows nothing about evil. The Bible also says: "God is light, and in him is no darkness at all" (1 John 1:5).

Now if the transcendent Ego is our ego and is all good, intelligence, love, harmony, truth, and vitality, then what is evil? What is sin? What is the autonomous ego of individuals? It is ignorance. Notably, it is the ignorance of God. When we live without the conscious harmony of God, when we try to live as if God did not exist, then we are living in sin. If we define sin in this manner (*sine Deo*), then sin is synonymous with ignorance. *Ignorance is the ignoring of that which is available to be known.* When we are ignorant of God, we judge by appearances, and as a result of that, we arrive at erroneous conclusions about the nature of existence and reality.

Ignorance is not passive but existential, which means that it is built into the human condition. We distinguish two kinds of ignorance, as mentioned earlier: negative ignorance and positive ignorance. Negative ignorance is when we don't know and we know we don't know. Positive ignorance is in evidence when we don't know but we think we know. Negative ignorance is existential. Positive ignorance is acquired through education. Buckminster Fuller calls our schools "ignorance factories." Let us put it this way: We are born naturally ignorant. Then we go to school and acquire an unnatural form of ignorance, based on miseducation. It is clear that the negative form of ignorance is much easier to heal than the positive one.

Interestingly enough, Jesus knew that because he had a running battle with a large and powerful group of positively ignorant people, namely, the Pharisees. These were the most educated elite group of his time, but they were miseducated as to the nature of Divine Reality. They had a legalistic approach to God. At one point Jesus said: "Except ye be converted, and become as little children [ye shall in no wise become enlightened] ye shall not enter the kingdom of heaven" (Matthew 18:3). He knew that in order to become enlightened, we must be willing to admit to negative ignorance. The Zen Masters and Buddhist scholars also understand this because they say, "Knowing can only come from not knowing."

The source of all ignorance is the tendency of man to judge by appearances. We draw erroneous conclusions based on false premises. The fact that there is such a great variety of psychotherapeutic schools demonstrates that they all have different assumptions about what man is. Every founder of a psychotherapeutic school has his own assumptions — either conscious or unconscious, explicit or implicit — about what man is. And if we start with a certain premise, we will inevitably arrive at certain conclusions determined by that premise. Thus the result is a multiplicity of psychotherapeutic schools. We cannot blame people for being Jungian, Freudian, Adlerian, Rogerian, etc. It does not help to blame and it is not fair to blame. We must understand how these things have come about, and then there will be no problem in communication.

The truth cannot be imposed on anyone. In psychotherapy it is absolutely futile to preach the truth to a patient. We are not receptive to the truth until we have suffered enough from the consequences of our ignorance. The therapist cannot impart the truth to a patient until such time when the patient has reached a point of receptivity. The purpose of suffering is to bring us to a point of receptivity to the healing, liberating, enlightening truth.

In Metapsychiatry we speak of God as omniactive Love-Intelligence. This is a dynamic concept of a cosmic Power which has the qualities of intelligence and love. This concept is eminently workable and helpful when we want to liberate people from their epistemic isolation. What do we mean by epistemic isolation? The epistemic isolation is built of the universally accepted habit of asking wrong questions, harboring opinions, and clinging to preconceived notions and invalid assumptions about life and the nature of reality.

The problem of epistemic isolation was beautifully portrayed in a recent television play called "The Cube." In this play a man is imprisoned in a room, the walls of which open and close to any visitor at any point. Visitors come and go. They taunt and torment the prisoner with their ideas. They leave through the walls at will, but the prisoner has no way of escaping. For him the walls of the prison have no opening. They are impermeable. He is hopelessly trapped and no one helps him.

Of course, none of his visitors come to him in the spirit of Christlike compassion and Divine Love, and no one helps him to know the truth of God which makes man free.

Compassion

We receive most of our thoughts from significant adults in our formative years. To a large extent we are what others have thought of us. The thinker and the thought are one. Since the thoughts are not our thoughts, our sense of selfhood is alien.

We are what we think, but our thoughts are not our own. Therefore, we are not acquainted with our true selves. When a transsexual, for instance, says, "I feel that I am a woman in a man's body, and I want to undergo a sex operation," he is in fact saying, "I have accepted the thought that femininity is fulfillment for me. I feel I should be a woman." These thoughts act as a dynamic force, or a highly charged dream in search of a dreamer. The dream creates the dreamer. After the sex operation, the dreamer and the dream are one. Anatomy is made to conform to the dream.

The devil is called the whisperer. The whisperer whispers into consciousness various suggestions about what should be, what is important, what could be pleasurable, what should not be, etc. These suggestions originate in the "sea of mental garbage," or the noosphere, and are mediated by significant adults in childhood and by the media. Since these suggestions are active in consciousness, we have a strong impression that they are our own thoughts. We accept responsibility for them and identify ourselves with them.

These thoughts, then, have the quality and dynamism of long-lasting posthypnotic suggestions. A hypnotized subject, who has been given a posthypnotic suggestion, finds it impossible to resist even the silliest command exactly because he has the feeling that he is acting out his own thoughts. The amnesia as to the origin of the suggested idea makes him a slave of the thought. In fact, the suggested thought makes the thinker. Thus the thinker becomes a behavioral expression of the suggested thought.

Recently, a forty-year-old man reported that he has an overwhelming desire to be a little boy and to be pampered by his mother. He is in the habit of periodically going on binges and indulging himself with sweets, consuming large quantities of chocolate and cookies. Recently, when he visited his mother, he was shocked to hear her say, "You are my sweet little boy." At that moment, it occurred to him that this idea is not his own, that it was suggested to him through his mother's thinking many years ago. This idea affected him somewhat like a posthypnotic suggestion, where the subject is under the influence of the hypnotist's thoughts, but he has the illusion that those thoughts are his own. Thus, this grown man has become what his mother was thinking about him.

Ordinarily, there is no way that man can be liberated from this hypnotism. What usually happens is that there is an exchange of one hypnotic suggestion for another. For instance, the man who indulged in sweets went through a period in his life which in Adlerian terms could be called "masculine protest." In his early twenties he developed an interest in guns, and toyed with the idea of becoming a soldier. These fantasies came to a sudden end when he accidentally shot one of his neighbors, wounding him slightly.

The human condition is fraught with hypnotic suggestions and various forms of mental bondage. We are all more or less hypnotized by our parents, and go through life either protesting, or submitting, or trying to escape in various ways, usually going from one error to another. Several methods of psychoanalytic therapy have been devised which were meant to liberate man from the hypnotic effects of his childhood experiences and influences. But what happens in such psychoanalytic therapies is that the hypnotism of the parents is replaced by the hypnotism of the psychiatrist and the particular theories he advocates. This is called "doctrinal compliance" (Ehrenwald).

Individually significant thoughts underlie modes of being-in-the-world. The only salvation, liberation, deliverance, or healing is the discovery of God as omniactive Mind, the source of all valid thoughts. And then the hypnotism disappears, and inspired wisdom, Love-Intelligence, and assurance appear because then we come to know ourselves as sons of God, and know that only what God thinks of us constitutes our true being. In proportion to our receptivity to this truth we are liberated from hypnotism.

When we say that only God's thoughts constitute our being, we don't say that thoughts which we have gleaned from certain books or lectures can liberate us. We must be humble enough to let God heal us. The fifth principle of Metapsychiatry says, "God helps those who let him." If we are trying to heal ourselves with the help of certain intellectual concepts, we are not letting God help us. It is somewhat like a child who insists on dressing himself when he cannot do it, but doesn't let his mother help him. The result is a stalemate.

We have to understand the difference between a "do it yourself" method and letting God heal us. The Bible says: "As many as received him, to them gave he power to become the sons of God" (John 1:12). The key word here is "receive." What does it take to receive God's thoughts? It takes humility, "shouldlessness," interest, but, above all, being still. Being still means not trying to figure things out and waiting for God's thoughts to reach consciousness. The universal Mind, which is Reality, is the source of a continuous flow of relevant, pertinent, intelligent, needed ideas, obtaining in consciousness, supplying every need, healing all hypnotism, and liberating from mental enslavement.

The qualities of forthrightness and humility are essential for receptivity to what we call God's thoughts, or what God is thinking toward man. "I know the thoughts that I think toward you, saith the Lord, thoughts of peace, and not of evil, to give you an expected end" (Jeremiah 29:11). The purpose of man is to come to know God and manifest Him in the world.

Returning to the gentleman we mentioned earlier, the way he lives now indicates that he is manifesting the thoughts of his mother, and his mother believes that she has created him for herself. She enjoyed him when he was a baby and she would like to preserve that happiness forever. And as long as he accepts this belief and shares this belief with his mother, he is the image and likeness of his would-be creator. But that is a very troublesome condition, especially when one is already forty years old. Now he needs to be liberated from this hypnotic spell and really come to understand that God is his creator and not his mother. She has not created him for herself. She was just an instrument in God's creative scheme of things. When he understands that, he will have a desire to manifest his full manliness, forthrightness, and love, and all the qualities of God as it becomes clear that he is God's idea and not his mother's idea. And that is salvation.

We all have to reach that point when we find it perfectly natural to live as God's manifest ideas. As long as we believe that we are creations of our parents, we cannot help but bear witness to their fantasies about us.

The only remedy for a victim of hypnotism is to awaken to a realization that the thought which is active in his consciousness is not his thought, and the expression of that thought is not what he truly is. "Awake thou that sleepest, and arise from the dead, and Christ shall give thee light" (Ephesians 5:14). This sentence actually affirms the fact that human experience is a dream and unenlightened man a dreamer, oblivious of Reality.

The Christ illumines the truth of our being as sons of God, or expressions of the mind, the will, the wisdom, the love, the spiritual good of God. God is the only true source of valid ideas. Only divine spiritual ideas constitute our true selfhood. "The Son can do [*think*] nothing of himself, but what he seeth the Father do [*think*]: for what things soever he doeth [*thinketh*], these also doeth [*thinketh*] the Son likewise" (John 5:19).

When we understand that the dream creates the dreamer, for instance, that Marxist ideas create communists and not the other way around, we can suddenly understand compassion. Compassion is not synonymous with sympathy, or with empathy, or with pity or sentimentality. Compassion is a transcendental form of love which says: "Father forgive them; for they know not what they do" (Luke 23:34).

Compassion sees that the human condition is a state of hypnotic counterfeit existence, and the evils of this world are vicious dreams appearing in the form of evil dreamers, acting singly or collectively. The history of the Nazi movement in Germany was one vicious dream engulfing an entire nation and expressing itself as the Second World War. It was a horrendous tidal wave of the "sea of mental garbage" sweeping over the world.

Compassion cannot be willed. It is existential. Man can decide to be sympathetic. He can make himself concerned and sad. He can will himself to feel pity. But true compassion is possible only when consciousness has awakened to the faculty of *spiritual discernment* of the difference between Reality and dream.

It is helpful to understand that, contrary to general belief, sympathy, pity, and empathy are actually pathogenic, which means they make a bad situation worse. When we sympathize we say, "I feel for you," which means, "I acknowledge and agree with you that you are in a bad way." When we pity someone we say, "I feel sorry for you," which means, "You have every reason to feel bad, miserable, and hopeless." If we empathize with someone we say, "I feel exactly the way you feel," which means, "Your misery is real because I share it with you." These three modalities of interaction remind us of the three "miserable comforters" who came to visit Job in his hour of trial. The Christ-truth is the only valid and effective comforter.

This process of awakening starts with the individual when he begins to forgive himself by realizing that his sins were never really part of his true being and that only good thoughts constitute his true selfhood. When he becomes able to have compassion for himself, his capacity to have compassion for others emerges spontaneously. Thus he can fulfill the commandment: "Thou shalt love thy neighbor as thyself" (Matthew 22:39).

Compassion is an essential ingredient of mental health, for without it one is constantly involved in judging, criticizing, condemning, and getting upset over the evils of the world. This, in turn, tends to disturb the homeostatic balance of the individual.

The compassionate man, however, is capable of *transcendent regard*, which is an ability to view life and people from a higher standpoint. I think it was Emerson who defined prayer as an endeavor to see life from a higher viewpoint. The higher viewpoint broadens our perspective beyond the interpersonal context of reasoning to the transpersonal.

Transpersonal psychology is possible only in the context of God, or the Christ-consciousness. It is quite clear that Jesus saw life and reality from a divine perspective and in the context of Divine Reality. The Bible says: "Let this mind be in you, which was also in Christ Jesus" (Philippians 2:5). We understand this to mean that the enlightened man is not a schemer, a manipulator, or a politician. He is not engaged in calculative thinking, but relies entirely on inspired wisdom and love.

Is There Nothingness?

There are many things in life of which we are not aware. And what we are not aware of is unconscious. This does not mean that there is an unconscious as such, but there is unconsciousness. There are thoughts which we prefer not to be aware of, and we can either repress these — just as Freud said — or we can suppress them, or avoid them, or try to escape from becoming aware of them. For instance, one of the most universal issues in life which we are all trying to escape from and avoid knowing about is the fear of nonbeing, or the dread of nothingness.

The manifestations of this universal fear can be seen in self-confirmatory ideation, activities, and pursuits. Translated into social experience, the fear of nonbeing manifests itself as the fear of being ignored, a fear of being unimportant, a fear of being a nobody or nothing, or of being unloved or unnoticed. This fear is so tremendous that very often we settle for almost anything in exchange. For instance, if we cannot be loved, we may settle for being hated. If we cannot be praised, we may invite criticism. If we cannot be beautiful, we may want to be ugly. If we cannot be considered smart, we may put on pseudo-stupidity just to avoid being ignored.

The fear of nothingness diverts our attention from what is important. The fear of nonbeing is called existential anxiety or, as the philosophers call it, "the dread of nothingness." St. Paul refers to it this way: "If a man think himself to be something, when he is nothing, he deceiveth himself" (Galatians 6:3).

Throughout life we are driven to make sure that we are something and not nothing. This unconscious urge is the basis for all self-confirmatory ideation. Psychopathology, and even pathology in general, has this common dynamism. Unenlightened man, whether educated or uneducated, is constantly preoccupied with the issues: "Do I exist? Am I real? Am I safe?" The basic desire to reassure ourselves of our own individual reality drives us in many directions, such as: to be successful, to be admired, to be loved, to be famous, to be hated, to be operated upon by surgeons, to be persecuted, to be pampered, etc. We seek self-confirmatory experiences in an infinite variety of ways.

We could say that ontologically we have a one-track mind, namely, to confirm the reality of our selfhood. It is paradoxical. Unenlightened man has an overriding desire to be acknowledged as existing. This kind of acknowledgment is reassuring and comforting. Unfortunately, the comfort is short-lived; no sooner do we get reassured that we are really somebody than the fear begins to mount again and we need new reassurances. The more we get, the more we want.

The question is, Is there an alternative? The philosophers Heidegger and Sartre, and most other existential philosophers who are not oriented toward God, offer us an interesting solution. They say: What is needed is to take a resolute stand, a "courageous resolve" to face up to the dread of nothingness and cope with it. But what happens if we do that? If we decide to conquer our fears, what does it mean? It means that we have made an act of self-confirmatory assertion: "I can cope with my fear of nonbeing; therefore I am being." These great philosophers are really mistaken, for we cannot heal self-confirmatory ideation with self-confirmatory ideation. We cannot fight fire with fire. The more we assert ourselves against our fears, the more fearful we become. This, then, is not a solution. This is no different from what psychoanalysis aims at, namely, ego control, which actually means self-confirmatory self-assertion against self-confirmatory ideation. It is like Auroborus, the mythical snake, swallowing its own tail.

A question then is, Is there no way out of this human dilemma? Yes, there is. Man has to come to understand that he is
not a self-existent personality, cast adrift in the world as Heidegger put it with his notion of *Geworfenheit* (being thrown).
This is not really so. The remedy to the problem of the self-
confirmatory mode of being-in-the-world is to understand its
meaning, which we have just explained as the dread of nothingness, and come to realize that we are not self-existent life
forms apart from the creator. We are manifestations of a creative power, underlying all of life in the universe, all the laws
of nature, the harmony, the beauty and infinite intelligence
discernible all around us. This is the power which expresses
itself through us. Therefore, we are not adrift in the universe
all on our own, but we are sustained, supported, governed,
cared for, and loved by this infinite power which we call
Love-Intelligence.

Now the question is, How can we come to realize that this
is really so? Our fears are self-evident. We also know that
self-assertion and various other actions can be consensually
validated. But when we talk about Love-Intelligence and Cosmic Power, this is not as easily validated. Various religions
have claimed the existence of God for thousands of years, but
this was just based on belief. To the vast majority of people on
earth God still remains a putative issue. Religions tell us: "If
you believe in God, a transcendent power, this will make you
feel better, and it will comfort you." Believing is better than
nothing, but believing is a long way from knowing.

In the history of Christianity there was a movement which
was concerned with coming to know the Reality of God. This
was the Gnostic movement. But this was considered a heresy
and its adherents were severely persecuted. Even today, if
someone wants to say something bad about a Christian or a
religious individual who wants to understand God, he can label him a gnostic to discredit him. It seems more respectable
to be an agnostic than a gnostic. The word gnostic is derived
from the Latin *cognoscere*, which means to know, to recognize,
to understand. And it is certainly not a sin to desire to know.

Of course, many people question the possibility of knowing God, and this seems to be a legitimate point.

In the history of religions there were unique individuals who claimed to have known Divine Reality, and this knowledge came to them through a special grace of God. These people were called mystics. Of course, it was difficult to ascertain whether they really knew or just claimed to know. And today it is still easy to claim to know and thus deceive people. So the issue of knowledge remains an important problem.

The question is, How can a finite mind know infinite Mind? Fortunately it is getting to be less and less a heresy to admit to a desire to know, and today there is less of a chance to be burned at the stake. Today there are new ways of coming to know more and more of Divine Reality. It helps to begin to call God new names. For instance, in Metapsychiatry we call God omniactive Love-Intelligence, Cosmic Consciousness, infinite omnipresent Mind, the source of inspired Wisdom, Love, creative Intelligence, and healing Power.

It is interesting to consider that Jesus chose to teach people about God through the process of healing. He was not a charlatan, nor was he a physician, really. He was a carpenter. But he wanted to help people to understand God, so he healed them of their illnesses. The question could be asked, In what way did the healing of diseases help people to understand God? Today, when a doctor prescribes a treatment and accomplishes a cure, this in no way facilitates the understanding of God. Jesus healed the sick, fed the hungry, and taught the ignorant; he supplied them with whatever they needed most. He did this with his great understanding of the human condition. He knew exactly what people were suffering from. He said: "I am come a light into the world, that whosoever believeth on me should not abide in darkness" (John 12:46) which means that he understood that all human problems arise from lack of understanding. Darkness stands for ignorance and fear. When we are in darkness, we don't know and we are fearful.

These were the two basic and essential problems of mankind two thousand years ago, and they are the same today. What we are suffering from is the darkness of ignorance and fear. All human approaches, all psychotherapeutic schools, as well as any other solutions that have ever been devised, are ineffective endeavors at coping with ignorance and with fear. They are ineffective because they are rooted in the same mistake, which is self-confirmatory ideation. When we are afraid, we are driven to say, "I am," and we can say it in a million ways. The more we say it, the sicker we get because it is not true.

The Bible says: Be still. Stop saying, "I am," and know that God is the only I am. ("Be still, and know that I am God," Psalm 46:10.) Jesus knew that there is no such thing as a personal ego, that God is the Ego of everyone. He was able to heal people and provide for their needs because he knew what they needed to know. If we come to catch a glimpse of this truth that God is our Ego, that we do not exist apart from God, in that moment all fear disappears, and when fear disappears, all the bad "fruits" of fear also disappear.

The universal remedy for problems is the abolishing of existential anxiety. When existential anxiety is relieved, self-confirmatory ideation becomes unnecessary and healing can take place. Healing is derived from the word "wholeness." Man cannot be whole until he is consciously in at-one-ment with his real Ego, which is God. When Jesus wanted to explain his own wholeness to the world, he said: "I and my Father are one" (John 10:30). I don't exist alone by myself.

There is no such thing as wholeness apart from God. In order to be whole, we must be united with God in consciousness. This is called conscious union with God, i.e., conscious awareness of the fact that our life, our vitality, our vigor, our intelligence, and our love are emanations of the Divine Mind. When we clearly understand this inseparability, this oneness of God and His creation, then we are whole; then existential anxiety disappears and we discover the "peace of God, which passeth all understanding" (Philippians 4:7), and there is no more self-confirmatory ideation. And that's when all pathology disappears because pathology is nothing else but a constant unconscious mental process of seeking to confirm our existence apart from God.

Here again we may ask the question, Is it really possible to know this? The Metapsychiatric method of coming to know is based on "two intelligent questions." Whenever we are confronted with a problem, we approach it with the following two questions: The first is: "What is the meaning of what seems to be?" And the second question is: "What is what really is?"

To illustrate, suppose we have a splitting headache. We do not ask, What is wrong with me? Why do I have this headache? Who or what is to blame for it? What should I do? Instead, we ask, What is the meaning of this seeming headache? If we ask this question and remain still for a while, pretty soon we may become aware of certain thoughts which reveal to us some resentfulness, vindictiveness, frustration, etc. This explains the meaning of the headache as a certain emotionally charged thought of a self-confirmatory nature. If we seek the meaning of phenomena, they will reveal themselves to us as self-confirmatory ideas. Thus we become aware of the fact that a symptom is a phenomenon, i.e., thought transmuted into symptom.

These self-confirmatory thoughts can be chronic and well hidden even for years, and often there is resistance against facing up to them. But if we are willing to face up to these mental processes and perchance be embarrassed by them, that constitutes effective repentance. Such repentance can proceed into forgiveness and reformation of character.

After this comes the second question which brings Divine Reality to our attention in a meaningful light. As a result of this process remarkable healings can take place, notwithstanding diagnostic labels. The second question reveals to us the allness of God and the wholeness of man, inseparable from the love of God.

A glimpse of the validity of this truth results in a sense of peace, assurance, gratitude, and love. And that is a sign of healing. When this occurs, we are aware of the fact that our thought processes have come into alignment with Divine

Reality, and the disappearance of our problems, the healing of them, gives us a sense of clear knowledge that God really is. This we call existential validation. In this manner we move from believing to knowing. We may even catch a glimpse of the fact that in Reality there is neither something nor nothing. God, Mind is all in all.

The "Is"

Contrary to prevailing opinions, discipline is not synonymous with self-control. Discipline is related to discipleship. A devoted disciple of a Master or a teacher finds it easy to live a disciplined life. A disciple enjoys living up to the standards of his teacher. To live a disciplined life on that basis is not arduous.

Discipline is not self-inflicted tyranny; it is enthusiasm and love for a value system. If there is no discipleship, then there is self-indulgence. The trouble with self-indulgence is that we lose contact with the source of what is. Either we are devoted to ourselves — our feelings, sensations, and possessions — or we are devoted to some higher values. "For where your treasure is, there will your heart [devotion] be also" (Matthew 6:21; Luke 12:34).

It is, however, important to be devoted to existentially valid teaching. Sometimes we may become devoted to something that is not valid, or to something that is personal. We call that a tragic blunder.

Sometimes there is an expectation of reward for one's devotion to spiritual values. However, God is not a reward-system. God does not reward us for being good, nor does He punish us for being bad. Children universally tend to think in terms of reward and punishment. There is an educational method in vogue nowadays called "operant conditioning." It is an attempt at behavior modification based on the principle of rewarding the good and ignoring the bad. This system seems to work in schools and in prisons and generally with immature subjects. However, it is clear that the price of such conditioning of necessity must be a fixation of minds on a very immature level. Behavior is modified at the price of mental stagnation.

Many traditional religious systems have fallen into similar patterns where God is presumed to be a rewarder of good behavior and a punisher of sin. This is a primitive concept of God and man, and it leads to certain difficulties. As long as God is presumed to be a capricious authority figure, there will always be a tendency to get around him. Enlightened man has a different view of God and His system. Instead of seeing God as a reward and punishment system, enlightened man sees God as an "Is system." What do we mean by an "Is system"? An "Is system" means that God is absolute Reality; and being in conscious union with it brings us a realization of perfect life. The right understanding of what really is abolishes all problems which seem to be.

If we consider all the strictures of traditional religions, we see that they are being constantly circumvented and compromised. There is a saying, "Laws are made to be broken." But if we understand God as an "Is system," it will make no sense at all to violate it. For instance, if we know that gravitation is, it is clear that no one in his right mind would want to challenge it by jumping out of the window. But suppose the law of gravitation would depend on a person. Then one would be tempted to try to circumvent it.

In Metapsychiatry we speak of theistic existentialism, which means a God-centered view of Reality.

The early Hebrew idea of God was that of a warlord, a tribal chief, or a judge, or a legal authority, who set down very complex laws and rules of behavior. The Bible represents a record of the continuing evolution of the concept of God from a punitive agency to a benefactor of mankind, until gradually God was seen as a benevolent father, and beyond that, as pure Love. God ceased to be a person and became a Reality. Today we are sufficiently advanced to be able to conceive of God as being.

Not a being, but Being itself, which is what is, a Life Principle. If we understand God as a Life Principle, then there is no one to reward us or punish us. There is only being in harmony with the Principle and thus prospering, or being out of step with it and suffering the consequences.

We like to speak of God not only as Life Principle but also as Love-Intelligence. Love and intelligence cannot be separated. There is no such thing as unintelligent love. Unintelligent love is not love. It is just ignorance. Love is intelligent, creative, life-enhancing, all-knowing, all-powerful, and omniactive. All these adjectives help us to gain a more precise understanding of God which is not a person but a power, a Reality, an "Is."

And in order to be in harmony with something, we must understand it. In order for man to be able to fly, he had to come to understand the principles of aerodynamics. In order to live in an intelligent, wholesome, and good way, we must understand God in an existentially valid fashion.

Unfortunately, the human race is just beginning to go beyond childish ways of thinking about God. This leads to many problems. Of late, we can see how some churches resist the struggle of women trying to gain equality with men.

When we understand God as an "Is system," we are not concerned with being religious but with being in harmony with what is, i.e., being enlightened. Since God is infinite consciousness, enlightenment means conscious union with Cosmic Consciousness, or at-one-ment with Love-Intelligence.

While traditional religions emphasize behavior, conduct, ritual, ceremonies, tithing, etc., the enlightened way is to focus on consciousness, which is in keeping with the teaching of Jesus, who laid great stress on the quality of thoughts and their manifestations.

An enlightened individual is one who is able to live in constant conscious awareness of omniactive Mind. This makes it possible to completely lose interest in fantasizing, daydreaming, scheming, influencing, manipulating, and being afraid. If we are full-time in conscious awareness of the good of God, then there is nothing else.

Jesus, speaking about observant religious people of his time, said: "Woe unto you, scribes and Pharisees, hypocrites! for ye are like unto whited sepulchres, which indeed appear beautiful outward, but are within full of...uncleanness" (Matthew 23:27), thus referring to the importance of maintaining an inner purity of thought.

How Mature Is God?

Forms of Maturity

1. *Organismic,* when the human body is fully developed.

2. *Psychosexual,* when the procreative faculties are developed with a capacity for human affection.

3. *Psychosocial,* when an individual becomes a useful member of society.

4. *Ethical,* when an individual develops a sense of fair play.

5. *Moral,* when an individual develops an appreciation of the Ten Commandments.

6. *Religious,* when the formal worshiping of God becomes sincerely appreciated.

7. *Existential,* when one becomes committed to being here for God. Such an individual is a beneficial presence in the world.

8. *Spiritual,* which is the realization of the Living Soul.

The process of spiritual maturity entails outgrowing the galloping evils of the "four horsemen." The "four horsemen" are: Envy, Jealousy, Rivalry, and Malice.

Envy is a desire to have what someone else has. Jealousy is a desire to be what someone else is. Rivalry is a desire to be better than someone else. Malice is ill will.

The first crime ever committed is described in the Bible in the story of Cain and Abel. This is a story of jealousy and rivalry resulting ultimately in murder. Here we have an immature god making comparisons between two brothers and favoring one over the other. This kind of parenting often leads to tragedy. The irony of this story is that the very god which instigated the rivalry between the siblings winds up blaming and punishing the jealous brother who is both a malefactor and a victim of his own immaturity. Immature people have immature gods. There is a saying that nations have the kind of governments they deserve.

We may very well ask, How can God be immature? Since time immemorial man has been suffering from his immature and invalid concepts of God. The Bible is a record of man's evolving, maturing ideas of God, from a vengeful, intimidating warlord, to a legal authority, a judge, an oriental ruler, a punitive agency, a merit system operating on the basis of reward and punishment, a moral disciplinarian, a loving father of Jesus Christ, the divine love of the apostle John, the disciple of Jesus, and finally to a cosmic Principle of Love-Intelligence in Metapsychiatry.

Man, who is an image and likeness of God, has a tendency to turn the tables on God and make Him over in his own image. Thus immature man conceives of immature gods.

One of the most prevalent ideas about God is that God is here for man. Man wants to find a way to "get a handle" on God through prayer, incantations, and ceremonies. Man wants to influence God and get God to serve him. This kind of effort of telling God what He should do is practiced either in solitude or collectively in congregations.

Metapsychiatry states that God is not here for man but man is here for God. Everything in the universe has the purpose of manifesting the glory of the Creator. We say that everything and everyone is here for God, whether they know it or not. To some people this is a shocking and revolutionary idea, not unlike the discovery that the sun does not revolve around the earth, but that the earth revolves around the sun.

Thus we come to see that spiritual maturity is not attainable unless we are given a mature and existentially valid concept of God. What do we mean by an existentially valid concept of God? An existentially valid concept of God makes it possible for man to overcome the "four horsemen" and to grow into an authentic, beneficial presence in the world.

The process of maturation can be studied with the help of the cross as a symbol. The cross consists of a vertical bar and a horizontal bar. Without the vertical bar there is only the horizontal bar. The horizontal bar symbolizes the conditions under which agnostic, i.e., Godless, man lives. He only knows human relationships where the basic issues are envy, jealousy, rivalry, and malice. These motives can be conscious or unconscious, but they are always present and play a dynamic role in all aspects of life, even in so-called "love" relationships. In the horizontal dimension of life love is mostly a cover-up for envy, jealousy, rivalry, and malice. Generosity is mostly bribery and manipulation. Admiration and praise are also disguised forms of envy and jealousy. Teaching is often a desire for mental domination, preventing learning. Information is misinformation. Giving is getting. Everything has an ulterior motive. Self-confirmatory ideation is ubiquitous. The apostle Paul put it very succinctly, "The good that I would I do not; but the evil which I would not, that I do" (Romans 7:19).

The biblical story of Samson and Delilah is rather instructive. Samson is described as a beautiful and intelligent man of great power and attractiveness. His qualities aroused a great deal of admiration, envy, jealousy, rivalry, and, finally, malice. Delilah, who was very much taken by him, discovered that all his power and attractiveness were located in his hair. It is safe to assume that Delilah envied the power of Samson's seeming personal mind, and this made it easy for her to betray him into the hands of his enemies, the Philistines. Therefore, she proceeded to seduce him and rob him of his power. Envy always aims at destroying whatever someone else has.

We can say that it is not uncommon to find a Delilah complex in women and even in men, where envy is consciously or unconsciously covered up as admiration or even sexual attraction. Such unconscious duplicity often results in tragic consequences to all who participate in it. Delilah's envy not only wanted to deprive Samson of his beauty, power, and mind, but she wanted to do it in such a way that Samson would not be aware, could not see what was happening to him; so he was attacked in his sleep and he was also rendered blind. When he became aware of what had been done to him, his rage was so overwhelming that he brought disaster on himself and everyone else around him.

When the horizontal bar is combined with the vertical bar we have the cross. The cross is an instrument of torture. It symbolizes the agony of religious man who tries to live in two dimensions at the same time. He tries to have a vertical relationship with God and, at the same time, continue his psychological relationship with his fellow man. His human inclinations toward envy, jealousy, rivalry, and malice are in constant conflict with the moral demands of his religion. He makes an effort to be a man for others (i.e., a beneficent person), but inevitably winds up being here for himself. Hypocrisy is inevitable.

When the horizontal bar is removed we have a vertical bar only. This vertical bar is a symbol of man's orientation toward God. In this phase of development man is committed to being here for God. This is not a religious commitment but an existential one. Here the individual progresses beyond religiosity into an actualization of being a beneficial presence in the world by manifesting Divine Love-Intelligence as a primary issue of life. "Commit thy works unto the Lord, and thy thoughts shall be established" (Proverbs 16:3).

In this phase of development man becomes increasingly healthy and blessed, and tends to prosper harmoniously in all his affairs. He lives effortlessly, efficiently, and effectively.

In the final phase of spiritual maturation even the vertical bar disappears and there is a realization of at-one-ment with God. There is a discovery of the Living Soul which was never born and never dies, which is "hid with Christ in God," or as the Zen Master speaks of it, "a realization of the Unborn." The Living Soul is a nondimensional entity of awareness within infinite Mind, or divine consciousness. In Hebrews 7:3, we read: "Without father, without mother, without descent, having neither beginning of days nor end of life; but made like unto the Son of God." When the Living Soul is realized, the sense of personhood disappears and with it all the human mockeries.

The Living Soul

In Metapsychiatry "Soul" is a word used to describe a non-dimensional entity which is alive, which was never born, and which never dies. It is synonymous with the Christ. It is a quality of consciousness attained through the process of studying and meditating on ultimate issues. When we realize that we are *living Souls*, we have beheld ourselves in the context of God. The Buddhists speak about the Buddha nature. Both these concepts point to the Christ consciousness.

The purported aim of Zen training is to realize one's own Buddha nature. The aim of Metapsychiatric study is to realize oneself as a living Soul which was never born and never dies, which is "hid with Christ in God," and which is the source of everything real and good and beautiful. All the spiritual qualities and ideas flow from God into this individual living Soul which we all are. When we say that everything and everyone is here for God, we mean that we are all living Souls at different levels of realization. When the Buddhists speak of the "unborn" it is the same thing as the living Soul, the ultimate nondimensional identity of everyone.

This reminds us of the Zen Master who asks: "Show me your face which you had before your parents were born." This koan liberates us from the fantasies of our parents. We have often spoken about the fact that we are unconsciously living out the fantasies of our parents. Now the koan says we have to realize our true identities, which are completely antecedent to any parental fantasies about us. In order to be really aware of one's true identity, one has to be free from parental and educational influences. In working with this koan one can reach a point of total freedom from other people's thoughts. Therefore, we seek liberation in becoming aware of ourselves as God has created us. This process of liberation is the freedom to be what God wants us to be. Our spiritual selfhood is hidden from ourselves and from the world, because few suspect it. Few can really understand it. It is a mysterious sense of identity beyond the comprehension of unenlightened man. It cannot be apprehended by the senses, but we can come to know it through the spiritual faculty of beholding. The beholder beholds his own true identity, which is devoid of all human influences. This is complete authenticity of being.

It is not advisable to attempt to visualize a living Soul. If we are eager to form images in our consciousness, that means that we are descending into the dimensional world, and we don't really understand ourselves as living Souls. We just imagine things. Whatever we can imagine will be purely imaginary. We will not be aware of Reality but only of fantasies. It is to escape from fantasies that we have to realize nondimensional Reality. The living Soul is pure wisdom and love and individualized spiritual life. It cannot be visualized and we cannot draw a picture of it. If we try, we lose it. We cannot even think about it. We have to be aware of ourselves as nondimensional units of awareness. God is infinite Mind. Infinity has no dimensions. We cannot measure infinity. It is nondimensional and everything in the context of infinite Mind is also nondimensional. The human mind cannot conceive of anything nondimensional. The human mind is an illusion, anyway. God is the Mind which makes it possible to be aware of Reality. Whatever can be imagined cannot be real. It is easy to kid ourselves that we are in touch with Reality when trying to visualize it.

When we speak of material man, we speak of the phenomenal world. In this world everything is an illusion, even the seeing of man as a dimensional form. When we ask, What sees man? we can only say, "The so-called 'carnal' mind sees dimensional reality." Dimensional reality can be thought of as a dream or a shadow. In order to be liberated from the problems of the phenomenal world, we have to reach a realization of nondimensional Reality which is unimaginable but discernible spiritually.

In the Bible it is described that God said: "Let there be a firmament — and let it divide the waters.... And God made the firmament and divided the waters which were under the firmament from the waters which were above the firmament" (Genesis 1:6, 7). Metapsychiatry interprets this as saying: The waters below the firmament are the "sea of mental garbage" in which unenlightened man lives and struggles, appears to be born, gets sick, and dies. This is what seems to be going on below the firmament. The firmament itself we understand to be the faculty of awareness, which we call spiritual discernment. This faculty makes it possible to be aware of the difference between the phenomenal world and noumenal Reality. Above the firmament is the infinite "ocean of Love-Intelligence." The firmament is the dividing line which is not structural, but a faculty of awareness. Until this faculty is awakened in us, we don't know Spiritual Reality. All we know is the "sea of mental garbage." When we start studying Metapsychiatry we discover that there are other dimensions to life, and then we gradually awaken to the faculty of awareness, i.e., spiritual discernment. The word "discernment" refers to a capacity to separate Reality from unreality. It is like separating the tares from the wheat. We are all familiar with the parable of the tares and the wheat (Matthew 13:24–30). When a farmer's employees discovered tares in the field of wheat, they came to him and asked, "What shall we do? The whole field is infested with this poisonous weed and everything is lost." But the farmer said, "Wait until harvest time. When the wheat ripens, then you will be able to discern the difference between the tares and the wheat and you will separate the two." When we reach the harvest time of our spiritual development, then the faculty of discernment emerges in consciousness and we have the ability to separate Reality from unreality. The spiritual and the material can now be clearly seen, and that constitutes the emergence of the firmament. From here on, we work and pray and meditate in the direction of rising ever higher to the point of beholding.

The faculty of beholding is the capacity to see Spiritual Reality. At this point we discover that we are living Souls, incorporeal nondimensional spiritual identities, living in the context of infinite Mind. We are not dealing any more with images but with realizations of our individual places in that Reality. Interestingly enough, at that point our lives begin to improve in every direction. We harvest the blessings of expanded awareness of spiritual consciousness. Our understanding of ourselves as living Souls becomes evident in healings, both of our bodies and of our so-called "temperament," as well as in our relationships with the world. Experiences become more harmonious. We find ourselves responding to daily challenges in more intelligent and effective ways. There is less strain in living. There is increasing effectiveness and new blessings.

The material world is seen as the shadow of Reality, a shadow of true substance. In proportion to our awareness of the perfection of life in the nondimensional realm, the shadow images cease to torment us; they disappear because there is nothing to feed them. A living Soul is unhampered by the inanities, the fantasies, the wants and not wants of the world. Therefore, Love-Intelligence can freely express itself in life. As a result, things become less complicated. There is less stress. Whatever is needed is responded to effortlessly, efficiently, and effectively.

Before the harvest time there is often a period of war between the spirit and the flesh. It is a conflict of interests. If there is conflict within us, that means that we have not yet reached a wholehearted interest in the spiritual life. We are just straddling the firmament, so to speak. This is where the flesh wars against the spirit. The Soul does not enter into issues below the firmament. The firmament, being the dividing line between the "sea of mental garbage" and the "ocean of Love-Intelligence," is aware of both so-called "worlds." The firmament is awareness. The firmament knows whether we live under the firmament or whether we sincerely seek to rise above it. Most of the struggle consists in turning away from ego-gratification. Ego-gratification is what drives the unenlightened world. Everything that is accomplished by unenlightened man is accomplished in quest of ego-gratification. Enlightened man is an instrument of omni-active Love-Intelligence, the creative principle of the universe.

The Prayer of "At-One-Ment"

Man is unavoidably prayerful at all times. Without realizing it, we live in a condition which requires us to pray in order to have a sense of direction in life. Without prayer we judge by appearances and tend to become disoriented. Our senses are not adequate to provide us with reliable information about Reality. We tend to wind up with misdirected modes of being-in-the-world. Whatever we cherish, whatever we hate, and whatever we fear are our gods, and we pray to them all the time.

Prayer can also be thought of as a mental hygiene principle. Sanity depends on being in touch with Reality. Thus, prayer is an existential necessity. We are not talking here about religious prayer, which is mostly petitionary. We define prayer as a constant conscious endeavor to be aware of our place in Reality.

The world is constantly intruding on our consciousness, creating disturbances, fears, confusion, and emotional upheavals. We misinterpret what we see. This results in discords and disasters. To live in harmony, we must learn to pray effectively. Effective prayer is based on *seeing* Reality rather than getting something from it.

In Buddhist literature we came across a prayer which could be thought of as "symbolic prayer." It speaks of a calm lake on a windless night which reflects the moon without distortion, so that it glows from the lake. This is a symbolic portrayal of man as a "place," or a consciousness which perfectly reflects the spiritual qualities of God. When human consciousness is filled with Love-Intelligence, God glows in it. Such an individual becomes a beneficial presence in the world. He finds his bearings in what we call PAGL (peace, assurance, gratitude, and love).

Metapsychiatry helps us to be keenly and painfully aware of the universal human tendencies toward self-confirmatory ideation and interaction thinking. Instead of being aware of our oneness with God and our contingency on Love-Intelligence to guide us and inspire us, we are constantly seeking to confirm our separateness from God. Every self-confirmatory thought is an assertion of our separation from God and leads to many kinds of problems. Misperceiving ourselves leads to misperceiving others, and this is essentially the nature of our ignorance.

The question now arises, How can we be aware of our complete oneness with God at all times? To understand this issue it is helpful to reexamine the biblical scene in which Moses asked God what His name was. According to the biblical text, God answered: "I AM THAT I AM." It seems that this is what Moses heard. This statement has led to many theological speculations and interpretations through the years. Judging by the consequences of these speculations, we must conclude that either the interpretations of various teachings have proved unsatisfactory, or that Moses may have misheard the message. As the record has it, he continued to relate himself to God as to a separate entity throughout the forty years of the Exodus. Shortly after this encounter with God, he was told to go to speak to Pharaoh on behalf of the children of Israel. Moses balked at the mission and said: "I cannot do this because I am slow of speech." Then God said: "I will be with thy mouth" (Exodus 4:12). Moses reluctantly obeyed, but he still did not understand his at-one-ment with God. The Bible also states that Moses was not allowed to enter the Promised Land. This may very well mean that he failed to become enlightened. He failed to realize his at-one-ment with God.

On reflecting on the problem of realizing our at-one-ment

with God, we begin to suspect that the original message may have been: "I *am the only I am*," rather than, "I am that I am." And indeed, this discovery opens up the door to effective realization of at-one-ment with God because it closes the door on all self-confirmatory ideation. It establishes in consciousness the awareness of man's inseparability from his Creator. Jesus, of course, understood this when he explained: "I and my Father are one" (John 10:30). "I am in the Father and the Father in me" (John 14:11).

The prayer of at-one-ment is a healing prayer because it abolishes the complications of unenlightened life, which is rooted in a sense of autonomous existence, independent and apart from God. It becomes clear that man does not have a relationship with God. He is an *individualized aspect of God*. His substance is Spirit. He is a living Soul, "hid with Christ in God" (Colossians 3:3).

Writings of Thomas Hora

Existential Metapsychiatry. New York: Seabury Press, 1977.
Forgiveness. Orange, Calif.: PAGL Press, 1983.
Healing through Spiritual Understanding. Orange, Calif.: PAGL Press, 1983.
A Hierarchy of Values. Orange, Calif.: PAGL Press, 1983.
The Soundless Music of Life. Orange, Calif.: PAGL Press, 1983.
Can Meditation Be Done? Orange, Calif.: PAGL Press, 1985.
Compassion. Orange, Calif.: PAGL Press, 1985.
God in Psychiatry. Orange, Calif.: PAGL Press, 1985.
Marriage and Family Life. Orange, Calif.: PAGL Press, 1985.
Commentaries on Scripture. Orange, Calif.: PAGL Press, 1987.
Right Usefulness. Orange, Calif.: PAGL Press, 1987.
Self-Transcendence. Orange, Calif.: PAGL Press, 1987.
What Does God Want? Orange, Calif.: PAGL Press, 1987.
Beyond the Dream. New York: Crossroad, 1996.
Dialogues in Metapsychiatry. New York: Crossroad, 1996.
In Quest of Wholeness.

Books Referencing Thomas Hora's Work (Partial List)

Andrews, Lewis. *To Thine Own Self Be True.* New York: Anchor Press/Doubleday, 1987.

Berends, Polly. *Whole Child/Whole Parent.* New York, Harper Magazine's Press, 1975.

Gourgey, Charles S. *Psycho-Spiritual Development: Metapsychiatry, Psychoanalysis, and the Journey to Reality.* Los Angeles: International College, 1985.

Linthorst, Ann. *A Gift of Love: Marriage as a Spiritual Journey.* Orange, Calif.: PAGL Press, 1986.

———. *Thus Saith the Lord, Giddyap! Metapsychiatric Commentaries on Human Experience and Spiritual Growth.* Orange, Calif.: PAGL Press, 1986.

———. *Mothering as a Spiritual Journey.* New York: Crossroad, 1994.

———. *Soul-Kissed: The Experience of Bliss in Everyday Life.* New York: Crossroad, 1996.

Linthorst, Jan. *A Primer on Metapsychiatry.* Orange, Calif.: PAGL Press, 1987.

Rubadeau, Joan. *Meditations from the Bible and the Works of Dr. Thomas Hora.* Orange, Calif.: PAGL Press, 1986.

————. *The Little Book of Good: Spiritual Values for Parents and Children.* Orange, Calif.: PAGL Press, 1986.

————. *Give Us This Day Our Daily Bread: Daily Life as Spiritual Devotion.* Orange, Calif.: PAGL Press, 1987.

Ryan, Timothy. *Metapsychiatry and the Quest for Wholeness: A Critical Assessment of Values in the Educational, Therapeutic and Healing Process.* Los Angeles: International College, 1982.

Tyrell, B. J. *Christotherapy.* New York: Seabury Press, 1975.

————. *Christotherapy II.* Ramsey, N.J.: Paulist Press, 1982.

PAGL Foundation Inc. is a tax-exempt organization incorporated for charitable and educational purposes. It provides an economic structure to benefit people all over the world through the allocation of funds to make available source materials for the study of Metapsychiatry.

More information on the works of Dr. Hora, related publications, and the PAGL Foundation may be obtained from:

Ruth Robins
P.O. Box 4001
Old Lyme, CT 06371
Tel.: 860-434-2999
E-mail: PAGLBooks@aol.com

Or visit PAGL Foundation's Web Site: http://www.pagl.org

Index